STUDIES IN LITERATURE, 1500–1800

General Editor
Robert W. Uphaus

ADVISORY BOARD
OF COLLEAGUES PRESS

John A. Alford, Michigan State University
Joan Ferrante, Columbia University
Richard Firth Green, Western Ontario University
Christopher Kleinhenz, University of Wisconsin
Stephen G. Nichols, Jr., University of Pennsylvania
Robert W. Uphaus, Michigan State University
Linda Voigts, University of Missouri-Kansas City
Frank Warnke, University of Georgia
Howard Weinbrot, University of Wisconsin
Siegfried Wenzel, University of Pennsylvania

MAN, GOD, AND NATURE IN THE ENLIGHTENMENT

Edited by

DONALD C. MELL, JR.
THEODORE E. D. BRAUN
LUCIA M. PALMER

COLLEAGUES PRESS

1988

Studies in Literature, 1500–1800: No. 2

ISBN 0-937191-03-5
Library of Congress Catalog Card Number 87-51123
Copyright © 1988 by Colleagues Press Inc.
All rights reserved

Published by Colleagues Press Inc.
Post Office Box 4007
East Lansing, MI 48826

Outside North America
Boydell and Brewer Ltd.
P.O. Box 9
Woodbridge, Suffolk IP12 3DF
England

Printed in the United States of America

CONTENTS

Acknowledgments — viii

Preface — xi

I. PHILOSOPHY

Vico's Frontispiece and the Tablet of Cebes — 3
DONALD PHILLIP VERENE

Vico, the Counter-Enlightenment, and Advanced Contemporary Thought — 13
GIORGIO TAGLIACOZZO

Kant and the Refutations of Idealism in the Eighteenth Century — 25
MANFRED KUEHN

The Conquest of Nature and the Ambivalence of Man in the French Enlightenment: Reflections on Condorcet's *Fragment sur l'Atlantide* — 37
DAVID LACHTERMAN

II. NATURE

Nature Is a Woman: The Duchess of Newcastle and Seventeenth-Century Philosophy — 51
SOPHIA B. BLAYDES

Wollstonecraft versus Rousseau: Natural Religion and the Sex of Virtue and Reason — 65
MELISSA BUTLER

"All Men and Both Sexes": Concepts of Men's Development,
Women's Education, and Feminism in the Seventeenth Century 75
    HILDA L. SMITH

Madamine! A Few of Mozart's Females or *Fanno così tutte?* 85
    JANE PERRY-CAMP

Paradox in Paradise: Nature and Art
in the Eighteenth-Century Landscape Garden 107
    COLLETTE HALL
    PETER PERRETEN
    JANE SHINEHOUSE
    DERK VISSER

III. SOCIETY

"Had Not Joseph Withheld Him": Portrayal
of the Social Elite in *Joseph Andrews* 123
    BRIAN MCCREA

Scottish Philosophy and Political Economy 129
    SPENCER DAVIS

"Government by Consent of the Governed"
in Eighteenth-Century Constitutional Theory 137
    LESLIE FRIEDMAN GOLDSTEIN

IV. RELIGION, MORALITY, AND LITERATURE

Early Eighteenth-Century Paraphrases of the Book of Job 151
    JAMES E. MAY

Man and God in Richardson's *Sir Charles Grandison* 163
    SYLVIA KASEY MARKS

The Pathetic and the Sublime: The Tragic Formula
of John Home's *Douglas* 173
    DAVID WHEELER

Contents

The Fear of Fiction 183
ROBERT W. UPHAUS

V. SCIENCE

The Scientist in Shirt-Sleeves: Charles Bonnet's
Letters on Parthenogenesis 193
VIRGINIA P. DAWSON

Linguistic and Biological Classification in the Eighteenth Century 205
W. KEITH PERCIVAL

Diderot's Comparative Linguistics: The Philosophe's English 215
BONNIE ARDEN ROBB

Paradigmatic, Narrative, and Genetic Histories,
or the Perils of Relying on Thomas Kuhn 225
JOSEPH MUSSER, JR.

Contributors 237

Index 239

ACKNOWLEDGMENTS

For permission to include materials published in other forms elsewhere, the editors wish to thank Vel Edizioni, Milano, *Il Foglio e l'Albero: L'intelligenza artificiale e la sessualita* (for Giorgio Tagliacozzo, "Vico, il contrailluminismo e il pensiere contemporaneo avanzato"); *The Journal of Politics* (for Leslie Friedman Goldstein, "Popular Sovereignty, the Origins of Judicial Review, and the Revival of Unwritten Law"); *Eighteenth-Century Studies* (for Joseph Musser, Jr., "Paradigmatic, Narrative, and Genetic Histories, or the Perils of Relying on Thomas Kuhn").

We are grateful to the University of Delaware for various favors and kindnesses. Provost L. Leon Campbell, Dean of the College of Arts and Science, Helen Gouldner, and former chair of the English Department, Zack Bowen, have approved a number of grants under auspices of the General University Research Funds that have made the preparation and publication of this book possible. Without their enthusiastic and constant support this volume could not be published.

We also want to acknowledge the invaluable help provided by numerous friends, colleagues, and associates both inside and outside the university. We wish especially to thank Jerry Beasley, Heyward Brock, Philip Flynn, William Frawley, Barbara Gates, and Leo Lemay for reading parts of the manuscript in its early stages and suggesting revisions. We wish also to thank Debby Andrews, Ken Gadomski, Richard Gordon, and John Quillen for their technical advice and thoughtful recommendations on computer matters; David Blatt, Matt Helms, and Diane Thena were responsible for keystroking the manuscript at the outset of the project, and Elizabeth Smith and John Johnson entered the final version of the book into DEC VAX-8600 computer, running the UNIX Operating System. Their work was always prompt and carefully prepared. Proofreading and copyediting were expertly provided by Margaret Pyle Hassert, Brad Howard, and Steve Reese. Deborah Lyall, Linda Russell, Violet Dawson, Margaret Sigmund, and Mary Imperatore handled the multifarious secretarial chores, accounting responsibilities, and massive correspondence, and we thank them all for their efforts. Robert Uphaus has expertly guided the book through press. We are grateful to him and his associates at Colleagues Press for their careful attention to detail during the many months of preparation and their excellent editorial suggestions during all phases of the volume's production. Finally, the contributors have always understood, accepted, and quickly responded to various editorial suggestions throughout the long preparation of this book, and we thank them for their patience, support, and cooperation.

PREFACE

Man, God, and Nature in the Enlightenment consists of twenty essays, whose subjects are as varied as the age itself. These subjects include: philosophy as practiced in several European nations, and the relationship of philosophy to metaphysical and epistemological speculations; religion (natural and revealed) and its profound influence on literature, art, and science; the social and psychological ramifications of conflicting philosophical concepts; political science in relation to economic theory and constitutional theories of governing, especially in America; the rise of feminism as a social and moral force encompassing interpretations of history, educational theory and practice, literature, and music; the impact of aesthetics on landscape gardening and architecture; changing attitudes toward language and linguistics in their international dimension; the challenge of the newly emerging romantic aesthetic of sensibility and pathos to didactic and formalistic conceptions of art, especially in the case of the drama and novel. It is the editors' hope that in the scope and vitality of its inquiry, in the interdisciplinary character and ambitious goals of the essays, and in the willingness of the contributors to confront received opinion and open new areas of investigation, this volume fittingly reflects the enlightenment spirit of *Sapere Aude* (dare to know).

The collection begins with Donald Verene's study of the frontispiece of Vico's *New Science*, in which metaphysics contemplates the triangular relationship of God, nature, and humanity. In his visual and verbal analysis of the emblematic configurations of the engraving, Verene not only introduces the volume's themes and establishes the overall philosophical contexts explored, but he also raises the important question of Vico's actual impact on enlightenment thought. He finds a specific rhetorical connection between the Earl of Shaftesbury's method of commentary on the Tablet of Cebes, in *Second Characters*, and Vico's commentary on his frontispiece. Verene sees in the connection a novel way for understanding Vico's metaphysics.

In a related essay, Giorgio Tagliacozzo dismisses the notion of Italian parochialism during the Enlightenment and speculates on the role Vico might have played in the Counter-Enlightenment reaction in Europe had the *New Science* been read at the time of its publication in 1725. He cites two important features of Vico's thought as having no clear counterparts in French and German philosophy of the period—its richly humanistic background, especially in the traditions of rhetoric and jurisprudence, and its use of the concept of the *verum-factum* (the identity of the true and the made) as a philosophical methodology. Tagliacozzo then notes the modernity of Vico, pointing out the many affinities that exist between his thought and the hermeneutics of such contemporary scholars as Isaiah Berlin, Hayden White, Edward Said, and Stephen Toulmin.

The next two essayists shift the philosophical setting to Germany and France respectively, and thus indicate the widespread presence throughout Europe of the philosophical debate over the question of man's nature and his relationship to God and to the world. Manfred Kuehn demonstrates that the controversies over German Idealism were of long standing before Kant's *Critique of Pure Reason*, while David Lachterman discusses, in the context of Condorcet's *Fragment sur l'Atlantide*, the conflict between the science of French politics and the politics of French science.

When Alexander Pope instructs the critic to "First follow Nature," he is using the word "Nature" in its enlightenment sense of what is natural, permanent, and representative in human nature and individual experience, both male and female. The critical urgency of the individual's struggle against social inequality is made fully evident in the next group of essays by Sophia Blaydes, Melissa Butler, Hilda Smith, and Jane Perry-Camp. Blaydes examines the philosophical works of Margaret Lucas Cavendish (1624?-1673), Duchess of Newcastle, finding in the last volume a revelation not only of the Duchess's philosophy but also of the general condition of women in the late seventeenth century. Butler, in her study of a major feminist from the late eighteenth century, discovers in Mary Wollstonecraft's criticism of Rousseau a serious challenge to his sexism, to his attitude toward natural religion, and to his denial of human perfectibility. Hilda Smith reviews the sexual biases of late seventeenth- and early eighteenth-century educational theory, which helped to assure that women, rather than receiving an education equivalent to men, were relegated to domestic life. Finally, in her account of the female characters in Mozart's operas, Jane Perry-Camp identifies an attractive female assertiveness, rather than servility. Perry-Camp contends that these characters typically possess dramaturgic energies by which they control, indeed alter, the course of the opera's action, most notably in the character of Susanna (*Le nozze di Figaro*).

When the eighteenth century described mimesis, or the creative process, as holding up a mirror to nature, the "nature" referred not only to the universal, permanent, and representative elements in men's moral and intellectual life, or to the imitation of classical models and authors. It also referred to actual landscapes, real gardens and scenery, as seen in Pope's *Windsor Forest*, the presence of his own garden and grotto at Twickenham in his Horatian poems, and in the abundance of descriptive poems and travel literature in the age. These external manifestations—especially in the landscape garden—provided eighteenth-century man not only with aesthetic pleasure but with iconographic and emblematic significance as well. The interdisciplinary inquiry of Collette Hall, Jane Shinehouse, Derk Visser, and Peter Perreten transcends the limitations of any single approach and makes use of diverse methodologies and differing forms of analysis. In their essay the authors contend that the English landscape garden developed out of a unique fusion of intellectual perceptions of art and nature. This "intertextuality" (as they call it) of philosophical speculation, travel accounts, model gardens, and illustrations of plants had at least some of its origins in America, France, and the Netherlands.

Man in his public aspects—his place, role, and moral responsibility as a member of society—is the topic of the three essays that follow. Brian McCrea, in his study of Fielding's *Joseph Andrews*, considers man in a social context, analyzing the various shifts of tone by which the novelist vindicates, even as he seems to criticize, the idea of a social elite group and status quo. Spencer Davis's essay focuses on an often-neglected aspect of the human sciences—the relation of economic man to the social order. Davis points out that the deductive abstract method characterizing classical economic theory, once attributed to David Ricardo, is now more appropriately associated with James Mill. Moreover, according to Davis, Mill's arguments for a doctrine of certainty, together with his dogmatism in the realm of social science, actually parallel those arguments employed by the Scottish commonsense philosophers in their religious quarrels with David Hume. Leslie Goldstein explores a variety of tensions between individuals and their political environment, as evidenced in American constitutional theory between 1776 and 1803. In Goldstein's view, the concept of government by consent of the governed changed during these critical years. She maintains that, in matters of judicial review, as popular sovereignty increased, the importance of unwritten law decreased.

In the next group of essays on religion, morality, and literature, James May begins by focusing on the figure of Job in the eighteenth century. Job, May argues, is represented in eighteenth-century paraphrases as the embodiment of "the true natural dictates of human reason," dictates derived from a theory whose primary justifications of God were based on the design of nature. On a less theoretical level, Sylvia Kasey Marks discusses an important form of contemporary moral dilemma as represented in Samuel Richardson's last novel, *Sir Charles Grandison*. This work, Marks shows, adapts the conventions of the Christian conduct book tradition in dramatizing the hero's response to calls upon his Christian duty in England and to challenges to his Protestantism in Italy. David Wheeler demonstrates that John Home's *Douglas* (1756) is a formulaic tragedy indebted to the ideas of the sublime as exemplified in the odes of Collins and Gray, and to an emerging sympathetic theory of tragedy advanced by Hume and Burke, among others. The play's adherence to contemporary literary tastes, Wheeler argues, accounted for its immediate though short-lived acclaim. Finally, Robert W. Uphaus speculates about the rise of the novel, emphasizing the context of the ostensible moral purpose of fiction. Uphaus cites numerous eighteenth-century discussions, especially those of Samuel Johnson, that focus on the conflict between mimetic methods of fiction and the moral ends of that fiction, and on the corollary fears that the claims and powers of mimetic fiction might eventually supplant the moral purposes.

The volume concludes with four essays that account for the wide interest in scientific investigation and assess the role of the natural scientist in the period. From this perspective Virginia Dawson examines French naturalist and entomologist Charles Bonnet's early correspondence with Réaumur and Abraham Trembley, concluding that the discovery of parthenogenesis was not merely a product of attentive observation of the mating habits of plant lice but can be related to a background of ideas with religious and philosophical implications. In his study of the relationship between taxonomies associated with linguistics and taxonomies used by natural historians in describing the natural world, W. Keith Percival explores the implications for language of man's belief in a divinely ordained order and a natural hierarchy. Eighteenth-century man asserted his humanity through language, Percival argues, by attempting to give rational order to divinely created biological phenomena in the same way that he conferred rational order on the development of languages. Two other linguistic studies, by Bonnie Robb and Joseph Musser, draw on the recent interest in semiotics, exploring the complex way that word patterns and metaphors associated with one field of inquiry or language structure often affect, sometimes adversely, our perceptions and understanding of another. In her exercise in the science of comparative linguistics, Robb takes up the subject of Diderot's language theories, noting that, although the great *philosophe* believed that French was best suited for clear and precise communication, his contacts as a translator with English are amply reflected in his theories of the origin of "natural" word order and—both lexically and syntactically—in his own expressive style. In the final essay, Musser focuses his attention upon historians of science. He finds that their rhetoric seems to rely on Thomas Kuhn's revolutionary paradigm, and he offers two additional and useful metaphors: scientific development as narrative and ideas as seminal. These metaphors, Musser argues, make greater allowance for continuous and subtle change, and for the transformation of a hypothesis by combination and revision rather than by revolution alone.

Preface

The essays in this volume were written as separate and independent pieces. We have made no attempt to impose on the essays some arbitrary kind of ordering that might impair the volume's intended variety or its diversity of approach or the integrity of the individualized responses to the enlightenment spirit. Nevertheless, since the concepts "Man," "God," and "Nature" are integral to the philosophical debate in the Enlightenment and since the relationships between these concepts (or some combination of them) provide an overall thematic focus for the collection, we have organized the essays so as to suggest possible connections, continuities, and interactions among the many disciplines, approaches, and topics represented in this collection. Although diversity of subject matter and theme seems at first to characterize these studies, *Man, God, and Nature in the Enlightenment* as a whole voices the single predominant truth of the age: mankind's persistent intellectual questioning and impassioned desire to know and understand the world.

Newark, Delaware
1987

D.C.M.

I. PHILOSOPHY

VICO'S FRONTISPIECE AND THE TABLET OF CEBES

DONALD PHILLIP VERENE

Giambattista Vico (1668-1744) is a thinker who has not had a place in his own century. He did not have a place in it during his lifetime, despite his efforts to make his ideas known to the thinkers of Northern Europe.[1] And he has been treated as "odd man out," or simply passed by in the philosophical history of his time.[2] He was Mastro Tisicuzzo, a gaunt figure on the streets of Naples going to and from the university, the author of the *New Science*, who some claimed was mad. Vico recorded popular opinion of himself at the end of his *Autobiography*; he says: "Among the caitiff semilearned or pseudo-learned, the more shameless called him a fool, or in somewhat more courteous terms they said that he was obscure or eccentric and had odd ideas."[3]

Vico's *New Science* became an Italian national and international book of the Risorgimento, held in high regard and proclaimed by Italian patriots, such as the poet Ugo Foscolo, in their travels in Italy and Europe. Vico's philosophical ideas were revived in the nineteenth century by Michelet in France, who also translated the *New Science* into French, as did the talented, exiled Princess Belgioioso (in 1844). Vico was revived in the twentieth century by Croce and Nicolini and James Joyce. Many other thinkers, such as Marx and Coleridge, and perhaps Rousseau, read the *New Science*. Attention to Vico's work has undergone Vico's own principle of *corsi* and *ricorsi*, yet Providence has never allowed it to pass into oblivion. Vico's thought is undergoing a widespread renewal in our own time, based on the relevance of his ideas for so many fields of the humanities and social sciences, led largely by English-speaking scholars but including many Europeans as well.

The great French historian of eighteenth-century thought, Paul Hazard, says: "If Italy had listened to Giambattista Vico, and if, as at the time of the Renaissance, she had served as guide to Europe, would not our intellectual destiny have been different? Our eighteenth-century ancestors would not have believed that all that was clear was true; but on the contrary that 'clarity is the vice of human reason rather than its virtue,' because a clear idea is a finished idea. They would not have believed that reason was our first faculty, but on the contrary that imagination was."[4] Hazard also says: "There was not an object that Vico touched without transforming it into gold."[5] Hazard's remarks highlight the fact that the key to Vico's strangeness, his "odd ideas," is his attachment to the imagination, what Vico calls *fantasia*. *Fantasia*, for Vico, is the power to make a truth. But it is not simply the power to make a poetic truth. It is the power to make truth in areas otherwise thought to be the province of reason, to make truth in metaphysics, in history, to make a social truth. *Fantasia* is the power through which the things of the civil world (*cose civili*) are made in their primordial beginnings, and it is the power through which we can ultimately come to comprehend their meaning.

Is Vico a child of the eighteenth century? Is he a child of the enlightened age? The answer is, yes and no. Isaiah Berlin sees Vico as a potential, but in no way an actual, leader of the Counter-Enlightenment. He says: "A thinker who might have had a decisive role in this counter-movement, if anyone outside his native country had read him, was the Neapolitan philosopher Giambattista Vico."[6] Berlin holds that Vico's importance in the history of the Enlightenment "consists in his insistence on the plurality of cultures and on the consequently fallacious character of the idea that there is one and only one structure of reality which the enlightened philosopher can see as it truly is, and which he can (at least in principle) describe in logically perfect language."[7]

Eugenio Garin attacks the thesis that Vico is essentially to be understood as "a late son of the Renaissance." He says: "Vico, far from being a man out of his time, belongs completely in the center of the great debate of the century, that witnesses the crisis of a 'criticism' of knowledge, and the necessity of distinguishing and organizing the tree of the sciences; to grasp the link between the investigation of nature and the investigation of man; to found and construct the new encyclopedia."[8] Garin does not remove Vico from the general humanist tradition, but, against the position of De Sanctis, he argues that Vico does not return to views of mathematics of a neo-Pythagorean and neo-Platonic or a Ficinian character. He says: "Vico, though in his own way, is exactly placed at the neo-humanistic turning point of the eighteenth century."[9] Both Garin and Berlin stress Vico's criticism of Cartesianism and of all ontological tendencies in mathematics. Vico's claim, in *De antiquissima Italorum sapientia (On the Ancient Wisdom of the Italians)*, that truths in mathematics are such because we make them, not because they reflect some rational structure in nature, demonstrates his concern with interpreting the "new sciences" of his time.

It is not possible here to solve the difficult question of the classification of Vico in eighteenth-century thought. My own view of the historical approach to Vico is closest to that of Ernesto Grassi, who has connected Vico to Latin and Italian humanism, not in terms of doctrines of neo-Platonic metaphysics but in terms of the Renaissance and ancient understanding of the connection of rhetoric and philosophy.[10] In this view, what Vico sets up against Cartesianism is a "topical philosophy," a sense of philosophizing that makes the rhetorical sense of the word basic to metaphysics and opposes this to the search for the "logically perfect language" as the means to describe reality.

This approach leads to the consideration of a single question: in what way does Vico structure and communicate his metaphysics? This is a broad question, and I can only answer it here in a broad way. To answer this question, Vico cannot be approached simply as a figure of his own time. We must approach Vico as a thinker having a way of philosophizing that we are only now discovering, or rediscovering, in our own time. Vico is a thinker of both the eighteenth and the twentieth centuries.[11]

My analysis is directed to the frontispiece and the first sentence of the third edition of the *New Science*, the *Scienza nuova seconda* (1730/44).[12] The 1744 or third edition of the *New Science*, a copy of which can be seen in the Vatican Library, was published with a full-page engraving of Vico and the frontispiece facing each other, that is, on opposed pages. These are followed by a forty-two-paragraph explanation by Vico of the meaning of the picture as an introduction to his work. Vico published this material instead of printing eighty-six pages of what probably would have proved to be very dreary correspondence with a Father Lodoli, disputing the original plan to publish the work in Venice.[13] The most curious suggestion regarding the frontispiece was made by the Jesuit father, Domenico Lodovico, who wrote a couplet which was printed below Vico's portrait in the third edition.[14] He sent Vico some bread and wine from the Jesuit house of the Nunziatella "suggesting that at the side of the alphabet in the symbolic frontispiece a little dwarf should be added, dumb with astonishment like Dante's mountaineer, and that beneath him should be written, 'with a significant diaeresis,' the name Lodo-Vico ('I praise Vico')."[15] The first sentence of Vico's *New Science* reads: "As Cebes the Theban made of moral, we present for view here a Tablet of civil things, as will serve the reader to conceive the idea of this work before reading it, and to bring it back most easily to memory, with such aid as the imagination may afford, after he has read it."[16] In the last paragraph of his introduction Vico says: "Last of all, to state the idea of the work in the briefest summary, the entire engraving represents the three worlds in the order in which the human minds of the gentiles have been raised from earth to heaven."[17]

The *dipintura* depicts three worlds (*tres mondi*): the world of nations, the world of nature, and the world of minds and of God. The female figure of

Metaphysic in the upper right dominates the picture and is connected by a ray of light to the eye of God in the heavens.[18] This ray reflects off a jewel on the breast of Metaphysic and shines down on the statue of Homer in the lower left. Metaphysic stands upon a globe, representing the physical world, balanced on a stone altar. Along the bottom line of the picture are a number of items lying on the ground in a row — including a balance, a purse, a sword, and a Roman fasces. More in the middle of the scene is a rudder, a plow, a cinerary urn, a tablet showing the ancient Latin alphabet, and a piece of Corinthian column; on the altar is a lituus, a vessel of water, and fire. All these objects are held within a cleared space of ground, behind which is forest and dark clouds having a bright clearing, from which radiates the eye of God.

Vico says: "All the hieroglyphs on the ground denote the world of nations to which men applied themselves before anything else. The globe in the middle represents the world of nature which the physicists later observed. The hieroglyphs above signify the world of minds and of God which the metaphysicians finally contemplated."[19] What is the basis of Vico's division of experience into three worlds? The *dipintura* of the frontispiece portrays the natural course of mind presented in the *New Science*. The first humans form nature into gods through their power of *fantasia* and in this way establish a basis for cultural activity. Thunder is formed as the god, Jove. Jove is the first name, the first *universale fantastico*, the first "imaginative universal."[20] Once in possession of the power of the name, all nature is transformed into a system of gods. Through their power of *fantasia*, God, nature, and man are interrelated to form the origin of the nation, *nazione*. From the original state in which these three elements are interrelated, each of these three elements is re-discovered as a separate world as the mind of the gentile peoples develops toward metaphysics. They first apply themselves to the creation of a civil world, then discover from its perspective the natural world of the physicists, and finally contemplate a science of the divine.

This course of mind that apprehends the three worlds depends upon the fundamental idea of Vico's early, metaphysical work, *De antiquissima* (1710).[21] This is Vico's principle of *verum-factum*, that the true and the made are convertible. What is true is that which is made. (1) The *verum-factum* principle applies in the world of minds and of God. God as maker of the world has perfect knowledge of the world. In the human mind mathematics is closest to divine activity in form because what is true in mathematics is so because it is made by the mind. (2) The *verum-factum* principle does not apply to our knowledge of nature. Since the objects to be known in nature are not made by the mind, there can be no conversion of the true and the made. Nature is an external. (3) The *verum-factum* principle is the key to our knowledge of the civil world. Because we are the makers of the world of nations, we can have a genuine knowledge of what is true of it.

Because we are ourselves the maker of this world, we can be the true knowers of it.

The *verum-factum* principle is tied to the very meaning of Vico's sense of science. Another distinction of Vico's *De antiquissima* is that between *scienza* (*scientia*) and *coscienza* (*conscientia*). *Scienza* is reserved by Vico to mean only those forms of thought in which *verum* and *factum* are convertible. When the object is not made by the knower, the *coscienza* is possible. *Coscienza*, the "witness conscience," is all that is possible in natural science as we normally think of it because its objects are not made by the mind that seeks to know them. Experiment in such science is important, Vico holds, because in experiments we do something like the making of the object. To understand Vico's *Scienza nuova*, his *New Science*, we must begin not with what *we* call science, but with what *Vico* called science. The new sciences arising from the Renaissance and the seventeenth century are by Vico's definition *coscienza*. Only the metaphysics of culture, like mathematical reasoning, can attain *scienza* because it imitates the divine activity of making itself in its ability to enact the *verum-factum* principle.[22]

What is this new science of metaphysics like, that models itself directly on the activity of the divine and not on the thought-form of the new sciences of nature? What does Vico mean in the very first words of the *New Science* by his comparison of his own work with the Tablet of Cebes the Theban? No commentator has carefully discussed this as a key to Vico's work. The tradition of the Tablet, or Table or Picture, as it is called, of Cebes is both complicated and broad. Cebes is known to present-day readers of Plato as one of Socrates's questioners in the *Phaedo*. Sixteenth-century humanists believed the first-century A.D. author of the Tablet had learned the way of virtue from Socrates himself, but the text is by no means authored by Cebes, the disciple of Socrates. A text of Cebes's Tablet existed in the sixteenth century in nearly every European language and Greek and Latin.[23]

Shaftesbury spent the last fifteen months of his life in Naples (1711–13), where he planned and produced some of his incomplete *Second Characters*, a work which was to include "an Appendix concerning the Emblem of Cebes."[24] Vico must have been in contact with Shaftesbury, as he was befriended by Vico's friends, Francesco Valletta and Paolo Mattia Doria, to whom Vico had dedicated his *De antiquissima*. Max Fisch believes that Vico's procedure of introducing his *New Science* by the engraving and commentary on it may have been suggested by what Shaftesbury was attempting in the *Second Characters*.[25] What does Vico mean by saying: "As Cebes the Theban made of moral, we present for view here a Tablet of civil Things"? Could it be that his new science of the true is enacted not by the methods of the natural sciences and logic but by the means used in the Tablet of Cebes?

The Tablet describes a group of pilgrims who are gazing at a picture in the temple of Saturn and ask an old man (usually called Genius) who is nearby to explain the meaning to them. The picture shows a great crowd of people standing outside a great circular wall, inside which are smaller concentric circles with various figures. The circles represent human life, and all who enter must first drink from the cup of Ignorance and Error. They must then move through Fortune and be challenged by Incontinence and Repentance in an attempt to achieve True Education. Their difficulty is to avoid taking False Education for True and thus fail to attain true happiness and knowledge. But before responding to their request to explain the meaning of what they are witnessing, the old man says to the pilgrims:

> Strangers, said he, I do not at all grudge you that satisfaction, but this you must understand, that the relation carries something of a danger with it.
> And what is that? said I.
> Why, said he, that if you give attention and understand the things that are told you, you will become wise and happy; but if you do not you will become fools and unhappy, vicious and ignorant, and will pass your days wretchedly.[26]

Cebes's Tablet and its dialogic explanation give us the course of the individual human life with its positive and negative forces toward moral education. Vico's Tablet or *dipintura* and his explanation give us the course of the life of the world of nations. Is Plato, one of Vico's "four authors,"[27] present here, with the analogy of virtue written in small letters and in large letters, as the individual is magnified as the state in the second book of the *Republic*? Vico's science was to be a moral conscience, a science to lead to true education. Consider the sentence with which Vico concludes the entire book of the *New Science*: "To sum up, from all that we have set forth in this work, it is to be finally concluded that this Science carries with it the study of piety, and that he who is not pious cannot be truly wise."[28] The interconnection of piety and wisdom cannot be achieved by the formulation of logical principles or metaphysical definitions. The formation of virtue in the person, like the formation of the civil world itself, depends upon memory, imagination, and ingenuity or genius. These are the powers behind rhetoric and poetic.

Vico was a professor of rhetoric. This is a fact that so many of his modern commentators forget. Croce forgot it, great thinker that he was, when he merged Vico with Hegel. Recent commentary has often missed the mark far wider than Croce. For Vico, memory, not reason, is the key faculty, and imagination is a part of memory. Vico says: "Hence memory is the same as imagination" (*Onde la memoria è la stessa che la fantasia*). And, "imagination is likewise taken for ingenuity or invention [*"fantasia" altresì prendesi per l'ingegno*].... Memory [*memoria*] thus has three different aspects: memory [*memoria*] when it remembers things, imagination [*fantasia*] when it alters or imitates them, and invention [*ingegno*] when it gives them a new turn or puts them into proper arrangement or relationship."²⁹ In his sentence opening the *New Science*, Vico says that the *dipintura* "will serve the reader to conceive the idea of the work before reading it, and to bring it back most easily to memory, with such aid as the imagination may afford, after he has read it." The key faculty for Vico's science is memory, which includes imagination and even ingenuity (*ingegno*).

Is there a danger in entering into the explanation of Vico's emblem and science similar to that advocated by the old man of genius, or *ingegno*, in the Tablet of Cebes? Would Vico also mean to imply a parallel to this warning? Could the danger be to half-understand Vico's science, to not really take him seriously, to assume that his notion of *scienza* is exactly opposite to that kind of knowledge sought in the sciences of nature? Is it dangerous to continue to think that what Vico is seeking in his new science is a science of the human world that is somehow parallel to the new sciences of the natural world? The danger is to commit the error of Vico's second axiom, "that whenever men can form no idea of distant and unknown things, they judge them by what is familar and at hand."³⁰ From this follows the conceit of scholars (*boria de' dotti*).³¹ Could this be to have drunk from the cup of ignorance and to have mistaken false education for true? We would then study Vico's work as if it were only a "science" and not a treatise on wisdom and piety.

I have suggested elsewhere that Vico's science stands in the long rhetorical tradition that Frances Yates calls "the art of memory" which includes the theatre of memory of Giulio Camillo.³² Vico's work is a theatre of memory. It stands in the Latin and Italian Humanist tradition that has been dismissed by rationalism and philosophical idealism as not "philosophical." Vico does not treat the interrelation of man, nature, and God as comprehensible through definitions, categories, deductions, or arguments. Instead we apprehend the three worlds of the *New Science* through an art of memory in which the specifics of human history are recalled in a universal way so that their ideal eternal history (*storia ideale eterna*) emerges to mind. All events are brought to mind as having a *corso*—a beginning, a middle, and an end—in which they live a life within the larger life of the *corso* of the nation. When the events of the human world are remembered in this way, using all three senses of Vico's memory, they are set off against the natural world. Our sense of the natural world is a-memorial. It is immediate reasoning in relation to the phenomenon. What is found in memory is always in contrast to what is not found there, what is found in reasoning from perception. Both memory and scientific reasoning show us the world of providence. The order in memory allows us to recreate the work of the divine within mind. In this we stand to the civil world the way God stands to the natural world of his creation.

Metaphysics is a rhetorical act for Vico, and we would do well today to understand it, because Vico attempts to establish in memory those central *topoi*, those common places that make up the roots of the human world out of which any nation comes, and to draw forth from these places the meanings of all particular events or "certains" in a nation's actual history. These *topoi* correspond to what Vico calls the common mental dictionary (*dizionario mentale commune,* or *vocabolario mentale*). From this language below language, Vico creates his total speech in which we are conducted toward true education in piety and wisdom.[33]

In conclusion, I have attempted to introduce a new element into Vico scholarship—the relationship of the *New Science* and the Tablet of Cebes— and to suggest the implications this has for the conduct of metaphysics. Vico is much too little studied in eighteenth-century scholarship. Paul Hazard is certainly right that had Europe listened to Vico, our intellectual destiny would have been different. It is still not too late to listen to Vico and to learn his special touch that transforms everything into gold.

NOTES

[1]Vico describes this in his *Autobiografia*, ed. Mario Fubini (Turin: Einaudi, 1970). English trans.: *The Autobiography of Giambattista Vico*, trans. Max Harold Fisch and Thomas Goddard Bergin (Ithaca, N.Y.: Cornell Univ. Press, Great Seal Books, 1963). Fisch's Introduction is a masterpiece of scholarly information for the student of Vico.

[2]For example, Ernst Cassirer, *The Philosophy of the Enlightenment*, trans. Fritz C. A. Koelln and James P. Pettegrove (Boston: Beacon Press, 1955), p. 209. In his systematic works on myth and symbol, Cassirer regards Vico as the founder of the philosophy of mythology, but he limits his comments on Vico's importance for the Enlightenment to one page.

[3]*Autobiography*, pp. 199-200; *Autobiografia*, p. 87.

[4]Paul Hazard, *La pensée européenne au XVIIIe siècle de Montesquieu à Lessing* (Paris: Librairie Arthine Fayard, 1963), p. 43. My translation.

[5]Hazard, p. 44. My translation.

[6]Isaiah Berlin, "The Counter-Enlightenment," in *Against the Current: Essays in the History of Ideas* (New York: Viking Press, 1980), p. 4.

[7]Berlin, p. 6.

[8]Eugenio Garin, "Vico and the Heritage of Renaissance Thought," in *Vico: Past and Present*, ed. Giorgio Tagliacozzo (Atlantic Highlands, N. J.: Humanities Press, 1981), p. 104.

[9]Garin, p. 109.

[10]Ernesto Grassi, *Die Macht der Phantasie: Zur Geschichte abendländischen Denkens* (Königstein/Ts.: Athenäum Verlag, 1979), and *Rhetoric as Philosophy: The Human Tradition* (University Park: Pennsylvania State Univ. Press, 1980). Grassi says: "In dessen Werk der Italienische Humanismus seinen letzten Höhepunkt erreichte: G. B. Vico" (p. 239). Karl-Otto Apel, in *Die Idee der Sprache in der Tradition des Humanismus von Dante bis Vico*, 2nd ed. (Bonn: Bouvier Verlag Herbert Grundmann, 1975), makes a similar point but through his metaphor connects Vico with Hegel: "*Vico* ist als Humanist ein Abschluss, wahrhaft die Eule der Minerva der italienischen Renaissancekultur" (pp. 320-21).

[11]Giorgio Tagliacozzo, "Vico: A philosopher of the Eighteenth and Twentieth Century," *Italica* 59 (1982), 93-108.

¹²Regarding the frontispiece see Margherita Frankel, "The 'Dipintura' and the Structure of Vico's *New Science* as a Mirror of the World," in *Vico: Past and Present*, pp. 43-51. See also Paolo Rossi, *Le sterminate antichità: studi vichiani* (Pisa: Nistri-Lischi Editori, 1969), ch. 5.

¹³*Autobiography*, p. 194; *Autobiografia*, p. 82.

¹⁴The inscription in the first edition of 1744 reads: "Vicus hic est: potuit vultum depingere Pictor; O si quis mores posset, et ingenium: R. P. Dominici Ludovico S. J." ("Here is Vico: the painter was able to depict his visage; oh that someone could depict his character and genius").

¹⁵*Autobiography*, p. 198 and p. 221, n. 201.

¹⁶*La scienza nuova*, 2 vols. (Bari: Laterza, 1978); English trans.: *The New Science of Giambattista Vico*, trans. T. G. Bergin and M. H. Fisch (Ithaca, N. Y.: Cornell Univ. Press, 1968), par. 1.

I have re-translated the above passage, not in disagreement with the excellent Bergin and Fisch translation but to bring out for the English reader certain senses reflected in my interpretation. The original is: "Quale Cebete tebano fece delle morali, tale noi qui diamo a vedere una Tavola delle cose civili, la quale serva di leggerla, e per ridurla più facilmente a memoria, con tal aiuto che gli somministri la fantasia, dopo di averla letta."

¹⁷*New Science*, par. 42.

¹⁸The source for this was probably Ripa's *Iconologia* (ed. Padova, 1611). See Rossi, pp. 184-85.

¹⁹*New Science*, par. 42.

²⁰Donald Phillip Verene, *Vico's Science of Imagination* (Ithaca, N. Y.: Cornell Univ. Press, 1981), ch. 3.

²¹*De antiquissima Italorum sapientia*, *Opere di G. B. Vico*, 8 Vols. in 11 (Bari: Laterza, 1911-41), I, esp. ch. 1, secs. 1-2. I agree with Guido Fassò, "The problem of Law and the Historical Origin of the *New Science*," in *Giambattista Vico's Science of Humanity*, ed. G. Tagliacozzo and D. P. Verene (Baltimore: Johns Hopkins Univ. Press, 1976), pp. 3-14, that the *historical* origin of Vico's *New Science* is the identity of *verum* and *certum*, not the *verum-factum* principle. I am here concerned with the systematic relationship.

²²Verene, *Vico's Science of Imagination*, ch. 2.

²³For a printing of these texts see *Cebes' Tablet: Facsimiles of the Greek Text, and of Selected Latin, French, English, Spanish, Italian, German, Dutch, and Polish Translations*, intro. by Sandra Sider (New York: Renaissance Society of America, 1979).

²⁴Shaftesbury, *Second Characters, or the Language of Forms*, ed. Benjamin Rand (Cambridge: Cambridge Univ. Press, 1914), pp. xviii and xxiii.

²⁵*Autobiography*, pp. 81-82.

²⁶"The Picture of Cebes, Disciple of Socrates," in *Second Characters*, p. 65. In lieu of Shaftesbury's planned "appendix," Rand prints this translation, which may have been done by Shaftesbury (see p. xviii).

²⁷*Autobiografia*, pp. 30-31 and 45-46; *Autobiography*, pp. 138-39 and 154-55.

²⁸*New Science*, par. 1112.

²⁹*New Science*, par. 819.

³⁰*New Science*, par. 122.

³¹*New Science*, par. 127.

³²Verene, *Vico's Science of Imagination*, pp. 181-92. See also Verene, "La Memoria filosofica," *Intersezioni* 2 (1982), 257-73.

³³Verene, "The New Art of Narration: Vico and the Muses," *New Vico Studies* (New York: Institute for Vico Studies and Humanities Press, 1983), pp. 21-38.

VICO, THE COUNTER-ENLIGHTENMENT AND ADVANCED CONTEMPORARY THOUGHT

GIORGIO TAGLIACOZZO

In his essay entitled "The Counter-Enlightenment,"[1] Isaiah Berlin says that Giambattista Vico "might have had a decisive role in this countermovement, if anyone outside his native country had read him." It is not my task here to discuss whether, where, when, or by whom Vico was read, or Berlin's further remark that "Vico was little read, and the question . . . is still uncertain . . . of how much influence he had had, before his *New Science* was revived by Michelet a century after it was written." I only want to comment on Berlin's view that Vico might have had, although he did not have, a "decisive role" in the Counter-Enlightenment.

I shall begin by underlining that Berlin's reference to Vico significantly occurs at a crucial point in his essay, i.e., between his listing, in Part I, of various types of opposition in different parts of Europe to the central ideas of the French Enlightenment and his discussion, in Part II, of the Counter-Enlightenment as a specific movement starting in Germany around 1760.

Berlin lists the following types of opposition to the central ideas of the Enlightenment: (a) the opposition by the "churches and religious thinkers of many persuasions"; (b) the persistence of the "relativist and skeptical tradition that went back to the Greek Sophists . . . [and was] strongly reasserted in the writings of such sixteenth-century skeptics as Cornelius Agrippa, Montaigne and Charron"; (c) a number of "sociological thinkers from Bodin to Montesquieu"; (d) David Hume's "revolutionary doctrines"; (e) Rousseau's and Mably's belief, in disagreement with the other opponents to the central ideas of the Enlightenment, that "the institutions of civilization were . . . a major factor in the corruption of men and their alienation from nature." After this enumeration, however, Berlin adds that, despite profound differences of outlook among the various types of opposition to the central ideas of the French Enlightenment,

> there was a wide area of agreement about fundamental points: the reality of Natural Law, of eternal principles by following which . . . men could become wise, happy, virtu-

ous and free. . . . One set of universal and unalterable principles governed the world for theists, deists and atheists, for optimists and pessimists, puritans, primitivists, and believers in progress. . . . Thinkers might differ about what these laws were, or how to discover them; . . . but that these laws were real, and could be known, whether with certainty, or only probability, remained the central dogma of the entire Enlightenment.

Berlin concludes Part 1 as follows: "It was the attack upon this [dogma] that constituted the most formidable reaction against this dominant mode of belief."

Berlin's reference to Vico occurs at this precise point. As the wording makes clear, Berlin sees in Vico the first thinker who not only opposed the basic tenets of the French Enlightenment but also reacted against its unopposed "central dogma." Berlin explains that Vico's attack consisted of: (a) his "revolutionary" denial of "the doctrine of a timeless Natural Law, the truths of which could have been known in principle to any man at any time, anywhere"; and (b) "his insistence on the plurality of cultures and on the consequently fallacious character of the idea that there is one and only one structure of reality which the enlightened philosopher can see as it truly is, and which he can (at least in principle) describe in logically perfect language."

After this brief *intermezzo* on Vico, Berlin devotes the rest of his essay to the Counter-Enlightenment as a movement condemning *all* aspects of the Enlightenment, whose father was the German Johann Georg Hamann. I shall now mention some key points of Berlin's discussion, as a necessary background for what I plan to say on Vico and the Counter-Enlightenment and on Vico and advanced contemporary thought.

Berlin points out the following:

(a) Hamann's theses rested on the conviction that all truth is particular, never general; that reason is impotent to demonstrate the existence of anything;

(b) Hamann took little interest in theories or speculations about the external world: he cared only for the inner personal life of the individual;

(c) Hamann is first in the line of thinkers who accuse rationalism and scientism of using analysis to distort reality. He is followed by Herder, Jacobi, Möser . . . [who in turn] were echoed by romantic writers in many lands;

(d) That to dissect is to murder is a romantic pronouncement of an entirely nineteenth-century movement of which Hamann is the most passionate and implacable forerunner;

(e) The influence of Rousseau . . . on this movement in Germany, which came to be called *Sturm und Drang*, was profound . . . Rousseau's idealization of more primitive, spontaneous human societies . . . appealed to Hamann and his followers. But even Rousseau did not seem to go far enough . . . Despite everything, Rousseau believed in a timeless set of truths which all men could read, for they were engraved on their hearts in letters more durable than bronze, thereby conceding the authority of Natural Law, a vast, cold, empty abstraction;

(f) While Hamann spoke in irregular, isolated flashes of insight, his disciple Gottfried Herder attempted to construct a coherent system to explain the nature of man and his experience in history;

(g) Herder believed that to understand anything was to understand it in its individuality and development, and that this required a capacity which he called *Einfühlung* ("feeling into") the outlook, the organic character of an artistic tradition, a literature, a social organization, a people, a culture, a period of history;

(h) Every culture, according to Herder, has its own *Schwerkpunkt* ("center of gravity") and unless we grasp it we cannot understand its character or value. From this springs Herder's passionate concern with the preservation of primitive cultures. . . . Herder rejected the absolute criteria of progress. . . . [For him] there is a plurality of incommensurable cultures . . .[and] every human society is to be judged by its own intellectual standards;

(i) [Analogous ideas were expressed by] Herder's contemporary, Justus Möser, [and by] Friedrich Heinrich Jacobi;

(j) Schelling was perhaps the most eloquent of all philosophers who represented the Universe as a self-development of a primal, nonrational force that can be grasped only by intuitive powers of men of imaginative genius. . . . This faith in a peculiar, intuitive, spiritual faculty which goes by various names—reason, understanding, primary imagination—but is always differentiated from the critical analytic intellect favored by the Enlightenment . . . becomes a commonplace used thereafter by Fichte, Hegel, Wordsworth, Coleridge, Goethe, Carlyle, Schopenhauer, and other antirationalist thinkers in the nineteenth century, culminating in Bergson and other antipositivist schools.

So much for the gist of Berlin's delineation of the Counter-Enlightenment and its wide European influences. Apart from obvious dissimilarities, on which it is impossible for me to dwell here, it is easy to recognize in the above a number of topics and ideas which have a clear affinity with some of those associated with the thought of Vico. This easily explains Berlin's view that "Vico might have had a decisive role in the Counter-Enlightenment."

As to the origin and nature of such affinities, a topic which has been debated in the past by a number of distinguished thinkers,[2] I want to mention here a recent, rather convincing explanation by a young American scholar, Allan Megill.[3] According to him, affinities between Vico and Herder should be attributed to the fact that both thinkers shared the tenets of "historism," the counterpoint tradition to the mainstream tradition in eighteenth-century historical thought, which preceded nineteenth-century "historicism." Megill demonstrates that "historism" was not born in the second half of the eighteenth century, as is generally thought, but at the very beginning of the eighteenth century and that its birth occurred *not* in the field of history, as a forerunner of "historicism," but in that of aesthetics. "Aesthetic historism," according to Megill, was a reaction against aesthetic neo-classicism which, in accord with the spirit of the Enlightenment, emphasized aesthetic laws analogous to those of Newtonian physics.

At this point, recalling Berlin's statement about Vico, the question occurs: *what* role would Vico have had in the Counter-Enlightenment, if his first *New Science*, published in 1725, i.e., five years before the birth of Hamann, had promptly become well-known to European, in particular, German, thinkers?

Such a question is too speculative to be confronted directly. However, it can perhaps be answered, at least in part, indirectly, by singling out the key features of Vico's thought which have no comparable counterpart in the thought of any figure of the Counter-Enlightenment. These, in fact, are the factors which, if active, might have caused the Counter-Enlightenment to embark on a different course and its widespread long-run influences to be different from what they have been.

In order to single out such features, I can only discuss here two fundamental ones; it is necessary to consider them within an overview of Vico's thought both in itself and in historical perspective.

Contrary to the old, frequent interpretation of Vico as a man behind or out of his time, recent studies[4] depict him as completely belonging to his century in his own particular way. Among such studies, besides the one by Megill just quoted, I have in mind the broadest and most authoritative one, prepared in 1978 for the Vico/Venezia international conference by Eugenio Garin.[5]

According to Garin, Vico was a participant in the counterpoint intellectual trend, opposed to the mainstream philosophico-scientific thought of its time, which originated and spread widely throughout Europe between the end of the seventeenth century and the beginning of the eighteenth. The trend consisted of a criticism of the philosophical foundations of the "new sciences" which had emerged in the seventeenth century, the physics-mathematics of Galileo and the physico-geometric philosophy of Descartes in particular; and, consequently, a return to the main themes of the humanists of the fifteenth century: "their 'philology'; the discussion of ancient fables and poetry; the reflections on language and imagination, on the customs of people, and on civil life." According to Garin, those themes, "trivialized in the sixteenth century, reemerged with new vigor in the eighteenth century"; and "it was within this intellectual context, extending to all Europe, that Vico returned to the humanistic discussions of letters and sciences, of the various disciplines, of rhetoric and poetry." Garin adds that such a return brought about a reduction in the supremacy of the sciences, and that the supremacy of the sciences was replaced by a greater attention to human disciplines, among them, jurisprudence (remember Vico's *Diritto Universale*). This, Garin points out, "did not imply a dogmatic rejection of the sciences of nature ... [In Vico] it was rather a new grounding of them, not conceiving them any longer as a structure existing in reality, but rather a construction made by man." In other words—Garin affirms—"the innovative thrust of [Vico's] thesis of the *verum-factum* (the identity of the true and the made) is not in the 'topos,' which was by then a commonplace, but in its methodological consequences.... [These], by breaking the Galilean link between physics and mathematics, make the latter, too, a theoretical construction made by man. On this ground ... [Vico] discovered the process through which man's entire world develops and is structured—the civil world, civil life and its patrimony: language, beliefs, customs, conceptions of reality, physics included."[6] Garin's words encapsulate the essence of Vico's philosophy: a philosophy based on, and unified by, a single principle, the *verum-factum, or "veri criterium est id ipsum fecisse."*

I am now in a position to affirm that nothing fully comparable to Vico's overall philosophy can be found either in the French opponents to the Enlightenment, to whom Berlin refers in Part I of his essay, or in any of the German figures of the Counter-Enlightenment. In particular, nothing comparable to Vico's overall philosophy can be found either in Hamann's "isolated flashes of insight" (to use Berlin's words)[7] or in the writings of Herder, by far the most important among the Counter-Enlightenment thinkers and the one who resembles Vico most. In spite of his "dominant influence" in many fields and on many thinkers, Berlin mentions "romanticism, vitalism, existentialism, ... social psychology, which he all but founded, ... social anthropologists, philosophers of language and of history, and historical writers in the nineteenth and twentieth centuries."[8] Herder did not succeed in what Berlin calls his "attempt to construct a coherent system to explain the nature of man and of his experience in history."[9] Herder did not succeed, let me add, because his thought lacked a unifying epistemological anchor comparable to Vico's *verum-factum*. Berlin calls Herder's thought "imprecise, often inconsistent,"[10] even though, as he also points out, Herder's thought was used by such writers as the Schlegels, Jacob Grimm, Savigny, and Hegel, "whose concepts of becoming and of the growth and personality of impersonal institutions begin their lives in Herder's pages."[11]

With the foregoing, I have outlined one of the two key features of Vico's thought which have no counterpart in the thought of any of the French opponents of the central ideas of the Enlightenment or of the German figures of the Counter-Enlightenment. In order to single out the second feature, it is necessary to go back momentarily to Garin's discussion of the European eighteenth-century return to the main themes of the fifteenth-century humanists. It will be noticed that in France the opponents to the central ideas of the Enlightenment, Rousseau included, introduced those themes within a cultural atmosphere little concerned with, and often hostile to, humanistic thought and, anyhow, in agreement with what was called above the "basic dogma" of the Enlightenment.[12] In Germany, Hamann and Herder shaped their views within a cultural atmosphere respectful of, but not imbued with, the classical and humanistic tradition and strongly pervaded by what Berlin has called "the inward-looking tradition of the Pietist movement."[13]

Obviously, Vico's cultural background differs radically from that of his French or German fellow-participants in the eighteenth-century European return to humanistic themes, described by Megill and Garin. Unlike them, Vico did not plant those themes on a heterogeneous or semi-heterogeneous soil. Thanks to his richly humanistic background, Vico was able to find and cultivate those themes within their natural soil: the humanistic tradition and especially humanistic rhetoric and jurisprudence.[14] This is the second key feature of Vico's thought which has no comparable counterpart in the thought of any of the French opponents to the Enlightenment or of any figure of the Counter-Enlightenment. This feature is strictly related to the first, as I shall explain in discussing their combined significance and potential impact.

In full harmony with the humanistic tradition,[15] Vico's philosophy is characterized by: (1) his constant polemic against Descartes, a polemic equivalent to the humanists' rejection of all kinds of philosphies based on a priori principles; (2) his thesis of the primacy of rhetoric over rational speech; (3) his interest in the nature of man in his concrete, emotive, history-bound evolution and in the problems of the origin of society and of the role of imagination. In brief, Vico's philosophy is characterized by a determined and forceful reassertion of the new conception of philosophical thought achieved by Italian fifteenth-century humanism. About the humanists' new conception of philosophical thought, Ernesto Grassi has written: "The new era of philosophy, the Copernical turning point, started neither with Descartes nor with Kant, but with Italian Humanism."[16] However, Vico went beyond reasserting the conception of the humanists, a conception which, until his time, had been expressed in various ways but had never been presented as an overall philosophy. Vico, thanks to his discovery of the philosophical core of rhetoric and jurisprudence, related to his methodological use of the *verum-factum*, was able to organize the tenets and methods of fifteenth-century humanists into a complete new way of philosophizing.[17]

At this point it will be obvious that, if the *New Science* had become well-known soon after its publication (which occurred some thirty years before Hamann's first Counter-Enlightenment writings), Vico might indeed have had a "decisive role" in the Counter-Enlightenment, or, as I would rather say, Vico might have had a pervasive influence on its birth, development, and consequences.

As we have seen, the Counter-Enlightenment and the ensuing history of philosophy missed the opportunity of making use of Giambattista Vico's thought. In view of this, one might wonder whether an analogous opportunity has occurred, is occurring, or will occur again, in the course of philosophical thought and, if so, when. It is my belief that such an opportunity exists at the present time. I shall explain this belief by listing a number of affinities between Vico's thought and advanced contemporary thought, and by pointing out what is missing in the latter that Vico's thought can offer.

(a) A basic feature of advanced contemporary thought is its anti-Cartesianism. Richard Bernstein has characterized this trend as follows:

> Most contemporary philosophers have been in revolt against the Cartesian framework. Descartes is frequently called the father of modern philosophy. If we are to judge by philosophy during the past hundred years, this title can best be understood in a Freudian sense. It is a common characteristic of many contemporary philosophers that they sought to overthrow and dethrone the father.[18]

Stephen Toulmin has written: "Many of the arguments by which Vico himself tried to hold back the tide of Cartesianism have been integrated into twentieth-century thought."[19]

(b) Interesting analogies exist between the early eighteenth-century epistemological crisis discussed by Garin in the essay mentioned above and the vast intellectual disorientation of our time: a disorientation linked to the exhaustion of analytic philosophy and, to an increasing degree, of the positivistic approach to the philosophy of science and to social science.[20]

(c) As the eighteenth-century epistemological crisis generated a return to themes of the fifteenth-century humanists, together, at least in Vico, with a new grounding of the sciences, so the contemporary crisis of analytic philosophy and of the positivistic approach to the philosophy of science and to social science has generated a return to humanistic themes and interests with a tendency toward a *rapprochement* between the humanities and the sciences. Nancy Struever, the distinguished humanist, has written: "The humanities should not oppose the sciences. And here it seems Renaissance Humanism is ahead of us: recall that in the Renaissance there was no opposition, no separation of the topics of scientific and humanistic inquiry."[21] Seen in this light, Vico is ahead of us.

(d) There is an intriguing parallelism between the humanistic themes that are in the forefront of today's scholarship and the themes, well-known to Vico, which were debated by fifteenth-century humanists. Among them, as will be recalled, Garin refers to " 'philology'; the discussion of ancient fables and poetry . . . ; the reflection on language and imagination, on the customs of people, and on civil life."[22] It is not difficult to think of parallel contemporary disciplines which present themselves under different names but in an almost one-to-one correspondence with them as to subject matter and even methodology.[23]

(e) As in the fifteenth-century humanists, and in Vico, there is a frequent mixing and overlapping of topics which are now generally considered as belonging to different disciplines, so, to quote Clifford Geertz, the distinguished anthropologist, "in recent years there has been an enormous amount of genre-mixing in social science."[24] A very telling example of this phenomenon has been offered recently by Jonathan Culler in the preface to his *On Deconstruction — Theory and Criticism after Structuralism*.[25] He writes:

> ... works of literary theory are closely and vitally related to other writings within a domain as yet unnamed but often called 'theory' for short. This domain is not 'literary theory,' since many of its most interesting works do not explicitly address literature. It is not 'philosophy' in the current sense of the term, since it includes Saussure, Marx, Freud, ... Goffmann, ...Lacan, as well as Hegel, Nietzsche, and ... Gadamer. It might be called 'textual theory,' but the most convenient designation is simply the nickname 'theory.' The writings to which this term alludes ... are a puzzling mixture.... There are no obvious limits to the subjects works of the theory may treat.

(f) Another key feature of contemporary humanistic thought is the strong presence of hermeneutics in social theory, philosophy, study of the classics, philosophy of history, aestheticsm, and literary criticism. The growing literature on hermeneutics includes among the authors many of the most influential thinkers of our time, who in turn refer to thinkers of the recent past such as Hegel, Marx, Nietzsche, De Saussure, Freud, Wittgenstein, and Heidegger, among others. A recent book distinguishes three main strands in it: hermeneutics as the theory and method of textual interpretation (Betti); philosophical hermeneutics or philosophy of culture (Heidegger, Gadamer); and "new hermeneutics," in which a fusion has taken place between elements of phenomenology, philosophy of language, psychoanalysis, and the critical theory of the Frankfurt School (Apel, Habermas, Ricoeur).[26] Another very recent book distinguishes "three faces" of hermeneutics: "analytic hermeneutics" (von Wright and Winch); "psychosocial hermeneutics" (Habermas); and "ontological hermeneutics" (Gadamer).[27] Because of its nature and range, contemporary hermeneutics presents marked analogies with the thought of Vico. The author of one of these books writes that "owing to the *verum-factum* principle — which lies at the root of his view that man can understand history because he made it himself — Vico could be considered the father of 'historical hermeneutics.' "[28] Another scholar, in a paper on "Contemporary Hermeneutics," has drawn a parallel between a fundamental aspect of Gadamer's and Heidegger's hermeneutics, on the one hand, and Vico's, on the other. He writes:

> In the thought of Gadamer and Heidegger, the concepts of common sense and tradition

are renewed as universal, although forgotten, features of all acts of interpretation and thus of the always unfinished growth of understanding . . . [Vico] gave articulation to the ancient humanistic and rhetorical theme in terms of will: what gives the human will its direction is not the abstract generality of reason, but the concrete generality that represents the community of a group, a nation, or the whole human race.[29]

(g) The above quotations are obviously quite significant. However, they do not go far enough. Vico's hermeneutics, unlike the hermeneutics of Dilthey, Heidegger, Gadamer, and Habermas, directs attention to the role of critical interpretation in understanding not only the humanities but also the natural sciences. Furthermore, Vico's hermeneutics considers both the humanities and the natural sciences as constructions of the human mind. In this sense, Vico's hermeneutics, unlike the hermeneutics developed by the four thinkers mentioned above, is not just "modern" but "post-modern."[30] I am aware that this view differs from the prevalent consideration of Vico as the progenitor of Dilthey's distinction between *Natur* and *Geist*, between scientific explanation and hermeneutic interpretation. However, my view appears to be supported by opinions recently expressed by scholars such as Stephen Toulmin and Eugenio Garin. Toulmin writes: "the general categories of hermeneutics can be applied as well to the natural sciences as to the humanities. . . . The natural sciences too are in the business of 'construing reality.'"[31] Garin states that "[Vico traced] with incomparable penetration the first elements of an encyclopaedia of knowledge." Garin also speaks of Vico's "philosophy of man as access to the world of nature." He underlines Vico's conception that "the way into the world of nature lies through the human world." And, finally, Garin emphasizes Vico's view that "the great systems of the world . . . [are] constructions of man, or rather of human imagination."[32]

The above list of *generic*, broad affinities between Vico's and advanced contemporary thought could almost be lengthened at will. Many further remarks in a similar vein could also be made. As examples: (a) A very long list of affinities of a *specific* nature between Vico and outstanding scholars in dozens of fields could be easily compiled. (b) Except for the existence of such affinities, how could the increasing presence of para-Vichian ideas in dozens of contemporary fields of study be explained? (c) How is it that a number of distinguished scholars, e.g., Isaiah Berlin, Hayden White, Edward Said, Stephen Toulmin, have been strongly influenced by Vichian ideas? How is it that Apel indicates Vico as a point of departure of the philosophy of language; that Gadamer finds in his thought the first non-traditional hermeneutics; that Habermas sees in his writings the true sense of *praxis*, in opposition to the imperialism of scientific and technical reason; that Cassirer sees in his theories the first description of the genesis of symbolic imagination? (d) How is it that a number of world-renowned thinkers who never mention Vico and may have never read his writings, e.g., Lévi-Strauss, Merleau-Ponty, Wittgenstein, Piaget, have been authoritatively shown to have important affinities with him? (e) How is it that Marx, Nietzsche, Freud, and Heidegger, four thinkers who have greatly influenced most of the key scholars of our time, have also been found to have affinities with Vico?

I am, at this point, in a position to draw final conclusions. We are, by now, able to realize that a situation exists today, in the relationship between Vico's thought and "advanced contemporary thought," which is analogous to, and at the same time dissimilar from, the situation that was prevailing a little over two centuries ago in the relationship between Vico's thought and that of the Counter-Enlightenment. The basic analogies consist in the facts that: (a) in both cases many thinkers independently, each in his field and only in that field, produced ideas resembling separate ideas contained in the writings of Vico; (b) in both cases no all-embracing structure of those independently-born ideas emerged; (c) in both cases many of Vico's ideas, taken individually, had counterparts in those of the "advanced thinkers" of the respective times; (d) in both cases Vico's thought offered something that in the respective time had not been achieved: a humanistic way of philosophizing. In turn, the main difference between the situation prevailing a little over two centuries ago and our time is this: while at the time of the Counter-Enlightenment Vico was practically unknown, today he is slowly becoming better known and more influential. This is what has made me affirm that the opportunity of making use of Vico's thought, missed by the Counter-Enlightenment, exists at the present time.

NOTES

[1] *Dictionary of the History of Ideas*, (New York: Charles Scribner's Sons, 1973), II, 100-12; rpt. in I. Berlin, *Against the Current* (New York: Viking Press, 1980), pp. 1-24.

[2] See, for example, F. Tessitore, "Vico nelle origini dello storicismo tedesco," *Bollettino del Centro di studi vichiani* 9 (1979), 5-34.

[3] "Aesthetic Theory and Historical Consciousness in the Eighteenth Century," in *History and Theory* 17 (1978), 29-62.

[4] See Tagliacozzo, "Vico: a Philosopher of the Eighteenth — and Twentieth — Century," in *Italica* 59 (Summer 1982), esp. 93-94 and notes 4-9.

[5] Eugenio Garin, "Vico and the Heritage of Renaissance Thought," in G. Tagliacozzo, ed., *Vico: Past and Present* (Atlantic Highlands, N. J.: Humanities Press, 1981), I, 99-116.

[6] Garin, p. 110.

[7] *Dictionary of the History of Philosophy*, p. 105; Berlin, p. 10.

[8] Berlin, p. 10.

[9] Berlin, p. 10.

[10] Isaiah Berlin, *Vico and Herder* (New York: Viking Press, 1976), p. 147n. and passim.

[11] *Vico and Herder*, p. 147 n.
[12] See Roger Hausheer, Introduction to Berlin's *Against the Current*, pp. xxv, xxxiii.
[13] *Vico and Herder*, p. 152. Berlin underlines "the human solidarity of these small groups, inspired by their burning Protestant faith; their belief in unadorned truth, in the power of goodness, in the inner light; their contempt for outward forms; their rigid sense of duty and discipline; their perpetual self-examination; their obsession with the presence of evil . . . ; and above all their preoccupation with the life of the spirit which alone liberates men from the bonds of the flesh and nature."
[14] See E. Grassi, *Rhetoric as Philosophy: The Humanist Tradition* (State College and London: Pennsylvania State Univ. Press, 1980), passim.
[15] See E. Grassi, especially Ch. 1, "Introduction: The Roots of the Italian Humanistic Tradition," and Ch. 3, "Historical and Theoretical Premises of the Humanistic Concept of Rhetoric."
[16] Grassi, pp. 66-67.
[17] Garin states: "Vico not only formulates a philosophy of history, he initiates a new anthropology and founds a genuine encyclopaedia of the sciences of man: where, in the boldest terms of the most audacious eighteenth century, he tackles, together with the religious phenomenon, the problem of the foundations of morality and law, linguistics and aesthetics." (n. 5, p. 114).
[18] Richard J. Bernstein, *Beyond Objectivism and Relativism* (Philadelphia: Univ. of Pennsylvania Press, 1984), Preface, p. ix.
[19] Stephen Toulmin, *Human Understanding* (Princeton, N. J.: Princeton Univ. Press, 1973), p. 23.
[20] See S. Toulmin, "The Charm of The Scout" (review of G. Bateson, *Mind and Nature: A Necessary Unity*), in *New York Review*, April 3, 1980, p. 40; R. Bernstein, *The Restructuring of Social and Political Theory* (New York: Harcourt Brace Jovanovich, 1976); S. Toulmin, "From Form to Function: Philosophy and History of Science in the 1950s and Now," *Daedalus* 1 (Summer 1977), 143-63.
[21] Nancy Struever, "Humanities and Humanists," *Humanities in Society* 1 (1978), 30.
[22] Garin, n. 5.
[23] It is sufficient to mention here the growing recognition in recent years, in the U.S. and Europe, of the importance of rhetoric and related disciplines not only in themselves but also within the framework of philosophical studies. This recognition is evidenced by the periodical *Philosophy and Rhetoric* as well as by such books as Samuel Ijsseling's *Rhetoric and Philosophy in Conflict—An Historical Survey* (The Hague: Martin Nijhoff, 1976): Grassi's *Rhetoric*, n. 15, and Donald P. Verene's *Vico's Science of Imagination* (Ithaca and London: Cornell Univ. Press, 1981).
[24] "Blurred Genres—The Refiguration of Social Thought," *The American Scholar* 49 (1980), 165-79.
[25] Ithaca, N.Y.: Cornell Univ. Press, 1982, p. 8.
[26] Joseph Bleicher, *Contemporary Hermeneutics* (London and Boston: Routledge and Kegan Paul, 1980).
[27] Roy Howard, *Three Faces of Hermeneutics* (Berkeley and Los Angeles: Univ. of California Press, 1982).
[28] Bleicher, p. 16, 27n.
[29] James Swearingen, "Philosophical Hermeneutics and the Renewal of Tradition," *The Eighteenth Century* 22 (1981), 196.
[30] On Toulmin and Vico, see L. M. Palmer, "Stephen Toulmin: Variations on Vichian Themes," *Scientia* 117 (1982), 89-96. On p. 90 Palmer notes that "unlike many Vichian scholars, Toulmin pays particular attention to the possible role that Vico's epistemic principles may play in the knowledge of nature."
[31] *Critical Inquiry* 9 (Sept. 1982), 93.
[32] Garin, pp. 113 and 110, 5n. On the hermeneutic dimension of natural science, the obvious figure of Thomas Kuhn as well as the marginally less obvious one of Paul Feyerabend come to mind. See Toulmin, "From Form to Function," pp. 154-56. Furthermore, the following passage by Karl R. Popper should be recalled: I oppose the attempt to proclaim the method of understanding as the characteristic of the humanities, the mark by which we may distinguish

them from the natural sciences. . . . Labouring the difference between science and the humanities has long been a fashion, and has become a bore. The method of problem solving, the method of conjecture and refutation, is practiced by both. It is practiced in reconstructing a damaged text as well as in constructing a theory of radioactivity. (*Objective Knowledge* [Oxford: Clarendon Press, 1972], p. 185).

KANT AND THE REFUTATIONS OF IDEALISM IN THE EIGHTEENTH CENTURY

MANFRED KUEHN

Examining the historical background of the "Refutation of Idealism," which Kant added in the second edition of the *Critique of Pure Reason* to the "Postulates of Empirical Thought in General" (B274-79),[1] will situate Kant's argument within the different traditions of refutations of idealism in the eighteenth century. The aim of this essay is historical explanation rather than systematic discussion and evaluation. However, it will make a significant difference to our understanding of the systematic issues, as does all truly historical work in the "history of philosophy." I hope to contribute to the clarification of Kant's argument and to the interpretation of transcendental idealism as a whole.[2]

The standard account of the prehistory of the "Refutation of Idealism" can be found in H. Vaihinger's now classic "Zu Kants Widerlegung des Idealismus" of 1884.[3] It is characterized by its almost exclusive emphasis upon the philosophy of Leibniz and Wolff as relevant for understanding Kant's conception of idealism. Vaihinger points out that, early in the history of their school of thought, idealism was not considered as a threat and was treated in a rather friendly fashion. Only later did it come to be seen as a dangerous philosophical sect and to be characterized in most unfriendly terms. Even Wolff himself started out by emphasizing the similarities of idealism to Leibniz's view, while he ended up considering it as both dangerous and absurd. After the sixties of the eighteenth century "it became a task of honour (*Ehrensache*) for any 'enlightened' philosopher to refute idealism, and the "Refutation of Idealism" thus became a standing paragraph in all textbooks of philosophy."[4]

Vaihinger argues that "this changing position . . . is functionally dependent upon the different interpretations of Leibniz's theory of monads."[5] While Leibniz and the early Wolff accepted this theory in its strictest form, the later Wolff and many of his students assimilated it to the theory of atoms. And the more they gave up the theory of monads, the more hostile they became towards idealism. From a strictly monadistic point of view, the idealist denied, in much the same way as did Leibniz, the reality of extended bodies, while from a more atomistic point of view idealism came to be seen as the denial of the world of bodies in general. Vaihinger claims that, because philosophers were unclear about the theory of monads and actually oscillated between a monadistic and an atomistic view, their refutations of idealism had to be "unclear and obscure." Kant's contemporaries, because they never clarified their relation to Leibniz, made a conceptual muddle of the problem of idealism.[6] And, since "Kant must not be isolated from his contemporaries," Vaihinger argues, his refutation must be understood against this confused rationalistic background:[7]

> As he accepted the basic principles of Leibnizian idealism, so he also brought with them, though in a different form, its internal contradictions.... However other aspects [of Kant and the Leibniz-Wolffians] may be different, in this one point we see Kant walk the Leibnizian line, and we can also explain the above shown contradiction historically in this way—to interpret Kant means to deduce him historically.[8]

Indeed, all the confusions and contradictions in Kant's argument can be traced back to this: "Kant did not overcome [the] contradictions of the Leibniz-Wolffian system," which on the one hand denies the material world of bodies, while on the other hand accepting it.

This picture is at best an oversimplification. First of all, the changes in German philosophy after 1750 cannot simply be identified with the changing attitude towards Leibniz's theory of monads. They went much further and often included a complete rejection of metaphysics in the Leibnizian style. Even his most faithful adherents had learned a great deal from other philosophical traditions. By 1770 English and French philosophers had become very influential in Germany. Most German thinkers were attempting to achieve a synthesis of rationalistic principles with an empiricist approach. Many had moved away much further from Leibniz and Wolff than Vaihinger seems willing to admit. Accordingly, the changing position with regard to idealism must also be related to these developments.[9]

Secondly, there are three different "traditions" in the "Refutation of Idealism." There is a tradition of metaphysical refutation, deriving mainly from Descartes. Then there is a tradition of sensationalist refutation, coming to Germany mainly from France and the French philosophers Condillac, Buffon, and Bonnet. And, finally, there is the Scottish tradition of a realistic refutation, transmitted to Germany through Reid, Oswald, and Beattie.[10] Because Kant's contemporaries knew and utilized elements of all three traditions in their refutations of idealism, we must take a closer look at all three traditions to determine the one which is closest to Kant's own refutation.

For Wolff, the problem of idealism is a metaphysical problem. It concerns the nature of reality as a whole. Whereas he understands himself as a "dualist"—i.e., as a philosopher who admits both material and mental substance—he sees in the idealist a "monist" who wants to reduce all of reality to mental substance, denying the existence of the world of body. He thinks the idealist's denial of the material world is based on the claims that (1) we cannot prove the existence of body and (2) if we assume material bodies, we necessarily contradict ourselves and create problems that cannot be solved. He mentions two such problems: (a) the union of body and soul and (b) the infinite divisibility of matter.

Wolff grants to the idealist that the existence of body needs proof, and that our perceptions of objects do not prove their real existence. Furthermore, he agrees with Descartes, Malebranche, and Leibniz that "the witness of the senses cannot amount to a proof" of the existence of external objects.[11] Although the senses give us the impression that objects exist exterior to ourselves, the mere idea of exteriority does not prove anything. Even if there were no objects whatsoever, we could still have mental episodes that would appear to be of external objects. The refutation of idealism must be based on rational argument and not on an appeal to sensation.

Wolff proves "the real presence of the world" by first demonstrating "on the basis of idealistic principles that there is a God and that he has created the world in order to reveal his own perfection."[12] Then he argues that, because the Leibnizian *systema harmoniae praestabilitae* increases the wisdom and splendor of God to the highest degree possible, there must be a real world of material substances.

This "proof" does not go beyond what Descartes and Leibniz had done, perhaps better, before Wolff. The real interest of Wolff's refutation of idealism consists in the preparatory stage, where he tries to lay to rest the idealist's scruples concerning the problematic character of the belief in a real world. According to Wolff's reconstruction of the idealist's position, the idealist does not claim that we cannot prove the union of body and soul, but rather that such a union cannot be made comprehensible, that is, that we cannot talk meaningfully about it.[13] Wolff refutes the strong claim of the idealist by offering a "meaningful," non-contradictory account of the union of body and soul. This is exactly what he does by citing "the *systema harmoniae praestabilitae*, or Herr von Leibniz's."[14] According to Wolff, this clearly shows that we can make sense of the union of body and soul if we assume that God has created two different universes, one material and the other spiritual, and that he has created them in such a way that there exists an exact correspondence between the events of the two universes. Thus, even if there is no influence of the one universe upon the other and even if we do not actually perceive the material bodies, we can still be sure of what we perceive because we can know that there must be something in the material universe which corresponds to what we see. The phenomena are thus "well founded" (*bene fundatum*). Even when the idealist rejects this system as being false, he cannot, according to Wolff, deny that,

> if reality were to be like this, then the union of body and soul would be comprehensible.... For this reason he can no longer say that the union between body and soul is a Gordian knot and so incomprehensible that it does not allow of a clear explication.[15]

One of the most convenient sources for an example of a sensationalist refutation of idealism is Condillac's *Traité des sensations*, whose first edition dates back to 1754. It may actually be considered as the attempt to disprove the claim that his principles are *"précisément les mêmes que ceux de Berkeley."*[16] Condillac tried to show in this work how he could talk of the existence of an external, material world, while holding that all our knowledge and all our mental operations are based upon sense perceptions or mere *"modifications de l'âme."* In this way Condillac offered a refutation of idealism on the basis of his own principles.

Condillac also seems to accept the view that the existence of a bodily world needs to be proved or at least that it must be explained how we can have awareness of such a world. He does not rely on reason so much as on sensation, and he takes the problem to be one of psychological or genetic explanation, believing that, if he could explain how the idea of exteriority naturally arises in the human mind, he would have solved his problem.

His explanation of the origin of the idea of exteriority is designed to prove how, even if we had only the use of our hands and the sense of touch, we would be able to discover our own body as well as the existence of other bodies external to ourselves. He therefore contrasts the feelings created by the touching of one's own body and the touching of another body; the former is a double affection of oneself, in the hand and another part of the body, and the latter involves only a single affection. He argues:

> Quand plusieurs sensations distinctes et co-existantes sont circonscrites par le toucher dans les bornes où le moi se répond à lui-même, elle [l'âme] prend connoissance de son corps; quand plusieurs sensations distinctes et co-existantes sont circonscrites par le toucher dans les bornes où le moi ne se répond pas elle a l'idée d'un corps différent du sien. Dans le premier cas, ses sensations continuent d'être des qualités à elle, dans le second, elles deviennent les qualités d'un objet tout différent.[17]

To show that the idea of exteriority arises somehow naturally in our consciousness does not prove anything about the independent existence of objects in themselves. Because it is commonly assumed that Condillac wanted to prove the latter, he has frequently been accused of committing a fallacy.

But it should be clear from this account that Condillac did not want to prove the independent existences of bodies. Rather, he is responding to those *"idéalistes . . . qui n'ayant conscience que leur existence et des sensations qui succédent au-dedans d'eux-mêmes, n'admettent pas autre chose,"* attempting to show that, contrary to what they claim, they must admit other objects because touch forces them to do so. This would mean that Condillac is not proving such a strong claim as "there exist external objects which are independent of, and numerically distinct from the self and its states," but is, somewhat like Wolff, disproving the strong claim of the idealist that "it is nonsensical to speak of external objects as independent and numerically distinct from the self and its states."[18]

While the rationalist refutation assumes that sense experience had no bearing on the problem of idealism, the sensationalist tries to show that it does have such a bearing and that the idealist can be shown to be wrong in his description of what we actually sense. The idea of exteriority has its origin in sensation. We can show how it develops from more simple sensations. Accordingly, for Condillac, idealism is no longer a metaphysical problem, but an epistemological one.

The Scottish refutation of idealism also presupposes that idealism is not so much a metaphysical but an epistemological problem. But whereas Condillac believes he can give a genetic account of our idea of exteriority, Reid considers such an undertaking not only unnecessary but also nonsensical. For Reid, we immediately perceive external objects. We only have to analyze our perceptions in order to discover this. And this is the reason why "Descartes, Malebranche, and Locke have all employed their genius to prove the existence of a material world . . . with very bad success."[19] For him, "the belief of a material world is older, and of more authority than any principle of philosophy."[20]

> Every operation of the senses, in its very nature, implies judgment or belief, as well as simple apprehension. Thus, when I feel the pain of the gout in my toe, I have not only a notion of pain, but a belief of its existence, and a belief of some disorder in my toe which occasions it; and this belief is not produced by comparing ideas, and perceiving their agreements and disagreements; it is included in the very nature of the sensation.[21]

The belief in the existence of the self is based on just such an immediate and natural belief. Inner experience is no more privileged than outer.[22] And all Reid tries to show is that our beliefs in the existence of the self and an external world are such that they cannot be disbelieved. Philosophers who have argued to the contrary actually prove this through their own conduct.

Reid backs up his theory of immediate perception by negative strictures against the so-called "ideal theory." This theory holds that we do not perceive things directly, but only by means of mediating mental entitities, such as impressions, ideas, or images of any sort. For Reid, the assertion of the existence of mediating mental entities between the perceiving subject and the objects is a hypothesis which is not only not supported by facts but is actually contrary to facts. Indeed, it amounts to a confusion of language. There are always two meanings for the particular terms of sensation in their ordinary usage. First of all, they are thought to refer to something actually to be found in the external world, and, secondly, they are also used to refer to the particular action that takes place when we sense something.[23] Thus, when we speak of the smell of a rose or the stench of a sewer, we clearly have something in mind that is quite independent of ourselves, something that confronts us whether we will or not. But we can also mean by "smell" or "smelling" what takes place when we are smelling. In other words, "smell" can mean an "act of the mind." This act of smelling has a beginning and an end. It is not a permanent characteristic or quality of ourselves. As an act of feeling it can "have no existence but when ... felt." There is nothing in sensation over and above the act of sensing or feeling. Philosophers have failed to attend carefully to this distinction and have, in fact, confounded the two meanings of "sensation" in various ways. In this way they created such mediating entities as "ideas."

> All systems of philosophers about our senses and their objects have split upon this rock, of not distinguishing properly sensations which can have no existence but when they are felt, from the things suggested by them.

But in doing so, the philosopher

> puts a different meaning upon the word, without observing it himself or giving warning to others, he abuses language and disgraces philosophy, without doing any service to truth: as if a man should exchange the meaning of the words *daughter* and *cow,* and then endeavour to prove to his plain neighbour, that his cow is his daughter, and his daughter his cow.[24]

This is exactly what philosophers are doing when they say that what we sense are not the objects but (ideal) sensations. And idealism can be traced back to this confusion of language.

Kant's "Refutation of Idealism" is intended to disprove what he calls "the problematic idealism of Descartes," which for him "merely pleads incapacity to prove, through immediate experience, any existence except our own." For the Cartesian, inner experience has epistemic priority. Its immediate experiences can supply us with absolutely certain knowledge, whereas outer experience is merely mediate and therefore doubtful. Against this, Kant wants

Kant and the Refutation of Idealism

to prove "that even inner experience, which for Descartes is indubitable, is possible only on the assumption of outer experience" (B 274-75).
The argument runs:
1. I am conscious of my own existence as determined in time.
2. All determination in time presupposes something *permanent* in time.
3. The permanent without me must be a thing without me and not merely a representation of a thing without me. (This follows from 1 and 2 as soon as it is understood that my consciousness of a representation presupposes consciousness of my own existence because the representation of an object must be either intuition or concept, and that means a perception or "representation with consciousness.")[25]
4. Therefore, the determination of my own existence in time presupposes the existence of actual things which I perceive outside me.
5. Therefore, I must perceive something outside myself in order to be able to determine myself in time.
6. Therefore, "the consciousness of my existence is at the same time an *immediate* consciousness of the existence of other things outside me" (B 276).

By attempting to show in this way that "inner experience in general is possible only through outer experience in general," or that outer experience is epistemologically prior to inner experience, Kant believes "the game of idealism has been turned against itself" (B 276).

Kant's approach in this argument is very unlike Wolff's. Indeed, according to Kant's classification, Wolff plays the idealist's game and therefore is himself a pseudo-idealist. For he accepts that inner experience, or the *mundus idealis*, is epistemologically prior to outer experience which needs to be proved by means of a rational argument that relies itself on inner experience. Furthermore, Kant disagrees with Wolff on the importance of sensation. Whereas Wolff believes that sensation has no say in the matter, Kant's argument depends upon an analysis of sensation—an analysis that turns around the logical relationship between inner and outer sensation presupposed by Wolff's Cartesianism.

Because Kant uses essentially epistemological arguments, he is closer to Condillac and Reid. But, since Condillac's view on the relationship between inner and outer sensation is just as Cartesian as is Wolff's, Kant's argument is directed against Condillac as well. His genetic account of the origin of the idea of exteriority also assumes that inner experience is prior to outer experience and that it is outer experience that needs to be explained. For this reason, Condillac would clearly have disagreed with Kant's view that we have immediate consciousness of the existence of other things external to us. Though both Kant and Condillac (as well as Reid) look at "empirically determined consciousness," Kant believes it is wrong to try to *infer* outer things in any way (B 276). Whatever Kant's "Refutation of Idealism" may amount to, it is meant to be neither a metaphysical argument against monism or for dualism in the Wolffian fashion nor a genetic or psychological account of the origin of our conception of exteriority in Condillac's sense.

If Kant is close to anybody, he is close to Reid. In "Refutation of Idealism" he attacks the Cartesian tradition in very much the same way as did Reid before him, namely by challenging the "special access theory" to internal sensation. Kant also tries to show that Descartes and his followers were led to skepticism and idealism because they gave priority to inner sense at the expense of outer sense. Reid held that our outer experience is just as immediate as is our inner experience and that the epistemological priority of inner experience is illusory. Kant agrees. Indeed, he takes Reid's approach one step farther. Whereas Reid claimed that outer experience was just as important and immediate as inner experience, Kant wants to prove that outer experience is more important than inner experience and that only outer experience can be truly called immediate. Thus, Kant may be said to start where Reid left off, i.e., with immediate perception.

But it might be argued that while Kant starts where Reid left off, he ends up contradicting Reid's account of the relationship between the natural judgments concerning the existence of the self and those concerning the existence of perceived objects. According to Reid, both are equally natural, necessary, and immediate. But the contradiction is merely apparent, since Kant nowhere claims that all judgments concerning the self can be shown to be dependent upon outer experience. It is only the experiential judgments concerning myself that are so dependent. The mere judgment, " 'I am,' which expresses the consciousness that can accompany all thought" is not reducible to outer experience. Indeed, it makes possible outer and inner experience. Since Kant differentiates between a transcendental or logical self and an empirical self, he can say that in one sense "I am" is independent of outer experience, while in another sense it is dependent upon outer experience.[26]

That Kant offers a "Refutation of Idealism" in the Reidian tradition is, I suggest, not an accident or a meaningless historical parallel. In other words, I propose that Kant knew what he was doing when he was employing a more or less Reidian analysis of sensation in his "Refutation of Idealism." Given the particular criticism of Kant's theory and its sources, it made perfect strategic sense for Kant to show in his refutation that his view of sensation was not only compatible with that of Reid but also that he could refute idealism better than Reid himself, because his theory was in fact a further development of Reid's.

To this it might be objected that Kant did not know Reid and that, even if he knew him, the famous passage in the *Prolegomena* shows that he could not possibly have learned anything from his "jejune appeal to common sense."²⁷ But neither objection is as strong as tradition has made it appear. First, a closer look at Kant's criticism of the Scot in the *Prolegomena* indicates that Kant himself claims he has read Reid and his followers, as well as their critic Priestley, and that this reading experience stands out from the many others in connection with Hume. How else could Kant claim that "it is *positively painful* to see how his opponents, Reid, Oswald, Beattie, and, lastly, Priestley, missed the point of the problem"? Could Kant say any more clearly that he had read Reid and found him important in thinking about Hume's problem?

Reid's *Inquiry* had appeared in German in 1782. Kant could have read it before he worked on the second edition of the first *Critique*, even if he had not known the work before then.²⁸ Indeed, it seems more than just likely that Kant would have availed himself of this opportunity, because between 1770 and 1780 Reid, Oswald, and Beattie were considered to be the enemies of Hume's skepticism and Berkeley's idealism.²⁹ Since Kant himself stood accused of being an idealist in very much the same way as was Berkeley, he had every reason to consult their arguments against his supposed predecessor.

If this had not been enough incentive, the fact that Johann Georg Heinrich Feder—the editor of the infamous review in the *Göttingische Anzeigen von gelehrten Sachen* and originator of the accusation—considered himself a follower of Reid would have provided another reason, if only to see how Reid's arguments squared with Feder's accusations about the idealism of the first *Critique*. Feder, who himself tended towards sensationalism, had made Kant's analysis of sensation the cornerstone of his criticism of Kant, claiming that "the Kantian system is based upon . . . sensations as mere modifications of ourselves (upon which Berkeley built his idealism as well) and upon [the concepts of] space and time."³⁰

Given this criticism and its background, it made perfect sense for Kant to focus on sensation, to show that he did not mix up these two and that he could not be construed as "contesting the rightful title of outer sense." His emphasis upon the immediacy of our consciousness of the existence of external objects—one of the most distinctive features of Reid's analysis of sensation—might have been intended to show to Feder that he, Kant, understood Reid better than did Feder, and that, insofar as Reid had anything of importance to say, it was *aufgehoben* in the first *Critique*.

All of this shows how wrong Vaihinger is in his identification of the historical background of Kant's "Refutation of Idealism." It cannot simply be identified with Leibniz-Wolffian philosophy; and whatever contradictions Kant's argument contains, they cannot be simply "historically deduced" from a Leibniz-Wolffian background. Insofar as Kant relies upon sensation, or more precisely, immediate sensation, he must be seen against a different background, and one that has not received much attention thus far.

Kant's reliance on the "immediate consciousness of the existence of other things outside me" is not just polemical strategy, dictated by the needs of the moment.[31] The doctrine of "immediate perception" is not a radically new doctrine first introduced in the second edition of the *Critique of Pure Reason*; it already plays an important, though little discussed, role in the first edition of this work. Accordingly, Vaihinger has a much better point than he perhaps realized when he pointed out in another publication that "Kant's relation to the Scottish school, the internal and systematic one as well as the external and historical one, would require a thorough monographic treatment."[32] It seems to me that Kant's doctrine of immediate perception would be a good starting point for such an investigation. In any case, only after we have understood that doctrine of Kant, will we be able to make ultimate sense of his "Refutation of Idealism."

NOTES

[1] Immanuel Kant, *Critique of Pure Reason*, trans. Norman Kemp Smith (New York: St. Martin's Press, 1965). All quotations whose page numbers are preceded by an "A" and/or a "B" are taken from this work. References to this work are given in the text.

[2] For a summary and discussion of these questions see, for instance, Moltke S. Gram, "What Kant Really Did to Idealism," in *Essays on Kant's Critique of Pure Reason*, ed. J. N. Mohanty and R. W. Shahan (Norman: Univ. of Oklahoma Press, 1982), pp. 127-56. See also Paul Guyer, "Kant's Intentions in the Refutation of Idealism," *The Philosophical Review* 92 (1983), 329-83.

[3] In *In Strassburger Abhandlungen zur Philosophie*, 1884, pp. 85-164.

[4] Strassburger, p. 110.

[5] Strassburger, p. 110.

[6] Strassburger, p. 111.

[7] Strassburger, pp. 112, 116, 122 ff. Vaihinger claims that Kant's transcendental idealism in the first edition is "in its essential characteristics" similar to Leibniz's system, and that, as a Leibnizian, Kant can indeed disprove "skeptical idealism" but not the "dogmatic idealism" of Collier and Berkeley.

[8] Strassburger, p. 139.

[9] See, for instance, G. Zart, *Einfluss der englischen Philosophie seit Bacon auf die deutsche Philosophie des 18. Jahrhunderts*, (Berlin, 1881). See also Manfred Kuehn, *Scottish Common Sense in Germany, 1768-1800: A Contribution to the History of Critical Philosophy* (Montreal and Kingston: McGill-Queen's Univ. Press, 1986).

[10] Wolff, Condillac, and Reid should be taken as representing these different approaches to the problem of idealism. I do not mean to claim that they were the only philosophers (or, with the exception of Reid, the most important ones of their school). Nor do I want to suggest that these three traditions were always completely distinct. Indeed, most philosophers were affected by all of them. The mature Kant is, as I shall try to show, an exception. He uses only one type of argument.

[11] Christian Wolff, *Ausführliche Nachricht von seinen eigenen Schriften* (Frankfurt, 1726), pp. 592 f.

[12] Wolff, pp. 597 f.

[13] Wolff, pp. 592, 594 ff.

[14] Wolff, pp. 594 ff.

[15] Wolff, p. 595. There are many other passages in which Wolff deals with idealism. See *Theologia Naturalis* (Frankfurt, 1736–1737), II, sects. 226n., 630; *Psychologia Rationalis* (Frankfurt, 1734), sects. 36–38, 42 f., 550 f., 614n., 709–11, as well as his *Vernünftige Gedanken von Gott der Welt und der Seele*, Preface.

[16] Denis Diderot, *Lettre sur les aveugles à l'usage de ceux qui voient*, in *Ouevres Completes*, ed. Assezat-Tourneux, 20 vols. (Paris, 1875–1877), I, 304 f.

[17] Condillac, *Ouevres philosophiques*, ed. Georges Le Roy (Paris: Presses Universitaires de France, 1947), I, 257.

[18] Diderot, *Lettre sur les aveugles*, p. 304.

[19] Thomas Reid, *An Inquiry into the Human Mind*, ed. Timothy Duggan (Chicago and London: Univ. of Chicago Press, 1970), p. 11.

[20] Reid, pp. 78 and 16.

[21] Reid, p. 268.

[22] Reid, pp. 24 ff. and 258 ff.

[23] Reid, pp. 39 ff.

[24] Reid, pp. 83 and 40.

[25] See, for instance, his *Stufenleiter* of representations in A 320–B 377.

[26] But the mere "I am" of logical consciousness is completely empty. It has no content. Insofar as the "I am" has content, it is empirically determined.

[27] See Lewis White Beck, "Kant's Strategy," in his *Essays on Kant and Hume* (New Haven and London: Yale Univ. Press, 1978), p. 6.

[28] But he might very well have known Reid's *Inquiry* in the French translation of 1768, which was available in Königsberg during the seventies.

[29] Kuehn, *Scottish Common Sense*, as well as Kuehn, "The Early Reception of Reid, Oswald and Beattie in Germany: 1768–1800," *Journal of the History of Philosophy* 21 (1983), 479–96.

[30] *Zugabe zu den Göttingischen Anzeigen von gelehrten Sachen*, 3. Stück, 19 Jan. 1782, 40–48. The result is "a system of the higher, or, as the author calls it, transcendental idealism, that is an idealism that comprises spirit and matter in the same way and transforms the world and ourselves into representations." Kant's arguments are those of a "Raisonneur" who leaves common sense behind "by opposing to each other two *genera* of *sense*: the inner and outer one, or by wanting to merge or change into each other these two. When the form of internal sensation is changed into that of external sensation or when it is mixed up with the latter, materialism, anthropomorphism, etc., result. And idealism is the product of contesting the rightful title of outer sense besides inner sense. Skepticism does at times the one and at other times the other in order to mix and shake everything into confusion. In some ways, our author does so as well. He does not recognize the rights of inner sensation. . . . But his idealism still more contests the laws of external sensation and the resulting form and language natural to us." The review closes in a somewhat Reidian fashion with an appeal to ordinary language, asking why and wherefrom Kant introduces his idealistic distinctions.

[31] Whether the refutation was successful as a strategic device is questionable, in any case. For in 1787, the very year it appeared, there also came out Friedrich Heinrich Jacobi's *David Hume über den Glauben, oder Idealismus und Realismus* with an appendix entitled "*Über den transzendentalen Idealismus*" in which Jacobi accused Kant of contradicting himself in his doctrine of the things in themselves, essentially offering the same Reidian inspired criticisms as Feder, though in a much more forceful way. Kant was not so successful against this version of the critique.

[32] H. Vaihinger, *Commentar zu Kant's Kritik der reinen Vernunft*, 2 vols. (Stuttgart: W. Spemann, 1881), I, 342.

THE CONQUEST OF NATURE AND THE AMBIVALENCE OF MAN IN THE FRENCH ENLIGHTENMENT: REFLECTIONS ON CONDORCET'S *FRAGMENT SUR L'ATLANTIDE*

DAVID R. LACHTERMAN

Condorcet's *Fragment sur l'Atlantide* (1793) is the third in a sequence of "Atlantean" texts. First came Plato's apparently incomplete *Critias*; then Bacon's *The New Atlantis*. Studying Condorcet's *Fragment* in the company of these two works allows us to throw light on some of the cardinal issues and dilemmas inseparable from the program of the scientific Enlightenment.

"Enlightenment" has long proved a polyvalent, even promiscuous concept. Let me briefly sketch the idea of the Enlightenment that sustains my analysis of Condorcet. It can best be pictured as a campaign pursued along two fronts simultaneously. On the first front is the campaign to conquer material Nature, first by discovering its laws and then by applying them to refashion Nature to suit human purposes—the campaign which Bacon inaugurates when the father of Salomon's House in *The New Atlantis* tells us: "The End of our foundation is the knowledge of Causes and secret motions of things; and the enlarging of the bonds of Human Empire, to the effecting of all things possible" and which Descartes epitomizes in his famous promise that through his new practical philosophy we shall become "maîtres et possesseurs de la nature."[1] On the second front is the campaign, undertaken simultaneously, to readjust or reattune our understanding of human nature and human affairs to conform with the programmatic aspirations and technical achievements of the new science. This reattunement is initially recognizable in the thinking of Hobbes and Spinoza and is flourishing in Condorcet's remark in his essay "On the Influence of the American Constitution in Europe":

> All errors in politics and ethics are based upon errors in philosophy and these latter are tied to errors in physical science. There is not a single religious system of supernatural extravagance which is not founded upon ignorance of the laws of nature.[2]

We should add that this means for Condorcet and most of his mentors the mathematical laws of nature. Mathematics, more by virtue of its powers of exact construction and systematization than of its deductive format, serves to hold these two fronts in strategic alignment.[3]

Measured by this conception of the Enlightenment, the urbanities of a Voltaire or a Hume provide a polite surface covering the audacious depths to which the would-be conquerors of Nature are ready to plunge.[4] It is only at these depths that the transformation of human self-understanding shows its enigmatic ambivalence: Does the conquest of Nature, whether conceived as infinite task or as an already fulfilled intention, signify a diminution or an enhancement of the human? This question is nearly coeval with the debut of the Enlightenment, receiving its most poignant articulations in Diderot, Rousseau, and Kant. At the outset, however, it had already been recognized by La Mettrie: "Everything is arbitrary and made by man's hand."[5] Does the energy of will directed upon the technical transformation of Nature equally impel human beings towards their own perfection, a condition all but indistinguishable from that artificial divinity Vico signals when he calls man the *Deus artificiorum*? Or is this same energy amplified and potentiated only in inverse ratio to the dwindling of pre-technical or pre-technological insight into the human? Can either perfection or imperfection continue to make sense if this insight is finally absent?

As it progresses, this collateral campaign takes its bearings from programmatic visions in which Pascal's claim that "man is produced only for infinity" assumes the more beguiling colors of a not-too-distantly realizable future, a future still marked out by endless horizons, the Baconian or Cartesian "infinity of artifices." That future is also securely anchored to political institutions that have been freed of any intransigent prejudice against the metamorphosis of social relations and human self-understanding underway in tandem with the conquest of nonhuman nature.

It is in this setting that Condorcet's *Fragment* is most naturally placed. His central preoccupations cannot be brought into full relief unless they are viewed against the backdrop of both Bacon's *The New Atlantis*—to which Condorcet expressly refers—and Plato's tale of the Old Atlantis. I shall point to two of the ways in which both Bacon (explicitly) and Condorcet (implicitly) oppose themselves to the Platonic archetype of their radically modern fables. First, while Critias' tale of the Old Atlantis ends abruptly, mirroring by its incompleteness the divinely devised disasters which put an end to Atlantis and ancient Athens alike, Bacon's Bensalem and Condorcet's union of enlightened nations are designed to endure, impervious to future assaults either of Nature or of the gods. The two versions of an enduring new "Atlantean" polity turn on the possibility of fusing a politics of science with a technical science of politics, so as to produce a coherently habitable whole, both in theory and in practice. When the *Critias* is read in concert with the *Timaeus* (to which it is the designated coda), *The Republic*, *The Statesman*, and *The Laws*, it is both a critique of any such fusion and an anticipatory challenge of those advocates who claim that limitless inventiveness and political order can somehow be yoked in harmony with one another to secure the intrinsic good of citizens.[6]

Our chain of interlinked texts begins with an aporetic questioning of the relation between the political and the technical; moves to a prophetic vision of their union, a vision not yet blind to the perplexities that would be generated by this union; and concludes in a strategy for institutionalizing that vision. This strategy would be effected by men and communities henceforth innocent of the perplexities brought to light by their own inherited dreams.

Measured by the fabulous perplexities of Plato's *Critias* ("The Old Atlantis") or by the seductive ellipses of *The New Atlantis*, Condorcet's *Fragment sur l'Atlantide* is bound to strike the reader as having more bathos than depth.[7] This is not due exclusively to the circumstances of its composition nor to Condorcet's eventual fate at the hands of the Jacobins, although these do lend a human color to the text. The more fundamental reasons for its lesser stature may be found in the confluence of three presuppositions by which the text is governed and which it never questions in a radical way. Condorcet does, however, expose the quandaries which follow in their wake.

First, none of the Platonic political writings challenge or provoke Condorcet as the *Critias* and *The Republic* challenged Bacon. For Condorcet, the quarrel of the Ancients and the Moderns has been decisively ended, with the Moderns triumphant. His task is to institutionalize that triumph, no longer to prophesy it. Accordingly, in the *Esquisse d'un tableau historique* Plato figures as a hero of the fourth Epoch. His essentially antisystematic skepticism is barely disguised behind the "hollow and frivolous hypotheses" to which his audacious imagination has led him. Moreover, Condorcet treats both Plato and Aristotle as writing an empirical science of political facts rather than "a true theory, founded on general principles drawn from nature and avowed by reason." It is Plato the mathematician who receives unalloyed praise. For example, Condorcet attributes to him the mechanical solution to the problem of duplicating the volume of a cube, while in fact Plutarch and other ancient sources tell us how vigorously Plato rebuked his pupils for offering constructions based on movements. Condorcet goes on to applaud those same pupils for "discovering the conic sections . . .; thereby, they opened up to genius that immense horizon where, until the end of time, it will be able to exercise its powers incessantly while with each step it sees boundaries recede behind it."[8] The Platonic mathematical tradition has become the protoform of Cartesian analysis and of its guarantee that solutions to more and more intricate geometrical problems can be constructed "*à l'infini.*"

Second, Condorcet presupposes that the Baconian dream of organized, global scientific research is nearing fruition simultaneously with revolutionary changes in the fabric of political life; needless to say, he would have been obtuse or jejune if this had not been his perception of the state of affairs in turn-of-the-century France, to say nothing of the rest of Europe and North America. The transition from dream to public reality on both fronts raises questions of organization and judicious planning at the same time that issues of a quite different sort appear fitfully, in the interstices of this dream. Above all, Condorcet must wrestle with the problem of the best alignment of universal political liberty among individuals with the optimal promotion of scientific progress among humanity as a whole. Ideally, the two projects ought to coincide at the point where the infinite perfectibility of scientific genius joins forces with the perfectibility of the moral faculties. "The degree of virtue to which a man can one day attain," he writes, "is as inconceivable to us as the degree to which the force of genius can be brought. Who knows, for example, if there won't be a time when our interests and our passions will have no more influence on the judgments which direct our will than, as we see, they have today on our scientific opinions."[9] In reality, their point of intersection is a concept of utility to which scientific and non-scientific individuals must be committed, even though "utility" fails to mask fully the heterogeneity of their basic desires.[10] At bottom, Condorcet must face the seemingly ineradicable difference between popular hedonism, sophisticated by each man's recognition of all other men's right to individual pleasure and utility, and the desire to know for its own sake, uncompromised by the passions of competition, ambition, and envy. Somehow, universal political liberty and the equally universal or imperial project of "apolitical" science must be made compatible with one another by principles of governance which are neither simply utilitarian nor simply scientific.

Third, unlike Bacon (but rather like Critias' old Atlanteans) Condorcet took mathematics to be the key to political insight and political organization. Mathematics lies at the heart of what he called the "social art" or "social science" intended to replace passion or narrowly-conceived self-interest by rationally measurable self-interest or utility in the decisions of the body politic. Although probability rather than naive geometry and arithmetic is now the armature on which the new "social art" turns, preoccupation with the precise is common to Critias' city-planners and Condorcet's decision-makers, each in his own way having forgotten or having obliterated the Platonic distinction between "the greater and the lesser" on the one hand, "the fitting and opportune" on the other—the distinction which animates the "kingly art" of the most thoughtful statesman.[11]

It is worth pausing briefly to take note of the most controversial formal result reached by Condorcet in his *Essay on the Application of Analysis to the Probability of Decisions Rendered by a Majority of Votes* of 1785.[12] This is better known to us today in the form of Arrow's Paradox of Social Choice, the mathematically established theorem that collective decisions in which each individual is concerned to secure the maximum number of votes cannot satisfy simultaneously the three conditions of non-dictatorship, the independence of irrelevant alternatives, and the so-called Pareto-condition (i.e., if 'a' is ranked higher than 'b' in the preference ranking of every individual, then 'a' should rank higher than 'b' in the collective or social preference). In cruder terms, enlightened, or at least mathematically precise, despotism more probably allocates to each person preferences closer to the top of his value-ranking than does majoritarian democracy.[13]

This technical result, which continues to perplex contemporary mathematical economists, brings home to us with remarkable clarity what might otherwise remain concealed in the happy formulation Keith Michael Baker gives of Condorcet's twin passions: "mathematics and the public good," namely the lability of their synthesis or contemporaneous fulfillment.[14] Let me try to capture this lability with the aid of all three presuppositions by which Condorcet's Atlantean vision is oriented.

Condorcet's mathematized social art or science is not only a research program to be carried out independently of public decision; it is also and more primarily meant to be an instrument for actual decisions, the heir to Leibniz's pacifying "*Calculemus!*" which puts an end to the fierce polemic of unenlightened passions.[15] In both instances, as research program and as public tool, mathematization capitalizes on specific assumptions sustaining Condorcet's global hopes. The first is the homogeneity of probability as a calculable measure in all domains of nature, including the human. As he writes in a manuscript note: "[All phenomena] are equally susceptible of being calculated and all that is necessary to reduce the whole of nature to laws similar to those which Newton discovered with the aid of the calculus is to have a sufficient number of observations and a mathematics that is complex enough."[16] Gilles Gaston-Granger's detailed study of Condorcet shows us, among other things, how necessary it is to abstract from the particularity of interests and characters (or souls) in order to furnish a uniform scale of mathematical probabilities. In this respect, human affairs are best observed and calculated from a nonhuman perspective.

However, this first assumption is buttressed by a second, viz., the essential homogeneity of human interests, such that the two in collaboration might be said to neutralize the difference between a human and a nonhuman perspective concerning the human and, in this way, to guarantee the universal applicability of mathematics:

> Since all men who inhabit the same country have more or less the same needs and since they also generally have the same tastes and the same ideas of utility, what has *value* for one of them generally has value for all.[17]

This passage from a contribution to the *Journal of Public Instruction* in 1795 inspires a number of considerations. First, we cannot fail to notice that *valeur* is on its way to becoming what it will thereafter remain—a quantitative and measurable term. The earlier attempt of the Physiocrats, Quesnay and Turgot, to discriminate between inalienable *biens* and alienable (or marketable) *valeurs* collapses, leaving only the latter as a yardstick of needs, tastes, and utilities.[18] Utilitarianism seems to be a direct product of mathematical homogenization. However, Condorcet still faces the difficulty of assuring the transnational uniformity of measurable utility, for the nationhood of each particular nation is a contingency spawned and sustained by custom and prejudice and thus is deeply at odds with the rational necessities of the mathematical social art. Enlightened imperialism seems to be the only way to extirpate an indefensible attachment to the local and ancestral while at the same time securing recognition for a single scale of value.[19] Condorcet's social art or science is cut from the same cloth as the contemporary effort, in which he also took part, to establish global units for the scientific measurement of time, distance, and so on. Both projects are impelled by the desire for "natural" invariance as a bulwark against the vicissitudes and revolutions of the locally or natively human. In the words of the report made to the *Académie des sciences* by the committee on which Condorcet served: a metric standard taken from Nature is "[t]he only means of excluding anything arbitrary from the system of measures and of being sure to preserve it unchanged, so that no other event, no other revolution in the order of the world can cast any uncertainty on it."[20]

So far, I have been trying to show how the mathematical basis of Condorcet's "social art or science" necessarily presupposes both the quantitative homogeneity and the qualitative uniformity of human interests. The course of history as sketched in the *Esquisse* should make us see how the political inequalities of the past have created the semblance of essential differences among men or among their desires. Liberty or the institutionalized equality of self-interest should therefore be trusted to dissolve this semblance. And yet, things stand differently in Condorcet's perception even of the revolutionized social future, and they stand differently because that future will continue to embody the difference between social utility and scientific discovery, however much the solution to the question of the best regime or the best life for mankind as a whole turns axially on the possibility of their coincidence or coalition.

In his *Fragment sur l'Atlantide* as well as elsewhere in his reflections, Condorcet is accordingly brought face to face with the tensions between his science of politics and his politics of science. He is thereby compelled to recollect or reenact (perhaps less thoughtfully) the Baconian dilemma, namely, the need to reconcile the few who are preoccupied with the kingdom of man over Nature, and the many who are concerned with the kingdom of man over man.²¹ These tensions come to sight in numerous ways, of which the following seem to me outstandingly revealing. First, while the social act of predicting and reaching collective decisions rests on the calculation of probabilities, the decisions to be made by the assembly of scientists are neither majoritarian nor mathematically predictable. On the contrary, Condorcet must take pains in the *Fragment* to establish non-mathematical procedures through which decisions and degrees of scientific research may be inoculated against the rivalries, enviousness, and other all-too-human passions of scientists themselves. Thus, he places the responsibility for electing senior administrators of science in the hands of their juniors, on the grounds that they can perceive the respective merits of proposed research programs with eyes unclouded by rivalry, envy, and other human passions.

Second, science is meant to become intramurally "apolitical" or free of the play of non-scientific passions, as far as that is possible, while also being extramurally insulated against the political in the form of national or international governments. Condorcet, like Bacon, sets his version of Salomon's House both physically and administratively apart from the life of the community. Unlike Bacon, he insists that the rulers of the community must judge, in the name of the body politic, which of the scientific projects "appears to merit either its concurrence or its munificence." This is intended to prevent the institutions of science from becoming genuinely apolitical.²²

The unavoidable interplay of the science of politics (Condorcet's "social art") with the politics of science (adumbrated in the *Fragment sur l'Atlantide*) and the disparity of interests that interplay involves stand out most clearly in Condorcet's reflections on the propriety of majoritarian voting in respect to matters reliably placed in the hands of enlightened scientists alone. In a key passage from his description of the penultimate epoch, Condorcet writes:

> Undoubtedly, there are matters on which the majority pronounces perhaps more often in favor of error and against the common interest of all; but, it still remains for the majority to decide which are matters concerning which it ought not rely immediately on its own decisions; it is for the majority to determine those whose reason it believes regulate [régler] the method that these ought to follow in order to reach the truth more surely; and the majority cannot abdicate the authority of deciding if their decisions have injured the rights common to all.²³

If the representatives of an egalitarian polity are unenlightened (or only on their way towards enlightenment) and, nonetheless, must select those whose reason should be substituted for their own and regulate the method used by those chosen, it is clear that the enlightened scientists must assume a transparently political policy if they are to persuade the majority that scientific discovery positively contributes to public utility or, less ambitiously, cannot "injure the rights common to all." Assuming that Condorcet is not writing disingenuously, we have to reckon with intersecting paradoxes. The unenlightened must be persuaded that enlightenment is the salient qualification for deciding matters lying beyond their (technical) competence; moreover, the unenlightened majority must give the appearance of wresting control of method from those who alone have mastered method—and this in direct contravention of Condorcet's insistence in the *Fragment* that, in matters of science, unequal weight must be given to more expert opinion. Egalitarian representatives have to juggle three distinct concerns: the preservation of rights common to all (and the embodiment of these in majority-decisions); public utility (present or prospective); and, finally, the advancement of scientific discovery. If these are capable of being harmonized with one another, it is not by any application of the calculus of probabilities but by the exercise of incalculably sagacious prudence.

In the absence of such prudence, the perception, on both sides, of an ineradicable heterogeneity of purposes or desires makes for a fragile compromise; the public powers are all the more mistrustful and envious of the aloof superiority of the enlightened scientists as the principle of equality among citizens takes root. The pride republican governors take in their egalitarian administration is "offended by the personal superiority that genius and enlightenment confer."[24] The scientists, for their part, recognize both that this superiority is the *sine qua non* of rational, progressive science and that only those with their desires impersonally fixed on the latter goal are suited for inclusion in an establishment distant from, but dependent on, the "concurrence or ... munificence" of their inferiors.

The desire for liberty—and hence the pursuit of self-interest or maximal personal utility which animates those who are naturally (or willfully) equal—goes against the grain of those for whom the infinite progress of discovery and invention is the sole good, even though it is acknowledged in these terms only by the superior or unequal few. The potential for conflict between liberty and progress now becomes self-evident, since the partisans of each principle subordinate all else to their chosen aim. Loyal Baconian or Cartesian as he is, Condorcet seems willing to place the "conquest and possession of nature" above the principle of civic liberty if and when the exercise of civil liberty retards the progress of science. Similarly, liberty of opinion does not, in the view of the scientist, include the opinion that the progress of science is not a good, if that opinion should become public policy.

However, Condorcet does strive to ameliorate this conflict and to mitigate the heterogeneity of desires from which it stems. "Utility," for him, plays a role akin to that of "generation" in Bacon's exemplary analogy between the philoprogenitive citizens of Bensalem and the fathers of Salomon's House.[25] While "utility" for the non-scientific many reduces to enlightened hedonism, for the scientific few it has global scope—the utility of mankind as a whole and into the indefinite future. When this difference in scope and meaning is ignored, each party gives the appearance of working towards a shared, univocal goal. The non-scientific many see in the "infinity of artifices" supported by their munificence the means for maximizing the self-interested pleasure of their senses and minimizing the contrary pains or malaise. The scientific few see in the applicability of their inventions incontrovertible epistemic validation of their discoveries. That this applicability is socially useful in the sense of enlightened hedonism is, so to speak, a bonus unaccountable by mathematical physics or by ethical standards independent of hedonism itself. In the end, Condorcet seems to appeal to something best, if not exhaustively, explained by a variant of that hedonism, namely, the painful embarrassment an individual scientist might feel if he fails to lend his talents to the utilitarian campaign on behalf of humanity as a whole, once this campaign has become an article of faith tying together the political many and the apolitical few into a single community. For Condorcet, this marriage of superiority with shame disguises and propagates the "natural" inequality of men and the heterogeneity of their desires.

In desperate concealment from his erstwhile republican interlocutors and avid to engineer the impending alliance of social egalitarianism with progressive science on his own artful terms, Condorcet seems to have had neither the time nor the temperament to think through to the end this or any of the preceding implications of his position. This reflective abstinence in the *Fragment sur l'Atlantide* as well as in the *Esquisse* to which it is appended marks the triumph, perhaps the Pyrrhic triumph, of his commitment not so much to technology as to technique, that is, to the view that the political or the human generally is a "problem" in the original mathematical sense, one for which there is a solution, constructive or insightful or both. And this triumph—if not commemorated then certainly domesticated as a home-truth for our own "Age of Enlightenment"—conceals the possibility that a pretechnical understanding of the technical may be more fruitful, even if less manageable, than a technical understanding of the technical. In less opaque terms, for Condorcet and his myriad progeny the political is "problematic," both mathematically and non-mathematically, just insofar as he and they seem intent on obscuring the place of the "polis" as the habitat of souls, that is, as the field in which diverse souls customarily exhibit their discrepant desires. We find ourselves living in a world quite thoroughly reshaped by Condorcet's "social art" and by the progressively operative science with which it is ambivalently, but persistently, allied. It is no longer immediately clear that *Aufklärung* can throw any more light on the quandaries, not the problems, by which such a world is held.

NOTES

[1] For Bacon, see *The Great Instauration and the New Atlantis*, ed. J. Weinberger (Arlington Heights, Ill.: AHM, 1980), p. 70; For Descartes, see *Oeuvres*. Compare L. Berns "Francis Bacon and the Conquest of Nature," *Interpretation* 7 (1978), 1-26; and R. Kennington, "Descartes and Mastery of Nature," in *Organism, Medicine, and Metaphysics* (Dordrecht, 1978), pp. 201-23.

[2] Condorcet, *Oeuvres*, ed. A. Condorcet-O'Connor and M. F. Arago (Paris, 1847; rpt. ed. Stuttgart-Bad Canstatt, 1968), Tome 8, p. 30. On Spinoza, see David Lachterman, "The Physics of Spinoza's Ethics," in *Spinoza: New Perspectives*, ed. R. Shahan and J. Biro (Norman: Univ. of Oklahoma Press, 1978), pp. 71-111; compare also A. Funkenstein, "Natural Science and Social Theory: Hobbes, Spinoza and Vico," in *Giambattista Vico's Science of Humanity*, ed. G. Tagliacozzo and Donald P. Verene (Baltimore: Johns Hopkins Univ. Press), pp. 187-212 and Pierre Jacob, "La politique avec la physique à l'âge classique," *Dialectiques* 6 (1974), 99-121.

[3] On the technical achievements in algebra, without regard to their wider philosophical and political implications, see Robin E. Rider, "Mathematics in the Enlightenment: A Study of Algebra, 1685-1800," (Ph.D. Diss., Univ. of California, Berkeley, 1980).

[4] For the *philosophes*, both Bacon and Descartes must be understood as revolutionaries and founders of empires; cf. D'Alembert, "Discours préliminaire" to 1778 edition of the *Encyclopédie*, Tome 1, p. xxvi, and Condillac, *L'Art de penser* II, 7. Condorcet, as well, praises Descartes for his audacity, which did more to bring men "to throw off the yoke of authority" than did the errors of his hypotheses (*Oeuvres*, VI, 169). These appreciations of the "revolutionary" direction of Cartesianism must be weighed carefully when the question of the philosophical provenance of the Enlightenment is at issue. At all events, in the picture offered here, the "party of humanity" is at the same time the party of modern mathematical physics.

[5] Cf. La Mettrie, *Anti-Sénèque, ou discours sur le bonheur, Oeuvres philosophiques* (Berlin, 1775), II, 13. On the tensions in the Enlightenment philosophy of history, see David Lachterman, "Descartes and the Philosophy of History," *Independent Journal of Philosophy* 4 (1983), 31-46.

[6] Little attention has been given to the theme of technical hypertrophy in this infrequently studied dialogue, even though it is evidenced in both the excessive innovativeness and the artificial geometrism of the Atlanteans' city-planning (see 115c-116b; 118c-3). Bacon's *The New Atlantis* is most illuminatingly and provocatively treated in H. B. White, *Peace Among the Willows* (The Hague: Martinus Nijhoff, 1968) and J. Weinberger, "Science and Rule in Bacon's Utopia: An Introduction to the Reading of the *New Atlantis*," *American Political Science Review* 70 (1976), 865-85. See also L. Berns, n. 1.

[7] For the text, see *Oeuvres*, VI, 597-660. Portions of this have been translated by Keith Michael Baker, *Condorcet: Selected Writings* (Indianapolis: Bobbs-Merrill, 1976), pp. 283-300. Important for the understanding of this text of 1793 and of its place in Condorcet's thinking generally are K. M. Baker, *Condorcet: From Natural Philosophy to Social Mathematics* (Chicago: Univ. of Chicago Press, 1975); Giles Gaston Granger, *La Mathématique sociale du Marquis de Condorcet* (Paris: P. U. F., 1956); Alexandre Koyré, "Condorcet," *Journal of the History of Ideas* 9 (1948), 131-52; and Frank Manuel, *The Prophets of Paris* (Cambridge, Mass: Harvard Univ. Press, 1962), pp. 81-96.

[8] "*Esquisse d'un tableau historique des progrès de l'esprit humain*," *Oeuvres* VI, 68, 74, 71. For Plato's objections to the mechanical or instrumental solutions of the Delian Problem, see Plutarch, *Vita Marcelli* 305 EF, and *Questiones Conviv.* 718 EF. Condorcet's *lapsus* in fact reveals the profound gap separating the classical from the radically modern understanding of "construction" in mathematics.

[9] Condorcet, *Ed. cit.* p. 628.

[10] Compare Rousseau, *Émile*: "As soon as we have contrived to give our pupil an idea of the word 'Useful,' we have got an additional means of controlling him." Jean-Jacques Rousseau, *Émile* (London: J.M. Dent, 1974), p. 141. It would seem that in the logic of modern self-understanding, this issue of homogeneity vs. heterogeneity is prior to the question of equality vs. inequality.

[11]For Condorcet on probability, see, in addition to the works of Baker and Granger cited above (n. 7), C. G. Gillespie, "Probability and Politics: Laplace, Condorcet and Turgot," *Proceedings of the American Philosophical Society* 116 (1972), 1-20; on the general setting, compare Ian Hacking, *The Emergence of Probability* (London: Cambridge Univ. Press, 1975). The mathematical aspect of Plato's *techne basilike* is discussed in *The Statesman* 283C-285B; see also Jacob Klein, *Plato's Trilogy: Theaetetus, the Sophist, the Statesman* (Chicago: Univ. of Chicago Press, 1977), pp. 172-77, and P. Kucharski, "La conception de l'art de la mesure dans la Politique," *Bulletin de l'Association G. Budé* 19 (1960), 459-80.

[12]Not included in the standard edition. For analysis of the Introduction, see K. M. Baker, n. 7, pp. 225-44.

[13]Kenneth Arrow, "Values and Collective Decision Making," in *Philosophy and Economic Theory*, ed. F. Hahn and M. Hollis (Oxford: Oxford Univ. Press), pp. 119-26. On some of the philosophical consequences of Arrow's theory and its sources in "classical" (i.e., modern) political economy, see A. Sen, "Rational Fools," in *Philosophy and Economic Theory*, pp. 87-109, and "Behaviour and the Concept of Preference," *Economica* 40 (1973), 241-59.

[14]Baker, *Condorcet*, n. 7 above, p. xii.

[15]Cf. Leibniz, *Philosophische Schriften*, ed. Gerhardt, VII, 200. Condorcet's attempt to work out his own version of a *characteristica universalis* is of considerable interest here; see G.-G. Granger, "Langue universelle et formalisation des sciences: Un fragment inédit de Condorcet," *Revue d'histoire des sciences* 7 (1954), 197-219.

[16]Cited from F. Manuel, *Prophets*, p. 65, taken from an unpublished manuscript by Condorcet in the Institut de France (p. 326, n. 19).

[17]*Oeuvres* I, 558.

[18]See M. Foucault, *Les mots et les choses* (Paris: Gallimard, 1966), pp. 202-14, on this debate among the Physiocrats.

[19]On what I am calling "enlightened imperialism," compare Bacon, *The New Organon*, Book I, Aphorism CXXIX. Bacon, however, is unlike Condorcet in expressly retaining a scale of heterogeneous "values" or ends of desire.

[20]See Maurice Crosland, " 'Nature' and Measurement in Eighteenth-Century France," *Studies on Voltaire and the Eighteenth-Century* 87 (1972), 277-309; the passage cited is on page 292.

[21]This comes through most clearly in Bacon's fables of the Sphinx (or, science) and of Orpheus (or, philosophy) in *De sapientia veterum*. According to the latter myth, men turn to the study of civil affairs only when they lose hope of succeeding in the "great work" of philosophy, viz., "The restitution and renovation of the things corruptible." Bodily resurrection (or immortal preservation) is the nobelest goal of science; "great and lofty services to the commonwealth" take second place to this aim. (*Works*, ed. Spedding and Ellis [New York: Hurd and Houghton, 1864], VI, 647-48).

[22]*Fragment sur l'Atlantide*, p. 657. It should be noted that Bacon, too, recognized the necessity of public munificence to the progress and fruition of the new sciences. See his "A Speech Touching the Recovery of Drowned Mineral Works," prepared for Parliament while he was Lord Chancellor.

[23]*Esquisse*, p. 177.

[24]*Fragment sur l'Atlantide*, p. 600.

[25]The "Feast of Tirsan" serves as the metaphorical meeting ground of the ordinary Renfusans ("ovine in nature"), who honor most those who can produce thirty living descendants, and the fellows of Salomon's House, who give birth to endless discoveries and inventions. The symbolism also evokes the issue of population control, of importance in the *Critias,* where the ancient Athenians are said to keep their population as close to 20,000 as possible (112D), and of express concern to Condorcet (Manuel, *Prophets,* p. 61 and n. 14).

II. NATURE

NATURE IS A WOMAN: THE DUCHESS OF NEWCASTLE AND SEVENTEENTH-CENTURY PHILOSOPHY

SOPHIA B. BLAYDES

Margaret Lucas Cavendish, the Duchess of Newcastle (1623?-73), often reminded her readers that women were part of God's creation. On one occasion, she offered a lovely prayer that is ostensibly from Nature to God:

> Eternal God, Infinite Deity,
> Thy Servant, NATURE humbly prays to Thee,
> That thou wilt please to favour Her, and give
> Her parts, which are Her Creatures, leave to live....[1]

Assuring God of her adoration, Nature prays for all of "Her" creatures:

> That in their shapes and forms, what e're they be,
> And all their actions they may worship thee...

Depicted as the all-encompassing and nurturing female, Nature seems to be reminding God that women are part of His creation and that they are among those creatures who adore Him and for whom Nature prays:

> For 'tis not onely Man that doth implore,
> But all Her parts, Great God, do thee adore....

Printed on the last page of the Duchess's *Philosophical Letters*, the prayer comes sometimes from Nature and sometimes from the Duchess herself, who is both the narrator of the poem and one of Nature's parts. Affirming in just a few lines the conventional view of a feminine nature—Mother Nature or Mother Earth—and masculine power—God the Father or the Creator—the Duchess also voices her fears that God will not favor her or give her "leave to live," although she is one of Nature's parts, and that He will not accept her "actions" as worship of Him. She feared that, because she was a woman, she would enjoy neither a long and healthy life nor lasting fame and honor after her death.

Unable to have children, the Duchess sought to fulfill her nature and to avoid oblivion in ways that were available to her. From 1653 through 1671 she wrote fourteen books that she published in twenty-four separate editions.[2] Exercising her gift from God, the Duchess applied her natural talents, writing poetry, fiction, and philosophy in order to instruct and entertain others in those ideas that she knew were virtuous and honorable. Yet, the honor and fame that she expected did not come, as her poem suggests, because she was a woman. Instead of being honored for her books, she was judged mad. If her fiction and poetry were disparaged—and they were—what chance did her volumes of philosophy have?

They had little, apparently, for she was accused on the one hand of plagiarism for using words that no woman could possibly know and on the other for being too original. In response, the Duchess wrote letters, poems, and dedications defending her books and her reasons for writing them. Such behavior from a noblewoman during the Restoration period was inappropriate. As Caroline Merchant noted recently, "Disorderly woman, like chaotic nature, needed to be controlled."[3] The ideal wife, Merchant continues, "combined goodness, virtue, intelligence, and common sense, but not too much 'learning and pregnant wit,' for 'Books are a man's prerogative.' "[4] The Duchess may have seen herself as the ideal wife, if we are to believe her many comments on the subject, but to Samuel Pepys, the Restoration diarist, she was a "mad, conceited, ridiculous woman" whose husband was "an asse to suffer her to write."[5] Dorothy Osborne, after reading the Duchess's *Poems and Fancies*, wrote to her future husband, Sir William Temple, that the Duchess "is a little distracted, she could never be so ridiculous else to venture at writing books."[6] The Duchess's errors, to write and to publish, are blamed first on her husband, and then on her apparent madness.

Over the centuries, the judgment of her age has prevailed. Only recently have most of the Duchess's books been read and studied, partly because they illuminate woman's condition during the Restoration.[7] Some readers have even found that some of her writing is as notable as her celebrated biography of the Duke.[8] No one, however, has examined each of her seven philosophic books individually for ideas or style. A brief discussion of a few of her ideas and her method of presenting them over fifteen years might help readers judge both the Duchess's sanity and her achievement.

A reading of the seven works in the order in which they were published reveals that the Duchess changed and developed as a writer and philosopher from 1653 through 1668. Her first three volumes—*Philosophical Fancies* (1653), *The Philosophical and Physical Opinions* (1655), and *Philosophical and Physical Opinions*, another edition (1663)—were written during the Newcastles' exile forced by the Civil War and then during their isolation from the Royalist mainstream after the Restoration in 1660. The fourth—*Philo-*

sophical Letters (1664) — was written after the Duchess had read other philosophers' works and had thus ended her intellectual isolation. Her last three philosophical works — *Observations Upon Experimental Philosophy, 2nd edition* (1668) — are careful responses to others' ideas and their methods as well as clarifications of her own. In the first three she was proud of her abilities, what she and her age considered natural reason. She was especially proud because she was untutored and thus independent of others' ideas. She remained proud in the next four volumes, even after she had read others and compared her ideas with their philosophies. It is through the comparisons that she affirmed herself and established her identity as a thinker.

The first woman to write for publication, the Duchess was the most radical of "Reason's Disciples," Hilda L. Smith's label for seventeenth-century English feminists.[9] In 1653, when the Duchess published her first philosophic work, she was the wife of the exiled commander-in-chief of the Royalist forces who was declared by Parliament the greatest enemy to Cromwell. Under those circumstances, one might question her haste to publish her thoughts on atoms, matter, and motion. She explains in *Philosophical Fancies* that the book occupied her idle time for three weeks while she was in England trying to salvage some of her husband's fortune. In a prefatory poem she writes:

> THOUGHTS, run not in such strange phantastick waies,
> Nor take such paines to get a *Vulgar Praise*.
> The *World* will scorne, and say, you are all *Fooles*,
> Because you are not taught in common *Schooles*.
> The World will think you mad, because you run
> Not the same *Track*, that former times have done.
> Turn foolish *Thoughts*, walke in a *Beaten Path*,
> Or else the *World* ridiculously will laugh. (sig. B3)

Her rejection of scholarship echoes, among others, sentiments expressed by Sir William Davenant and Thomas Hobbes, both friends of her husband. They, too, disdained books for the development of either poetic wisdom or practical leadership. In his "Preface" to *Gondibert* (1651), Davenant emphasizes the need for original, not imitative poetry.[10] Hobbes's introduction to *Leviathan* (1651) repeatedly states that wisdom comes not from books but from self-study and that is what leads to knowledge of "Man-kind."[11] Like them, the Duchess upheld the natural and free exercise of one's faculties. Thus, she was in the mainstream of the tradition of writers in the seventeenth century that honored reason and sought to solve problems through it.[12]

An octavo of 112 pages, *Philosophical Fancies* is her smallest and shortest book. Only seventy-one of those pages contain her philosophic discussions. The others have prefatory poems, epistles, and dedications. The volume ends with a five-page list of questions she could have posed and answered if she had had time. Irritating as the mix of materials is today, such prolegomena and epilogues, as we know, were common in the seventeenth century. Davenant outdoes his heroic poem *Gondibert* with a prefatory letter to Hobbes that is not only long but also of greater interest than the poem. He appends Hobbes's answer and an epilogue as well.

The Duchess opens her philosophic discussion with a prose passage:

> There is no *first Matter*, nor *first Motion*; for *matter* and *motion* are *infinite*, and being *infinite*, must consequently be *Eternall*; and though but *one matter*, yet there is no such thing, as the *whole matter*, that is as one should say, *All*. And though there is but one *kinde* of *matter*, yet there are *infinite degrees* of *matter*, as *thinner* and *thicker*, *softer* and *harder*, *weightier* and *lighter*; and as there is but one *matter*, so there is but one *motion*, yet there are *infinite degrees of motion*, as *swifter* and *slower*; and *infinite changes of motion*.... (pp. 2–3)

The next passage ends simply: "the *Minde*" is "*Matter moving*, or *Matter moved*" (p. 2). Like other philosophers of her day, Gassendi and Descartes among them,[13] she declares herself a materialist. Her language, if not her concerns, might have amused or annoyed her readers. Even today, we find her redundant and foolish. We forget that the young Duchess was not alone in her concerns or their mode of expression. She is writing in a way that would have been acceptable if she had not been a woman. Her error is that she insists upon an original vocabulary. For example, in her paragraph "Naturall *or* Sensitive War," she writes:

> ALL *Naturall War* is caused either by a *Sympatheticall Motion* or an *Antipathetical Motion*. For *Naturall Warre*, and *Peace* proceed from Selfe-preservation, which belongs to the *Figure*; for *nothing* is annihilated in *Nature*, but the particular *Prints*, or *severall shapes* that *Motion* makes of *Matter*; which *Motion* in every *Figure* strives to maintain what they have created: for when some *Figures* destroy others, it is for the maintenance or security of themselves: and when the Destruction is, for Food, it is *Sympatheticall Motion*, which makes a particular Appetite, or nourishment from some *Creatures* to others; but an *Antipatheticall Motion*, that makes the *Destruction*. (p. 14)

Behind the passage lurks the familiar Hobbesian theory of the state, which begins in the *Leviathan* with the observation that man, who is by nature self-seeking and hostile toward others, seeks to establish a contract with a sovereign for protection.[14] The Duchess's idea is not so radical; it is her language that is an impediment. Such notions demand certain terms that the Duchess did not use.

The small volume includes her early atomist theory and introduces her interest in remedies and recipes. Again, part of a familiar concern, medicine and cookery were included in many more-honored books. Sir Kenelm Digby included recipes and cures as part of his "chemical secrets" in his philosophic treatises. In one case, he informs his readers through a kind of rebus or pictorial code "How to fix silver into gold by mercury and mercury precipitate." Today, we may be amused by his charming errors.[15] Despite the similarities in some methods and ideas, Hobbes, Digby, and the Duchess evoked different responses from their readers. They still do. Hobbes informs; Digby amuses; and the Duchess annoys. One might question whether the judgment of the Duchess arises—and arose—from criteria that are repressive. In a recent study, Marcie Kaplan notes that most psychologists and psychiatrists assess a woman's mental health and social stability so that

> the typical psychologically healthy woman is more submissive, less independent, less aggressive, more emotional and emotionally expressive, more excitable and more concerned about appearance. If a woman rejects this stereotype, she is an unhealthy woman. . . .[16]

Is it possible that the Duchess's contemporaries judged her by her unconventional behavior and that today we judge her according to her nonsensical philosophy that conformed to the notions of her time?

In 1655 the Duchess published her second volume, *The Philosophical and Physical Opinions*. The work includes the Duchess's "physical" or medical comments that she had omitted from the first book. More ambitious, the book is still another that the Duchess completed in isolation. Testifying to that isolation are a number of defenses of her original genius and her honesty, evidently prompted by the response to her first philosophic book. In the first of many such testimonials, the Duke writes, "If you have read any such things before, i'le be bold to burn the Book" (sig. A2ᵛ). Defending her against the contradictory charges of plagiarism and originality, the Duke argues that "in natural Philosophy, one opinion may be as true as another, since no body knows the first cause in nature of any thing" (sig. A2ᵛ). After defending her gifts and her books, the Duke moves to the real cause of the attacks on his wife: "here's her crime, a Lady writes them, and to intrench so much upon the male prerogative, is not be forgiven . . ." (sig. A2ᵛ).

The Duchess defends herself on the altar of nature. In language that is clear, rational, and authoritative, yet laden with homely imagery, she describes her condition and her proximity to philosophic ideas. Comparing her situation to those of other women, she writes:

> as many others, especially wives go from church to church, from ball to ball, from collation to collation, gossiping from house to house, so when my Lord admits me to his

company, I listen with attention to his edifying discourse, and I govern my self by his Doctrine; I dance a measure with the muses, feast with the Sciences, or sit and discourse with the arts. (sig. A4)

In easy, colloquial terms, the Duchess emphasizes the nobility and predictability of her situation; she is, after all, following the example of her husband, her lord, whose will she accepts. He is her model and her law. Her case is more poignantly stated when she explains:

Since nature is so generous to distribute to those that fortune hath cast out, and education hath neglected, why should my readers mistrust nature should be sparing to me, who have been honourably born, carefully bred and nobly married to a wise man. . . . (sig. A4^v)

Insisting upon her own sense of decorum and fulfillment of her natural role, she writes, "I am my Lords Scholer." Although a woman, the Duchess claims that she has received wisdom as God's bounty, which she exercises according to ideals learned first from her family and then from her husband. Expecting censure yet seeking praise, the Duchess suggests that her book may be worth reading. Emphasizing the credos of her age and class, she insists that "my head is so full of my own natural phancies, as it had not roome for strangers to boord therein, and certainly natural reason is a better tutor than education" (sig. B2).

Particularly noteworthy in her second book of philosophy is a passage that relates to John Locke's theories. To the Duchess, "remembrance is but a pattern taken from the Memory, and the memory but a pattern taken from the objects" (p. 116). It is an important point because she feared that only memory provided immortality, and that memory, like everything else, was matter that would turn to dust.

The third volume of her philosophy was published in 1663 and continues to be a product of her isolation. When the Newcastles returned to England from exile in 1660, they were neglected by their restored monarch. Isolated and with more time than she had expected to have, the Duchess reviewed and restated her theories in a folio of five hundred pages. She abandoned some, like the atomist ideas. Even so, she claims in this volume that "the best Natural Philosophers are those that have the Clearest Natural Observation, and the Least Artificial Learning" (sig. d2^v), which, of course, places her among the best. Introducing each of her ideas with the qualifier, it "seemeth to human sense and reason," she explains that "Natural Philosophers go and study not beyond Sense and Reason; and according to the proportion of that Sense and Reason that I have, I shall declare my Philosophical Opinions" (p. 27). Just as she had in the other volumes of philosophy that she published within a ten-year span, the Duchess emphasizes her originality and her virtue as an uneducated, natural philosopher. She sees herself as one of nature's creatures, endowed with reason and writing talent. In each she relies upon her reason for her conclusions, which she expresses in direct, simple language. Isolated first as an exiled Royalist in Europe and then by the court and king in England, she produced books that served to isolate her even more.

By 1664, when the Duchess published her fourth book of philosophy, *Philosophical Letters*, she had read four philosophers of her day, Descartes, Hobbes, Henry More, and Van Helmont. Although she had disclaimed knowledge of others' philosophies in her previous works, now she reveals that she will present her arguments that have arisen from her study of them. A lengthy commentary on the four *Philosophical Letters* demonstrates that the Duchess abandoned her proud isolation, educated herself, acquired a more conventional philosopher's vocabulary, and discovered a frame of reference for her own ideas. Using the genre that she found most congenial, the informal friendly letter, the Duchess presents her arguments with the philosophers in a series of clear statements. Through an order imposed by the form, the Duchess carefully explains her ideas so that her fictitious correspondent can readily understand each point. She intends to dispute with the philosophers, she writes, "according to the ability of my Reason . . ." (p. 3). Explaining that each philosopher seems to espouse his own truth, she states with justifiable self-righteousness, "All what I speak, is under the Liberty of Natural Philosophy, and by the Light of Reason onely, not of Revelation; and my Reason being not infallible, I will not declare my Opinions for an infallible Truth . . ." (p. 17). She will not declare her opinion as truth, as the philosphers have; she will instead suggest that her views have as much validity as another's, even a man's.

Reflecting the form of others' speculative philosophies, *Philosophical Letters* has four sections. In the first, twenty-nine letters discuss Hobbes's *Leviathan*. Too detailed to summarize, the Duchess's appraisal includes Hobbes's views of perception, motion, and imagination. In her arguments with Hobbes, the Duchess is surprisingly effective and sensible. For example, she states that Hobbes in his chapter on reason defines reason to be "nothing else but *Reckoning*: I answer, That in my opinion Reckoning is not Reason itself, but onely an effect or action of Reason . . ." (p. 36). By the thirtieth letter the Duchess writes that she has begun to read Descartes. Intending "to pick out onely those discourses which I like best" (p. 97), she soon argues with the philosopher over his views of mind and matter—she insists that they are inseparable (p. 111)—and over his notion that only man has reason. By the forty-second letter, the Duchess summarizes the philosophies of Hobbes and Descartes and then restates her own beliefs:

> First I am for self-moving matter, which I call the sensitive and rational matter, and the perceptive and architectonical part of nature, which is the life and knowledge of nature. Next I am of an opinion, that all Perception is made by corporeal, figuring self-motions, and that the perception of foreign objects is made by patterning them out. . . . (p. 127)

The second portion of the book opens with an attack on Henry More and his book *Antidote*. If, as More states, everyone believes in a god, why does More write a book that is designed to prove the existence of God? "[U]nless," she writes, "it be to shew Learning and wit: In my opinion, to prove that, which all men believe . . . is the way to bring it into question" (p. 137). She argues with More's view that man is a superior being. Like Mother Nature in her poem, the Duchess notes the excellence of "the rest of natural Creatures . . ." (p. 147). Emphasizing her materialism as she reviews More's philosophy, the Duchess denies his view of "Incorporeal substance" and in doing so corrects one of her early errors:

> When I did write my first conceptions in Natural Philosophy, I was not so experienced, nor had I those observations which I had had since; Neither did I give those first Conceptions time to digest, and come to a maturity or perfect growth, but forced them forth as soon as conceived, and this made the first publishing of them so full of Imperfections, which I am much sorry for; but since that time, I have not onely reviewed, but corrected and altered them in several places. . . . (pp. 232-33)

After reviewing others' philosophies, the Duchess reconsidered her own. She does not hesitate to inform her readers of her changes and the reasons for them.

Her education, however, did not prepare her for the chemistry of Van Helmont, whose work she reviews in the third section of the book. Unable to understand much of it, the Duchess accuses the scientist of making "such a mixture of Divinity, and natural Philosophy, that all his Philosophy is nothing but a meer Hotch-potch, spoiling one with the other" (p. 248). Relying upon her own natural reason, the Duchess is able to point out convincingly that Van Helmont's views are not so enlightened as they appear. At one point, she notes, Van Helmont attributes the trembling of the earth to the judgment of God for man's sins (p. 264). He also writes of a gold-making stone. The Duchess cannot resist chiding him: "I wish with all my heart, the poor Royalists had had some quantity of that powder; and I assure you, that if it were so, I myself would turn a Chymist to gain so much as to repair my Noble Husbands losses . . ." (p. 285).

The last section of the book restates some of the Duchess's ideas and confirms her change from an original, isolated writer who claimed a unique and uninformed approach to the world of ideas into a philosopher who correlates her work with that of others. She discarded some notions and reaffirmed others. Still a materialist, she finds no distinction between the world of matter and reason. She emphasizes that natural philosophy is above those dissensions caused by theology and law. *Philosophical Letters*, the product of her self-education, also reveals the Duchess's antipathy toward the new sciences, for she insists that one discovers truth through reason, not through experiments.

In 1666 the Duchess published *Observations upon Experimental Philosophy*, considered by some to be her most important scientific treatise.[17] In another five hundred folio pages, the Duchess offers a critique of experimental science that she calls "this brittle Art" (sig. b). She accuses the experimental scientists "in these latter times" of busying "themselves more with other Worlds, then with this they live in" (sig. b^v). As a natural philosopher, she writes:

> I confess, I have but little faith in such Arts, and as little in Telescopical, Microscopical, and the like inspections, and prefer rational and judicious Observations before deluding Glasses and Experiments. . . . (sigs. b-b^v)

She even recommends her "Pastime" to others; "if all Women that have no imployment in worldly affairs, should but spend their time as harmlessly as I do, they would not commit such faults as many are accused of" (sig. c^v). She encourages her readers to avoid those writers who

> confound both Divinity and Natural Philosophy, Sense and Reason, Nature and Art, so much as in time we shall have rather a Chaos, than a well-order'd Universe by their doctrine: Besides, many of their writings are but parcels taken from the ancients; but such Writers are like those unconscionable men in Civil Wars, which endeavour to pull down the hereditary Mansions of Noble-men and Gentlemen, to build a Cottage of their own; for so do they pull down the learning of Ancient Authors, to render themselves famous in composing books of their own. (sig. c2)

This, her fifth philosophic work, she explains, addresses "our Modern Experimental and Dioptrical Writers" just as she had presented "some famous and eminent Writers in Speculative Philosophy" (sig. d^v) in her fourth. Dismissing her first three works in favor of her *Philosophical Letters* and this volume, the Duchess informs her readers:

> as for Learning, that I am not versed in it, no body, I hope, will blame me for it, since it is sufficiently known, that our Sex is not bred up to it, as being not suffer'd to be instructed in Schools and Universities; I will not say, but many of our Sex may have as

much wit, and be capable of Learning as well as men; but since they want Instructions, it is not possible they should attain to it; for Learning is Artificial, but Wit is Natural. (sig. d2ᵛ)

Expending time and effort to learn what others had written, the Duchess still prefers the untutored, natural wit to the learned, artificial instruction that men enjoyed. In an effort to reach all readers, the Duchess applauds simplicity in language, just as she honors naturalness in philosophy. She suggests to her readers, "If you do write Philosophy in English, and use all the hardest words and expression which none but Scholars are able to understand, you had better write it in Latine . . ." (sig. d2ᵛ). She advocates her own approach, which is to shun artificial, difficult language so that one's writing "may be the better understood by all, learned as well as unlearned . . ." (sig. e).

The text of *Observations* contains a clear, often amusing, view of experimental philosophy. The Duchess derides the "toys" of men — microscopes, telescopes — and experiments, equating such activities with women's work (pp. 102–03). She also writes of the ancients, whose wisdom she praises. Yet, "I, being a woman," she writes, "do fear they would soon cast me out of their Schools . . ." (p. 2). After reviewing Thales, Plato, and Aristotle, among others, in the second part of the book, she ruefully observes that they will have lasting fame even though their reasoning is often faulty, "For Fame doth all, and whose name she is pleased to record, that man shall live, when others, though of no less worth and merit, will be obscured, and buried in oblivion" (p. 32).[18]

In 1668, *Observations* was brought out in a second edition, but unlike her other works, this seems to be a reprint rather than a reworking. One might theorize that her books had been burned in 1666 in the Great Fire of London that destroyed the publishing industry for a brief time. In 1668 not only was the volume reprinted but altogether six of the Duchess's books came out in new editions.[19] The only change in the second edition of *Observations* was that she omitted some of her lengthy explanations.

That same year, 1668, the Duchess published her last philosophic work, *Grounds of Natural Philosophy*, which she dedicated to "all the Universities in Europe" (sig. A2). Less discursive and thus more controlled now, even without the added control of the epistolary form, *Grounds* presents most of the same ideas that the Duchess had expressed in her other, earlier works. Her approach to matter remains the same. She writes:

> Matter is what we name *Body;* which Matter cannot be less, or more, than Body; Yet some Learned Persons are of opinion, That there are substances that are not Material Bodies. But how they can prove any sort of Substance to be no Body, I cannot tell. . . . (pp. 1–2)

The Duchess continues in the work to refer to other philosophers and their ideas, but she dismisses any of their ideas that contradict her observations or defy her natural reason.

From her discussion of matter, the Duchess moves through 232 pages that she divides into thirteen sections. First, she explains her philosophy and her basic vocabulary so that her ideas will be clearly understood by her readers. Then she addresses topics that range from men to dropsies and appearances to vegetables. More provocative is the lengthy passage that the Duchess has appended to the thirteen sections. The appendix, about one hundred pages long, is divided into five parts that cover topics that obsessed her. She refers to her own oppressive illnesses. Under some stress, the Duchess considers God, sin, society, birth, dreams, Hell, and other worlds. Finally, using a philosophic format, she presents a discussion between various parts of her mind. She discusses her restoration to health after illness and to life after death. Seeking, it appears, reassurance of her immortality, the Duchess considers her own return from death, her husband's after his death, and the return to life of her dead family. Although a work of philosophy, *Grounds* becomes in its last pages an expression of the Duchess's greatest fears. As she had in her poems, plays, and fantasies before, the Duchess here lets her imagination momentarily satisfy her. The last section of the work becomes an expression of her desire for survival, restoration, and immortality.

It is that final hope for immortality that drove the Duchess throughout her life to write and to publish what she wrote. To the Puritans, the king, and his court, she was mad, a rebel against society. Yet, it is possible that she believed she was fulfilling the role that was hers by birth, breeding, and marriage. Born to an aristocratic family, the Duchess enjoyed an idyllic, pastoral childhood despite her father's death while she was an infant. Her desire to write and to instruct was bred in her by her family, especially her mother who applied sweet reason in her role as head of the family. Later, with a husband who was as supportive and reasonable as he was attractive, the Duchess could pursue in an intellectual and social vacuum activities she had enjoyed as a child.[20] Consistent with her breeding and her experience, the Duchess did not defy convention through her published philosophy. Instead, she fulfilled her nature; and her books, especially her philosophic books, explain what her nature was.

The Duchess's philosophical works offer evidence that their writer had a mind capable of instruction, albeit self-instruction. Her readings of other philosophers and her discussions with her husband reveal the plight of the intelligent seventeenth-century woman. She could not attend their schools, but she could nonetheless learn from the philosophies of men. After 1664, most of her foolish redundancies lessened, her vocabulary became more conventional, and her faith in her basic natural philosophy was affirmed. She did abandon her earlier atomist theories and her notions of the uncorporeal world, but she found that her disdain for experimental philosophy intensified so that she continued to attack what she now perceived even more clearly to be the foolishness of vain pursuits.

Is that all one can say of her philosophical works, that they permitted her to develop and change? Clearly there is more merit to them than that. At the very least, some of her seven volumes should be important in the history of philosophy. Placing her books beside those of such figures as Sir Kenelm Digby reveals that her prolixity and her topics are typical of other philosophers who were not derided. What was it after all that she proclaimed but a faith in reason, proclaimed also by Descartes and Locke, among others, a fundamental materialism, considered also by Hobbes, and a skepticism toward the experimental sciences, echoed by Henry More. That the history of science proves her wrong on some of her notions is beside the point. That was not why she was ridiculed and rejected.

There is no mystery to her rejection. She was a woman who dared to trespass into the world of learning, traditionally the man's preserve. There is, however, a mystery to her motives. One explanation is that she did not defy the laws that dictated the behavior of seventeenth-century noblewomen. Rather than defiance, each of her books conveys the impression of a wife who is obedient to her husband's wishes and a woman who expects to be judged by a code of honor and truth that she remembers from her past and sees again in her husband. A thoughtful, ambitious woman, the Duchess found that her self-imposed isolation, of which she had been so proud, had become her prison. In an effort to attract fame and honor during her lifetime and immortality after death, the Duchess sent copies of her books to universities in England and Europe. Her wishes were in part fulfilled, but not as she had expected. Safely stored for centuries, the volumes survived so that we can now read some of them and wonder.

Of the seven volumes, the last three might interest today's reader the most because they provide more of a seventeenth-century context for the Duchess's ideas. Of the three, however, the last volume would intrigue those readers who are fascinated by the revelation of a person through literary forms, philosophical treatises, and biographical statements. To read the Duchess is to learn about woman's condition in the late seventeenth century and, in particular, the condition of one intelligent noblewoman. Not always easy to read, the Duchess is a natural philosopher who is able to express basic ideas in clear, homely language and to argue with some of the more prominent figures of her day. As such, she is refreshing. She is also a woman who seems to be out of tune with her times. It seems from her poem on Nature that the Duchess learned a bitter lesson during her lifetime. Like Nature, she was endowed with talents. However, like Nature, she was not free to exercise them because she was a woman.

NOTES

[1] *Philosophical Letters* (London, 1664), p. 543. Subsequent references will be cited parenthetically in the text.

[2] *Poems and Fancies* (London, 1653, 1664, 1668); *Philosophical Fancies* (London, 1653); *The World's Olio* (London, 1655, 1671); *The Philosophical and Physical Opinions* (London, 1655, 1663); *Nature's Pictures* (London, 1656, 1671); *Playes* (London, 1662); *Orations of Divers Sorts* (London, 1662, 1662, 1663, 1668); *Philosophical Letters* (London, 1664); *CCXI Sociable Letters* (London, 1664); *The Description of a New World* (London, 1666, 1668); *Observations upon Experimental Philosophy* (London, 1666, 1668); *The Life of . . . William Cavendishe* (London, 1667); *Grounds of Natural Philosophy* (London, 1668); *Plays never before Printed* (London, 1668). Subsequent references to each of the works will be cited parenthetically in the text.

[3] Caroline Merchant, *The Death of Nature: Women, Ecology, and the Scientific Revolution* (1980; rpt. San Francisco: Harper and Row, 1983), p. 127.

[4] Merchant, p. 166.

[5] *The Diary of Samuel Pepys*, ed. Robert Latham and William Matthews (Berkeley: Univ. of California Press, 1976), IX, 123. For another commentary on Pepys's response to the Duchess, see the article by Samuel I. Mintz, "The Duchess of Newcastle's Visit to the Royal Society," *JEGP* 51 (1952), 168-78.

[6] *The Letters of Dorothy Osborne to William Temple*, ed. G.C. Moore Smith (1928; rpt. Oxford: Clarendon Press, 1947), p. 37.

[7] See, among others: Virginia Woolf, *The Common Reader* (1925; rpt. New York: Harcourt, Brace and World, 1953); Gerald Dennis Meyer, *The Scientific Lady in England 1650-1760*, California Univ. Publications in English Studies, Nos. 11-12 (Berkeley: Univ. of California Press, 1955); Alison Adburgham, *Women in Print* (London: George Allen and Unwin, 1972); Patricia Meyer Spacks, *The Female Imagination* (New York: Knopf, 1975); C. Merchant, *The Death of Nature: Women, Ecology and the Scientific Revolution* (1980; rpt. San Francisco: Harper and Row, 1983); and Hilda L. Smith's *Reason's Disciples: Seventeenth-Century Feminists* (Urbana: Univ. of Illinois Press, 1982). A contemporary of the Duchess, Lucy Hutchinson, is said to have imitated the life of the Duke by the Duchess in an effort to write the life of her Puritan husband, Colonel John Hutchinson; see *Beyond Their Sex: Learned Women of the European Past*, ed. Patricia H. Labalme (New York: New York Univ. Press, 1980), p. 165.

[8] See among others: Clara Whitmore, *Women's Work in English Fiction* (New York: Putnam, 1910); Henry Ten Eyck Perry, *The First Duchess of Newcastle and Her Husband as Figures in Literary History* (Boston: Ginn, 1918); B. G. MacCarthy, *The Female Pen: Women Writers, Their Contribution to the English Novel 1621-1744* (Dublin: Cork Univ. Press, 1946); Douglas Grant, *Margaret the First* (Toronto: Univ. of Toronto Press, 1957); Jean Gagen, "Honor and Fame in the Works of the Duchess of Newcastle," *The Bulletin of the West Virginia Association of College English Teachers* 4 (1977), 44-52; "Memory is a Future," *Enlightenment Essays* 10 (1979), 102-19; "The Poetry of the Duchess of Newcastle: A Pyramid of Praise," *The Bulletin of the West Virginia Association of College English Teachers* 6 (1981), 26-34; Philip Bordinat, "The Duchess of Newcastle as Literary Critic," *The Bulletin of the West Virginia Association of College English Teachers* 5 (1979), 6-12.

[9] *Reason's Disciples*, p. 75.

[10] Sir William Davenant, "Preface," *Gondibert* (London, 1651), pp. 9, 34-36.

[11] Thomas Hobbes, *Leviathan*, ed. C. B. MacPherson (1651; rpt. England: Penguin, 1977), pp. 82-83.

[12] Robert E. Schofield, *Mechanism and Materialism: British Natural Philosophy in an Age of Reason* (Princeton, N.J.: Princeton Univ. Press, 1970), p. 3.

[13] Merchant, p. 192.

[14] Hobbes, pp. 223-24.

[15] Sir Kenelm Digby, *The Closet of the Eminently Learned Sir Kenelme Digby, Kt.* (London, 1669), p. 1.

[16] Wray Herbert, "Curing Femininity," *Science News* 124 (September 1983), 170.

[17] Gerald D. Meyer, "Science for Englishwomen, 1650-1769, the Telescope, the Microscope, and the Feminine Mind," Diss. Columbia 1951, p. 29.

[18] Bound with the volume is *The Description of a New World*, a work of both literary and philosophic interest. A fantasy, it is literally worlds from the discourse that precedes it. The Duchess explains in her preface to it that she appended the fanciful story to the more serious work because "The end of Reason, is Truth; the end of Fancy, is Fiction . . ." (sig. a3ᵛ).

[19] *Observations* . . ., 2nd edition; *Description of a New World*, another edition: *Poems and Fancies*, 3rd edition; *Orations*, 2nd edition; and the Latin translation of the life of the Duke, *De Vita*. . . .

[20] "A true Relation of my Birth, Breeding, and Life," in *Natures Pictures* (London, 1656), pp. 156-57.

WOLLSTONECRAFT VERSUS ROUSSEAU: NATURAL RELIGION AND THE SEX OF VIRTUE AND REASON

MELISSA A. BUTLER

"In every age," Mary Wollstonecraft wrote, "there has been a stream of popular opinion that has carried all before it and given a family character, as it were, to the century."[1] The metaphor may be mixed; nevertheless, there are two good reasons for using this passage as a starting point in reconsidering Wollstonecraft's work. First, it warns us about reading too much of contemporary feminist theory back into the eighteenth century. Second, it invites us to examine some of the "family characteristics" which her work shares with other writers of the age.

As we look back in search of feminist perspectives, or "a woman's view" on the eighteenth century, we might beware of searching too hard for strong ancestral resemblances to ideas we cherish today. If we allow ourselves to become preoccupied with tracing the lineage of those ideas that give a "family character" to our own age, we risk losing an opportunity to make contact with the milieu that shaped older notions. To twentieth-century critics, who see Wollstonecraft's *Vindication of the Rights of Woman* as the first great feminist work, her real originality consists in the fact that she "recognized the similarity between the plight of oppressed womankind and that of oppressed mankind and concluded that the solutions were identical."[2] Evaluations of this sort clearly place Wollstonecraft in a modern perspective—a perspective shaped by streams of nineteenth- and twentieth-century opinion.

The themes of this volume—God, man, and nature—summon us back to the ideas that gave a "family character" to Wollstonecraft's century. They invite us to consider the arguments that she adopted to appeal to her contemporary audience. As one commentator noted, her work was "as much a page torn from the journal of the French Revolution as Paine's *Rights of Man* or Condorcet's *Sketch*."[3] Though Wollstonecraft often stood against the stream of opinion of her day—she attacked Burke, Rousseau, Gregory, Fordyce, and a host of other opinion molders of the time—she did so in an eighteenth-century voice speaking with the clear accents of rationalism.

This essay attempts a re-examination of some aspects of her conflict with Jean Jacques Rousseau as expressed in *The Vindication of the Rights of Woman*. Although Wollstonecraft concerned herself primarily with his analysis of the position of women, she did not limit her criticism to a narrow discussion of gender roles. Rather, her attack on Rousseau took place on several levels. She argued that Rousseau had not only misconstrued the nature of woman but misunderstood God and man as well. Her opening arguments against him turned not merely on questions concerning woman's nature nor on details about the education of Emile and Sophy; rather, the debate began with an assault on his version of natural religion and his denial of the value of human perfectibility. It is a mistake to think that Wollstonecraft merely wished to modify and extend to women Rousseau's views on man's nature and education. Her challenge went much deeper than that. Indeed, she adopted a different theology and also rejected Rousseauistic pessimism and nostalgia — or, to use her language, "sensibility" — in favor of "reason."

"Reason," of course, was a central concept for eighteenth-century writers. Its place in Wollstonecraft's scheme was clarified at the very beginning of *The Vindication of the Rights of Woman* when she set out her "first principles":

> [T]he perfection of our nature and capability of happiness must be estimated by the degree of reason, virtue and knowledge that distinguished the individual and direct the laws which bend society and that from the exercise of reason, knowledge and virtue naturally flow is equally undeniable, if mankind be viewed collectively (*VROW*, 40).

"Reason" Wollstonecraft defined as "the simple power of improvement, or more properly speaking, of discerning truth" (*VROW*, 94). She believed that reason alone established human preeminence over the rest of creation. Yet her faith in reason was not without certain limits. She was aware that reason was often used in service of prejudice. In fact, prejudice seemed especially likely to adopt the guise of reason in arguments concerning women. Wollstonecraft charged that many men, Rousseau among them, made a "great show of reason" when they discussed woman's place. The show was necessary because their "arguments were supposedly deduced from nature." Wollstonecraft's task, then, was to provide the substance instead of the mere show of reason. For her, despite occasional half-hearted attempts at a kind of casual empiricism ("I've seen more girls than Rousseau has"), the strongest, most convincing arguments were to be made by using reason to lead back to God and then to proceed from there to explain His divine plan. Wollstonecraft might have applauded Rousseau's efforts to undermine absolutism and orthodoxy in religion.[4] No doubt she would have supported the task Rousseau assigned to the Savoyard vicar in *Émile*, namely, establishing the principles of natural religion by "yield[ing] nothing to human authority nor the prejudices of our native land" and by following the light of reason alone.[5] Yet she disagreed strenuously with several important elements of Rousseau's version of natural religion.

Before discussing the specific areas of disagreement, it might be helpful to summarize Rousseau's natural religion as outlined in *Émile*. There, through the character of a Savoyard priest, Rousseau presented the principles of natural religion reached by agreeing to "admit as self-evident all that I could not honestly refuse to believe and to admit as true all that seemed to follow directly from this" (*Émile*, 231). His method led him to conclude (in Cartesian fashion) that he existed and had sense impressions; that the natural state of matter was rest; therefore, a body in motion implied a mover; and that, since there was movement in the universe, there must be a mover. He was not able to explain complicated mechanisms such as the order of the universe, but he was able to "admire the workman in the details of his work" (*Émile*, 237). He reasoned that blind chance could not have led to the harmony he perceived about him; and so, he came to believe that "the world is governed by a wise and powerful will"—a God (*Émile*, 239).

Beyond these observations, Rousseau's vicar could say little about God, except in relation to himself. His search for his place in the order of things led him to discover his own species and its particular excellence, namely, its greater power to act and will and use intelligence: "Man was lord of the earth" (*Émile*, 240). Yet, as Rousseau's vicar looked around, he found confusion and disorder in place of the harmony and proportion of nature. These ills, he reasoned, must have been produced by mankind. The distressing discovery of man's responsibility for evil led him to the altogether happier discovery of the soul. This came about as he reflected upon man's nature and realized human nature had two principles: the first led to the study of eternal truths, to the love of justice and true morality; the other led "downward to himself" and "made him a slave of the senses and of the passions" (*Émile*, 241). Rousseau concluded that man was free to act and was animated by an immaterial substance. Since man acted freely, his actions were not part of the system set out by Providence. Man had been made free to choose good and refuse evil.

Further reflection on the disorder and evil in the world led Rousseau's vicar to reason that the soul must survive the body. He argued that it would be unfair of God to give man the idea of good and order or to implant the idea that, if one were just, one would be happy, and then default on that promise. Since, in life, he had observed that "the wicked prosper and oppression continues," the soul must live on for God to keep faith with men (*Émile*, 245).

Next, Rousseau attempted to deduce principles of conduct from this simple theology. How was man to choose between courses of action? He should consult only himself, but even within himself he might hear conflicting voices—namely, the voice of reason and the voice of conscience. For Rousseau, it was conscience, not reason, that truly raised man above the beasts. Reason often deceived men. Reason spoke of self and had to be explicitly rejected as a sufficient foundation for virtue. On the contrary, man should let conscience—"the innate principle of justice and virtue by which in spite of our maxims we judge our own actions or those of others to be good or evil"—be his guide (*Émile*, 252). This was a principle of the heart, a principle of feeling. It grew out of the earliest stirrings of natural pity through which man related to others. The decrees of conscience were not judgments but feelings. How was a man to choose between actions? How was he to know if reason was deceiving him? Rousseau's answer was twofold: first, move slowly, wait until the first beams of judgment no longer dazzled, until the eyes had become adjusted to the light of reason which then illuminated rather than blinded; or, second, rely on the first feelings (*Émile*, 254).

Wollstonecraft took issue with Rousseau's version of natural religion at several points. First, she rejected the idea that human beings were responsible for the existence of evil in the world. God, it would seem, was at least a co-conspirator. Wollstonecraft could not imagine how human beings, who were but "helpless creatures . . . called from nothing," could "break loose and boldly learn to know good by practicing evil, without his permission" (*VROW*, 42). Implicit in this comment was the key to Wollstonecraft's whole understanding of the role of evil and its relation to reason. Quite simply, for her, evil was a part of the divine plan. The existence of evil gave mankind the opportunity to "rise to excellence by the exercise of powers implanted for that purpose" (*VROW*, 42).

Ultimately, the power that enabled human beings to rise to excellence was reason. Consideration of the role of reason in religion introduces several more contrasts between Rousseau and Wollstonecraft. The first concerns the relationship between reason and arguments for the immortality of the soul. Although Wollstonecraft appreciated the beauty of Rousseau's arguments for spiritual immortality, she herself reached the same conclusion by a very different route. For Rousseau, souls must live on as a matter of justice— "the good will be happy, because their maker, the author of all justice, who has made them capable of feeling, has not made them that they may suffer; yet they have suffered in this life and it will be made up to them in the life to come" (*Émile*, 247). Wollstonecraft presented her best argument for immortality in highly mechanistic terms—"everything looks like a means, nothing like an end or a point of rest" (*VROW*, 94). This unfinished quality in human development led her to accept immortality. She believed that reason unfolded only gradually. This drove her to her conclusion, for she maintained that "were man created perfect, or did a flood of knowledge break in upon him when he arrived at maturity, that precluded error, I should doubt whether his existence would be continued after the dissolution of the body" (*VROW*, 94). Thus, for Wollstonecraft, "the stamen of immortality is the perfectibility of human reason" (*VROW*, 94). This approach to the question of immortality implicitly placed a different and much greater demand on God. In Wollstonecraft's view, the deity did not simply restore balance and harmony as he did for Rousseau; rather, he gave play to man's efforts to achieve the full development of human powers, to the point the humans might become fit to "enjoy a more godlike portion of happiness" (*VROW*, 43).

Wollstonecraft also differed from Rousseau by insisting that reason was what established human beings' preeminence over creation. For Rousseau, it was not reason, but conscience that separated men from beasts:

> Conscience! Conscience! Divine instinct, immortal voice from heaven; sure guide for a creature ignorant and finite, indeed, yet intelligent and free . . . apart from thee, I find nothing in myself to raise me above the beasts—nothing but the sad privilege of wandering from one error to another, by the help of an unbridled understanding and reason which knows no principle (*Émile*, 254).

Conscience, for Rousseau, was a kind of moral instinct. As such, his idea of "conscience" seems analogous to what others had termed "common sense," "sensibility," or "untaught feeling." Wollstonecraft had already had occasion to reject all of these "mysterious instincts" which supposedly "reside in the soul and instantaneously discern truth, without the tedious labour of ratiocination."[6]

In contrast, it was clear to Wollstonecraft that "only the power of exercising understanding" raised humans above the level of brutes; and it was this exercise of reason that produced the "first glimmerings of morality" (*VROM*, 77). There could be no moral purpose served by merely extolling "good dispositions," described as "instincts." To her, it was clear that virtue was not a matter of instinct. She literally despaired at the thought of this: "If virtue be an instinct, I renounce all hope of immortality" (*VROM*, 77).

How did Rousseau's and Wollstonecraft's views on natural religion relate to their debate on the position of women? Wollstonecraft's review of Rousseau's natural religion, combined with her analysis of his educational principles, led her to charge him with "inconsistency" in his description of "Sophy, or woman." She attacked him vigorously for abandoning his own principles. He had, after all, asserted that "the morality of our actions consists entirely in the judgments we ourselves form with regard to them" (*Émile*, 250). Moreover, where matters of religion were concerned, Rousseau argued that "no man is free from a man's first duty; no one has a right to depend on another's judgment" (*Émile*, 270). Yet, when Rousseau described Sophy, his ideal woman, he maintained that "her conduct should be controlled by public opinion and her religion ruled by authority" (*Émile*, 340). Women, in general, were unable to make judgments in matters of religion and so "they should accept the judgments of father and husband as that of the church" (*Émile*, 340). For Rousseau's Sophy, the details of religion were too difficult. Consequently, she was instructed by her parents to wait until she had grown up, when her husband would teach her what she needed to know about religion. Rousseau thus absolved women from "man's first duty," for he assured his readers that should a woman follow a false religion out of obedience, "the docility which leads [her] to submit to nature's laws would blot out the sin of error in the sight of God" (*Émile*, 340).

Wollstonecraft reviewed Rousseau's plans for Sophy and asked quite pointedly, "Is this a preparation for immortality?" (*VROW*, 142). Submission and obedience might possibly render women blameless, but they certainly did not elevate the sex. Reliance on another's judgment, or reliance on opinion, dulled women's moral senses. Women, as rational creatures, should be "incited to acquire virtues which they may call their own, for how can a rational being be ennobled by anything that is not obtained by its *own* exertions?" (*VROW*, 92).

In Rousseau's scheme of things, however, man and woman cultivated different talents appropriate to their different natures and roles in the world. Thus, as Rousseau argued, one should "consult the women's opinions in bodily matters, in all that concerns the senses; consult the men in matters of morality and all that concerns the understanding" (*Émile*, 306). Women and men naturally complemented each other: "woman should discover an experimental morality, man should reduce it to a system. Woman has more wit, man more genius; woman observes, man reasons. Together they provide the clearest light and the profoundest knowledge which is possible to the unaided human mind" (*Émile*, 350).

In Rousseau's own system, where reason was less important, and conscience more so, women needed only to consult "the inner voice which is [their] guide." Women would need to reconcile conscience with respect for public opinion. To perform this task, reason was needed, but not the glorious sort of reason Wollstonecraft exalted. Rousseau questioned whether women were capable of solid reason at all and whether the exercise of reason could ever be "compatible with becoming simplicity" (*Émile*, 345). He concluded that the reason that taught a woman her duties was quite simple. It revealed to her "the natural and self evident consequences of her position," namely "the obedience and fidelity which she owes to her husband, the tenderness and care due her children" (*Émile*, 345).

In contrast, given the primacy of reason in Wollstonecraft's system, she could never have accepted Rousseau's version of the complementarity of the sexes, since, reduced to its simplest terms, this approach gave reason to men and sensibility to women. Unlike Rousseau, Wollstonecraft had rejected sensiblility as a possible ground of morality: "Sensibility is not reason" (*VROW*, 109). Sensibility could not lead either to virtue or immortality.

For Wollstonecraft, the path to virtue and immortality was the same for men and women. Whereas Rousseau had emphasized woman's end as "pleasing man," Wollstonecraft resolutely maintained that "the first object of laudable ambition is to obtain a character as a human being, regardless of distinction of sex" (*VROW*, 34). There was no difference between the sexes in their goals. In addition, there was no difference between the sexes with regard to the means of attaining their goals. If women had souls (and Wollstonecraft assumed that she could get her audience to agree to that much), they must have the capacity to save their souls; and, she noted, "there is but one way appointed by Providence to lead *mankind* to either virtue or happiness." That way was through reason. Further, she argued that there was not "a shadow of reason to conclude that [men and women's] virtue should differ in respect to their nature. In fact, how can they, if virtue has only one eternal standard?" she asked (*VROW*, 59).

Rousseau, on the contrary, had followed others in insisting that there was indeed a distinction between the virtues of man and of woman. Woman's virtues included obedience, chastity, modesty, neatness; man's virtues included boldness, frankness, uprightness, and courage. Yet Wollstonecraft decried all such schemes which set up strength on one side and weakness on the other and called both virtues. In particular, she rejected Rousseau and all other writers who endeavored to distinguish between the virtues of man and of woman. Indeed, Wollstonecraft argued that "the cold arguments of reason give no sex to virtue" (*VROM*, 112). Those who saw women's chief business as inspiring man's love or serving as a repository of oxymoronic qualities — "fair defects," "amiable weakness," "beautiful weakness," etc. — clearly implied that nature had made an eternal distinction between the qualities that dignify a rational being and the animal perfections, "so that women's duty and happiness must clash with any preparation for a more exalted state" (*VROM*, 112).

What Wollstonecraft wished to effect was nothing less than a "revolution in female manners." By asserting that virtue had no sex, she was herself effecting part of the revolution. The very word "virtue" in its etymology is derived from the Latin stem *vir* for "man," that is, male. The common phrase "manly virtue" was, in a sense, a redundancy. Throughout her writings, Wollstonecraft herself was somewhat hampered by terminology. She wrote against Burke "in manly fashion" to condemn those "emasculated by effeminacy." In the *Vindication of the Rights of Woman*, she openly challenged and appropriated elements of a male-dominated terminology. She commented that people inveighed against "masculine" women, "but if it be against the imitation of manly virtues, or more properly speaking, the attainment of those talents and virtues, the exercise of which ennobles the human character, and which raise females in the scale of animal being, when they are comprehensively termed *mankind*; all those who view them with a philosophic eye, must, I should think, wish with me that they may every day grow more masculine" (*VROW*, 33).

Though Wollstonecraft acknowledged no difference between men and women with respect to the kind of virtue or reason or knowledge they acquired, she did recognize a difference in degree. Female development had been retarded by all those men who, like Rousseau, had sought to impede and degrade the sex by considering them as women only, and not as human creatures. As Wollstonecraft reviewed the status of women in her own age, she realized that

> [woman] has always been either a slave or a despot . . . each of these situations equally retards the progress of reason. The grand source of female folly and vice has ever appeared to me to arise from narrowness of mind; and the very constitution of civil government has put insuperable obstacles in the way to prevent the cultivation of the female understanding (*VROW*, 96).

At this point we return to another difference between Rousseau and Wollstonecraft—one that is critical for her analysis of the rights of woman, namely, her views on the perfectibility of man. Wollstonecraft's case for the rights of woman was not, by and large, an empirical case. She did not attempt to cite examples to prove that women are or can be the intellectual equals of man. She refused to make a case for the exceptional woman and was interested instead in the general improvement of the sex as a whole. Consequently, her argument was made against the way the sex had been treated as a whole. Yet her appeal was not simply to the generosity of men, nor was it even to their sense of justice. Wollstonecraft made an argument geared to appeal to the "interest" of men who might well have thought that it was in their interest to oppress women. Her argument was that until "women are more rationally educated, the progress of human virtue and improvement in knowledge must receive continual checks" (*VROW*, 77).

Against Rousseau, who denied that there were progressive improvements in virtue or knowledge, this argument had little force, as Wollstonecraft realized. But, it was not her purpose simply to develop a complete critique of Rousseau's views of women. Had that been the case, we might have expected a full-blown analysis of the *Second Discourse*. Instead, she used the ideas which gave a "family character" to her age to appeal to a contemporary audience beyond Rousseau. Her faith in reason permitted her to reject Rousseauistic sensibility and nostalgia. Her belief in progress allowed her to realize that, in the final analysis, the greatest difference between herself and Rousseau consisted in the fact that "Rousseau exerts himself to prove that all *was* right . . . I [exert myself to prove] that all will *be* right" (*VROW*, 43).

NOTES

[1] Mary Wollstonecraft, *A Vindication of the Rights of Woman* (New York: Norton, 1967), p. 52. Hereafter cited as *VROW*.
[2] Ralph M. Wardle, *Mary Wollstonecraft: A Critical Biography* (Lawrence: Univ. of Kansas Press, 1951), p. 157.
[3] H. N. Brailsford, *Shelley, Godwin and Their Circle* (New York: Henry Holt and Company, n.d.), p. 206.
[4] Eleanor Flexner, *Mary Wollstonecraft: A Biography* (New York: Coward, McCann and Geoghegan, 1972), p. 163.
[5] Jean Jacques Rousseau, *Émile*, trans. Barbara Foxley, (New York: E.P. Dutton, 1911), p. 278.
[6] Mary Wollstonecraft, *A Vindication of the Rights of Man* (Delmar, New York: Scholars' Facsimiles and Reprints, 1975), pp. 68-69. Hereafter cited as *VROM*.

"ALL MEN AND BOTH SEXES":
CONCEPTS OF MEN'S DEVELOPMENT, WOMEN'S EDUCATION, AND FEMINISM IN THE SEVENTEENTH CENTURY

HILDA L. SMITH

In the seventeenth century, both works about education and the institutions based on these works were predicated upon the developmental stages of young males. Contemporary feminists, such as the Duchess of Newcastle, Bathsua Makin, and especially Mary Astell, when criticizing these writings and institutions for the exclusion of women, noted their broader implications for justifying and perpetuating educational inequality between the sexes. To understand the basis for these feminists' criticisms, it is necessary to examine their response to educational theory directed towards men which defined in major ways male and female characteristics generally.

I propose to deal first with general education treatises and then with the response of women writers, as exemplified in the thought of Mary Astell. I will argue that these women, who may be regarded as the first feminists, were the earliest to understand clearly that attitudes towards male education were at the root of the exclusion of females from equal institutions and opportunities. Seventeenth-century educational theory and individual textbooks for the young directed to male teachers and students pursuing a classical education advance a scheme for universal human behavior in male terms. This was, of course, no universality at all.

The assumption existed, both linguistically and experientally, that "children" and "boys" were synonymous terms. Educational writers spoke consistently of a boy's education as preparing him to acquire mature habits in language which implied that male experience comprised the whole of human experience. Such was not the case for educational writings about girls. The terms "children" and "girls" were not used interchangeably, nor was it assumed that girls' lives as adult women reflected universal experience. Thus, the developmental continuum from boyhood to manhood and from childhood to adulthood were wholly overlapping, and what boys did determined the universal behavior for childhood. Girls' and women's experience, on the other hand, was seen as particularistic, having relevance for that sex only.[1]

Hoole's *Children's Talk*, for example, was intended to teach schoolboys to speak Latin with as great a facility as they did English. In a dedication to two London citizens, a Mr. Joseph and a Mr. Humphrey, Hoole, a grammar school teacher, made clear how "boys" and "children," "parents" and "men," were interchangeable terms:

> Your desires are (worthy Sirs) to have your Sons gain a faculty of speaking Latin, as well as English; . . . but the many difficulties that attend the work . . . , and with Children not thoroughly grounded, many of whose Parents being illiterate or . . . do not care . . . to have their Sons brought up in a Scholar-like Way hath made most of our Profession . . . not at all . . . undertake the Task.[2]

These "sons" or "children" possessed difficulty because they had not reached the age of "discretion," a condition presumably applicable to both sexes. One result of this terminology was the assumption that all children grew up to be men. When speaking about age differences, educational writers contrasted the terms "children" and "men," but only "girls" with "women."

Hezekiah Woodward's *Childe's Patrimony* was a solemnly religious program for educating boys to follow God and to respect the will of their heavenly as well as earthly father. The bulk of the book dealt with boys' education and followed the pattern of assuming children were boys. Woodward wanted to ensure a properly religious development from infancy to old age which erects "faire Edifices to the Lord, which are the Children of Men." Woodward devoted a single chapter to girls' education, and here the term "child" was dropped and the word "girl" employed. The goal of this work was to provide parents and teachers with a text preparing the child as he "goeth along from infancy to Childhood, thence to youth, and so on till he brings his childe to a growne, yea an old man, full of dayes."[3]

This continual exchange between male experience and the universal is evident as well in works that argued education should be extended beyond the ranks of the gentry. Christopher Wase's *Considerations Concerning Free Schools as Settled in England* argued the need for bringing learning to the boy destined for the plow. By necessity, his work addressed the class limitations inherent in the English educational system but ignored limitations based on sex. Here, as elsewhere, the term "scholar" was restricted to males, whether young or mature. Wase contended that "the right bred scholar sees reason not to magnify himself against the industry of other honest laborers and Artists, since God hath charg'd his support in good measure on part of their labors." He invested women's efforts in education with typically feminine characteristics describing Queen Elizabeth's endowment of grammar schools and colleges as the acts of "a tender Mother" in her efforts to establish educational institutions for "the Children of her Country," though only males were involved. Here was a striking example of the particularity imposed on women's behavior, while universality was tied to men: the national policy of a queen was described in terms of motherhood, while males attending grammar schools and colleges became the children of the country.[4]

The writings of more prominent figures also fit this pattern. John Milton's education writings reveal its contours well. Milton's most important essay focusing solely on the issue of education was the "Tractate of Education," published during 1644. Milton, who believed reforming education was "one of the greatest and noblest designs that can be thought on, and for the want whereof this nation perishes," proposed a national educational program involving schools that housed approximately 150 students in towns throughout the country. These schools, which combined grammar school and university studies, were to include traditional training in classical languages, the study of ancient Near Eastern languages, and courses in philosophy, theology, history, and rhetoric, etc., as well as a strong component of military training. It was a rigorous program, seemingly little suited to large numbers of the English population.[5]

Critical of current preparation in the classical languages, Milton wanted his students to learn a language thoroughly before they were asked to write or speak difficult passages. He had little use for language training for its own sake and stated that, if someone knew "all the tongues" of the earth, but not their solid teaching, he should no more "be esteemed a learned man as any yeoman or tradesman competently wise in his mother-dialect only."[6] Milton's educational plan was built upon a progression of learning languages well, then studying history, geography, and the Bible, and finally tackling rhetoric, theology, and philosophy.

His educational system, although a national program, gave no consideration to girls. Its goal was to produce "brave men and worthy patriots," to teach students "to delight in manly and liberal exercises," and to "scorn all their childish and ill-taught qualities."[7] Such an elaborate plan, which served the needs of only one sex, reiterates the general identification of scholarship with men and their duties in life. It demonstrates why Mary Astell felt compelled to demand a rigorous general education for women and why she thought it obtainable only in a separate institution.

John Locke's *Some Thoughts Concerning Education* also focused on the education of boys but revealed a greater sensitivity to the fact that he was doing so. In his first chapter, which has the charming title of "Health, Tenderness, Warmth, Feet," Locke includes the following:

> I have said *He* here, because the principal Aim of My Discourse is, how a young Gentleman should be brought up from Infancy, which, in all things will not so perfectly suit the Education of *Daughters*; though where the difference of Sex requires different Treatment, 'twill be no hard Matter to distinguish.[8]

Locke was at least more cognizant of the sexual boundaries implicit in his educational proposals than were his contemporaries. Seemingly, he also favored more similar treatment for boys and girls. In a letter to the mother of children he tutored, he stated the principles of female education, "wherein there will be some though no great difference, for making a little allowance for beauty and some few other considerations of the sex, the manner of breeding of boys and girls, especially in their younger years, I imagine should be the same." There is here, as there is in his *First Treatise*, an understanding of the importance of sex division in organizing society.[9] It is to be regretted that Locke did not write more systematically on the topic of female education, for he may have undercut the seventeenth-century link between "standard" behavior and male education.

Why did educational theorists and practitioners generally express such a link in their writings? Was it merely a question of oversight — of course they weren't writing about girls or women, so why should they come to mind when making educational generalizations? Did it represent common usage, so that authors gave little thought about generalizing boys to children or speaking of boys but not girls as scholars? Or, did it represent a much more fundamental and systematic way of categorizing human beings and human behavior generally?

The Athenian Mercury, a late seventeenth-century periodical whose editors were especially interested in the education of women, included the phrase "all men and both sexes." Such a phrase sounds strange to our ears until we realize that "all" was a word which referred to condition and not sex. Further, when one reviews the literacy statistics gathered by David Cressy, on ecclesiastical court witnesses, one notes that the men were divided by all kinds of conditions, but women from servants through duchesses were combined. This does not reflect a society where women were all of one class, but one in which sex was a separate category of human division. In some ways these distinctions are still with us, if less systematically and overtly than during the 1600s. It is no accident that Chartists during the 1840s spoke of universal suffrage when they were speaking of extending political rights to additional males. "Universal" was a term connected to condition or class, not sex. And today, when speaking of youthful understanding, we are apt to speak of a "schoolboy vision" of the world, for age divisions are still readily connected to male experience.[10]

Christopher Wase included a representative listing of these divisions which indicated their self-exclusive nature: "All ages, sexes, ranks, relations in every condition, all capacities, ly [sic] under some duty towards God and man." They echoed a 1596 division of prospective students into "burgesses, artisans, labourers, women or girls." Occupations or sex denoted a person's status, but not both. To understand why women were so easily excluded from the best of education in the seventeenth century, we must realize how the relationships among sex, age, and condition established male development (including education), leading to maturity and wisdom. Women's education, segregated from this progression, trained women for their limited function within English society. Authors, in dividing human behavior, used three distinct ways to categorize people: age, condition, and sex. When authors were engaged in defining the first two, they ignored the third; condition and age were divisions allotted to males. It is not that people in the seventeenth century, or any other up to the most recent year, failed to note that women aged or that there were poor as well as rich women, but when writing about condition they did not focus on sex.[11]

A small group of seventeenth-century feminists, writing from 1650 through 1710, took issue with the English education system. Among them, the Duchess of Newcastle resented identification of serious scholarship with the university, while Bathsua Makin proposed advanced secondary training for girls, comparable to the best grammar schools. Elizabeth Elstob pursued her Anglo-Saxon studies outside the university but was angered that women were denied access to linguistic training. On the continent, Anna van Schurman was pursuing a scholarly career and corresponding with Makin concerning the need for women to have a serious education. All of these women understood the connection between dominance within society and male monopoly of educational institutions. Mary Astell, building upon the earlier educational writings of Newcastle, Makin, and Hannah Woolley, continued this demand for advanced education and carried the effort a step further through the practical proposal of a women's college.

Astell realized that denying women the best of scholarship was based on degrading their God-given talents, defining them as something other than scholars, and denying them the possibility of developing toward independence of mind and station. It was not just that a few women were denied the right to join the philosophic and scientific ranks during the 1600s, but that all women were omitted from a universal continuum of age and condition where education and public responsibility led to enhanced status and rewards.

Astell saw women's advancement dependent on their access to a quality education. Convinced that none of the institutions currently available to women provided adequate training, she proposed a college for females who wanted to immerse themselves in the best philosophic, theological, and historical works. Astell deplored what customarily passed for a woman's education: the socially correct training of boarding school or tutor, emphasizing dance, a little polite French, music, and fancy needlework tied to elementary reading; or the more religious and solemn education of the Puritans which stressed domestic competence, religious piety, and familial duty; and even the more liberal education of a Fénelon that would include science and philosophy but simplified for the ladies. Mary Astell desired women to employ their minds in the same ways and with the same texts as the most learned men.[12]

Her college did emphasize Christian belief and good works, but this did not prevent her from allying Christian values with the best education. In fact, her Christianity was at the heart of her reasoning. God had created both men and women with rational souls, and it was both sacrilegious and foolish to subvert God's will by denying women the ability to employ their reason to the fullest. Further, Christianity demanded that each person be responsible for her or his salvation, and women could not rely on the wisdom or goodness of husband or minister to guarantee their faith. Only through a thorough understanding of religious texts could they resist the temptations by which those who possess simple piety are endangered. She realized these views diverged from the typical religious advice for women. Women might be, Astell granted, "taught the Principle and Duties of Religion, but not acquainted with the Reasons and Ground of them; being told 'tis enough for her to believe, to examine why, and wherefore belongs not to her."[13] Astell's views clearly ally her with the intellectual values of her century, both the scientific revolution and rationalism expressed by philosopher and popular writer alike. Francis Bacon had stated, "The Inquiry, Knowledge, and Belief of Truth is the Sovereign Good of Human Nature," a view central to Astell's thought. Astell's contribution was to remind scholars that the pursuit of truth was as central and important for females as for males. Her principal intellectual mentor was Descartes. She agreed wholeheartedly with his assertion of the primacy of the individual mind, his distinctions between faith and reason, his assurance of God's existence and benevolence, and his methods of systematic thought. In her *Serious Proposal to the Ladies, Part Two*, she outlined in detail the process by which an individual should proceed from clear and concise ideas, to the conclusions formulated through continual testing of first principles, and ultimately to truth. In her school, women were not encouraged to memorize, nor to repeat lessons by rote, but to grapple with ideas and develop their minds in order to think clearly and rationally about any new subject they might encounter. This open-ended approach to training women to deal systematically with the range of human experience set her work off from standard religious and educational tracts directed towards women.[14]

Mary Astell argued that pursuit of scholarship was a means to alter women's lives, their images of themselves, and society's views of them. Astell never tolerated a smattering of learning or culture for her sex. She complained, "there is a sort of Learning indeed which is worse than the greatest Ignorance: A Woman may study Plays and Romances all her days, and be a great deal more knowing but never a jot the wiser." Unlike many religious writers,

Astell was not centrally concerned with the immoral nature of romances. Rather, she wanted women to stretch their minds by reading the most challenging works: those works "writ with Order and Connexion, the Strength of whose Arguments can't be sufficiently felt unless we remember and compare the whole System."[15]

In arguing for the pursuit of scholarly excellence among women and in establishing a challenging and heavily Cartesian program of study in her college, Astell had few counterparts. She argued that no restraints should be placed on the female mind in studying philosophy, theology, history, or government, and that great harm had been done to the quest for excellence by associating its attainment with a single sex. Traditionally, genius has been intertwined with masculinity, leaving women some claim to creativity and much to a kind of untutored "intuition," but little to abstract and systematic intelligence built upon a unique or original view of the universe, of human behavior, or of mechanical or mathematical operations. This stereotype has held over time whether or not women were admitted to institutions of higher education, were taught math and science, or had access to machinery or technology, and whether or not common wisdom held that philosophy and theology were beyond their capacities. Mary Astell understood the power of this view; it had reverberations for women's lives and education generally, channeling women's training into the concrete, the simplified, and the pietistic. She stated that a woman was drawn away from serious education not only by lack of opportunity but by being taught "to think marriage her only preferment, the sum total of her endeavours, the completion of all her hopes, that which must settle and make her happy in this world." This vision of marriage as the completion of women's lives contrasted with men's development through successive stages leading to greater independence and responsibility.[16]

In her integrated understanding of women's education, frivolous lifestyles and marriage, Astell viewed men as beneficiaries. Not by accident were women poorly trained and placed in an inferior position within marriage. In concluding a general plea for women to improve their lives through education, she assumed that women would appreciate her proposal but believed men would "resent it to have their enclosure broke down, and Women taste of that Tree of knowledge they have so long unjustly *Monopolized*." Excusing her partiality to women, she noted the partiality of men to their own sex and insisted that "Women [are] as capable of learning as men are, and that it becomes them as well."[17]

Mary Astell has been interpreted as a conservative feminist by Joan Kinnaird in an article on Astell's political and religious thought and in an essay by Regina Janes. However, I think there needs to be a reassessment of the strength and fundamental quality of her feminism, taking what she said about women in isolation from her general political and religious values. We are much less apt to question the breadth or depth of a writer's feminism if she holds Marxist (or even Freudian) values that limit viewing the world wholly from a women's perspective, than if her constraints are due to orthodox religious or political beliefs. One can hold conservative views—be a royalist and Tory as was Astell—and maintain quite radical views vis-à-vis the relationships between men and women.[18]

Still further, historians of women generally have questioned the legitimacy of feminist theory when it is concerned only with the interests of the elite, of middle and upper-class women. Certainly the pursuit of wisdom is an effort of elites, one requiring sufficient leisure and income to make the attempt feasible. Plainly, it was middle- and upper-class men who were able to develop intellectual talents and attain positions of independence and responsibility. Dale Spender, in her introduction to *Women of Ideas*, has argued convincingly that education is essential to establishing equality between the sexes. It is important that women formulate theories about the relative positions of men and women for the benefit of their sex as a whole. As Spender expresses it, " 'Theory' has been used to construct a division between those who know and those who do not, and, like most divisions in our hierarchical society, it is not a division of equal parts."[19] It seems incontrovertible that education, thought, and the written word are powerful instruments in defining worth within a society, and that fair access to equal education is essential for any group seeking to establish its own identity.

Yet, did Mary Astell's devotion to the issue of high-level scholarship represent her personal scholarly interests or was it tied to an understanding that denying the right to excel to the few was denying the right to social and intellectual development for all women? How, in other words, did men and women's education reflect their differing roles within society and a distinct process through which each must pass to become an adult? Astell's arguments for advanced training for women were not limited simply to a question of justice: that women should be able to employ their minds as were men. It was linked, as well, to her view that a man's education evolved from society's acceptance of his position as an independent male, who would become the religious and political head of his family. To deny women the same education as men was to prevent them from maturing to an independent and responsible position, to keep them perpetually childlike, and to deny them a direct relationship to God. Educational progression enabled men to achieve public recognition of their theological, political, and intellectual competence. It is thus essential to understand the theories which outlined educational process in ways that excluded women and which were tied to the functions of manhood. It was against the established attitudes, principles, and institutions that early feminists struggled. Women in seventeenth-century England, most notably Mary Astell, saw with astonishing clarity the implications of male-centered educational theory and institutions and took the first steps towards denouncing them and offering an alternative.

NOTES

[1] A survey of texts dealing with boys' education during the second half of the seventeenth century provides copious evidence for this assertion. For example, Hezekiah Woodward, *A Childes Patrimony Laid Out Upon the Good Culture of Tilling over his whole Man* (London: J. Legatt, 1640); William Walker, *Some Improvements to the Art of Teaching* (London: Printed by J.M. and are to be sold by Tho. Sawbridge, 1676); Christopher Wase, *Considerations concerning free schools as settled in England* (Oxford, 1678); Obadiah Walder, *Of Education. Especially of Young Gentlemen*. In Two Parts. Fourth Impression (Oxford, 1683); Charles Hoole, *Childrens Talk, English and Latin* (London, Printed for the Company of Stationers, 1697). Although there are numerous late seventeenth-century educational tracts, these were selected from a listing of rare educational works held by the National Institute of Education.

[2] Hoole, Epistle Dedicatory, n.p.

[3] Woodward, Preface, n.p.

[4] Wase, p. 12; 42-43.

[5] John Milton, *Milton on Education. The Tractate of Education*, Ed. and with an Intro. and Notes by Oliver Morley Ainsworth (New Haven: Yale Univ. Press, 1928).

[6] Milton, *Tractate*, pp. 51-54.

[7] *Tractate*, pp. 57-62.

[8] John Locke, *Some Thoughts Concerning Education* (1705), in *The Educational Writings of John Locke*, Intro. and Notes by James L. Axtell (Cambridge: Cambridge Univ. Press, 1968.)

[9] Locke, p. 117. The letter to Mrs. Clarke is included in an appendix to this edition of Locke's educational writings. It combines in an interesting, if not always clear, manner his chivalric concerns for the "softer sex" with an understanding of the essential equality of the sexes in areas relevant to education. Locke states: "I acknowledge no difference of sex in your mind relating ... to truth, virtue, and obedience" and thus would have "no thing altered in it from what is writ of sin" (p. 344). He continues, though, with the need for girls to have dancing masters; the greater hazards from exposing them too much to sun, wet, or cold; and the impropriety of employing corporal punishment against them. The latter he would preclude fathers administering: "Only I think the father ought to strike very seldom if at all to chide his daughters. Their governing and correcting, I think, properly belongs to the mother" (p. 346).

[10] For this phrase and a discussion of the views of the editors of *The Athenian Mercury* concerning women's education, see Hilda L. Smith, *Reason's Disciples* (Urbana: Univ. of Illinois Press, 1982), pp. 192-201.

[11] Wase, *Considerations*, p. 5.

[12] Mary Astell, *A Serious Proposal to the Ladies for the Advancement of their True and Greatest Interest*, Parts I and II. (New York: Source Book Press, 1970). This reprint includes the fourth edition of Part I of the *Serious Proposal* appearing originally in 1701 and the 1697 edition of Part II. The best general coverage of women's education during the seventeenth century appears in Josephine Kamm's *Hope Deferred: Girls' Education in English History* (London: Methuen, 1965), and Dorothy Gardiner's older work, *English Girlhood at School: A Study of Women's Education through Twelve Centuries* (Oxford: Oxford Univ. Press, 1965), continues to be useful. There is no thorough study, however, of girls' education during the 1600s because of the lack of institutional records.

[13] *Serious Proposal*, Part I, p. 12.

[14] *Serious Proposal*, Part II, pp. 78-131. Francis Bacon, *The Essayes or Counsels, Civill*

and Morall. (London: Printed by John Haviland for Hanna Barret and Richard Whitaker, 1625), p. 3.

[15] *Serious Proposal*, Part I, p. 19.

[16] Mary Astell, *Some Reflections upon Marriage*, 4th ed. (London, 1730), p. 78-79.

[17] *Serious Proposal*, Part I, p. 20.

[18] Joan K. Kinnaird, "Mary Astell and the Conservative Contribution to English Feminism," *Journal of British Studies* 19 (Fall 1979), 53-75; Regina James, "Mary, Mary, Quite Contrary; or, Mary Astell and Mary Wollstonecraft Compared," *Studies in Eighteenth-Century Culture* 5 (Madison: Univ. of Wisconsin Press, 1976), 121-40; *Reason's Disciples*, pp. 117-39. For a contrasting view, which places Astell's work into a strong feminist ideology of the late seventeenth and early eighteenth centuries, see Jerome Nadelhaft's "The Englishwoman's Sexual Civil War: Feminist Attitudes Towards Men, Women, and Marriage, 1650-1740," *Journal of the History of Ideas* 43 (1982), 555-78.

[19] Dale Spender, *Women of Ideas and What Men Have Done to Them from Aphra Behn to Adrienne Rich* (London: Routledge & Kegan Paul, 1982), p. 18.

MADAMINE! A FEW OF MOZART'S FEMALES OR *FANNO COSÌ TUTTE?*

JANE PERRY-CAMP

Wolfgang Amadeus Mozart's notorious ineptitude in matters of local politics is well documented, and has led some critics to argue that he had little understanding of people as real-life characters. The continuing debate over Mozart's level of awareness in the case of women has apparently been an offshoot of this thinking. However, a close examination of the female characters of Mozart's worlds, both real and fictional, reveals that his women are more than mere romantic representations of ideals; they are fully realized human beings possessed of such traits as fear, courage, loneliness, and sorrow. Hence, we are drawn to view his females as inhabitants of a rather Don Giovannian laboratory.[1]

To name all the women of Mozart's worlds is obviously beyond the scope of a single essay, and space demands that only a selection of his females be offered in a catalogue much more modest than Leporello's. It is necessary, then, to establish certain criteria for choosing a workable number of female characters from the more than fifty who populated his works. This study, therefore, will treat only those females who meet these two requirements: first, the personality of the character must remain basically unchanged throughout the course of the opera as with the case of Don Giovanni; and second, the figure, again like Don Giovanni, must have a catalytic effect on the opera's action.

Of the two characteristics sought, the first is the more troublesome, for some of the most interesting Mozart results from the musical treatment of developing personalities. Interesting, too, is Mozart's penchant for characters that grow rather than deteriorate, a penchant precisely parallel to the sonata language of late eighteenth-century musical style, the so-called Viennese classical style. When one of Mozart's characters seems dissolute at the end of the drama, it is usually because he or she has been so all along—for example, Elettra and the Queen of Night (both of whom we shall meet again). But narrowing the list of fifty female characters to seven does permit the luxury of a focused, in-depth look both at the humanity and dramatic power of Mozart's women.

GIUDITTA (JUDITH)

> from *La Betulia liberata*, K. 118/74c (actually a dramatic oratorio, not an opera proper; libretto by Pietro Metastasio [1698-1782]; commissioned in Padua, 13 March 1771; circumstances of first performance uncertain: perhaps during Lent of 1771 or 1772 in Padua, perhaps 23 May 1775 in Munich)

GIUNIA (JUNIA)

> from *Lucio Silla*, K. 135 (*opera seria*; libretto by Giovanni de Gamerra [1743-1803], revised by Metastasio; first performed in Milan, 26 December 1772)

ZAIDE

> from *Zaide* (or *Das Serail*) K. 344/336b; (a fragment of a *Singspiel*; libretto by Johann Andreas Schachtner [1731-1795]; not performed until 1866 in Frankfurt but begun in Salzburg, Autumn 1779)

ELETTRA (ELECTRA)

> from *Idomeneo, Rè di Creta*, K. 366 (*opera seria*; libretto by Giambattista Varesco [c. 1736-1805]; first performed in Munich, 29 January 1781)

SUSANNA

> from *Le nozze di Figaro*, K. 492 (*opera buffa*; libretto by Lorenzo da Ponte [1749-1838]; first performed in Vienna, 1 May 1786)

VITELLIA

> from *La clemenza di Tito*, K. 621 (*opera seria*; libretto by Metastasio, revised by Caterino Mazzolà; first performed in Prague, 6 September 1791)

THE QUEEN OF NIGHT

> from *Die Zauberflöte*, K. 620 (*Singspiel*; libretto by Emanuel Schikaneder [1751-1812]; first performed in Vienna, 30 September 1791)

Our catalogue's roll is thus set; in view of the thorough-going sexism of Leporello's catalogue, one might detect some irony in a catalogue of Mozartean women—not men—who gain and maintain an upper hand. At the same time, we need only remind ourselves that catalogues are inherently neutral as well as useful. Further, ample precedent exists in the Mozart family's habitual use of such genderless devices, from father Leopold's meticulous records of his son's compositions (1764-1768) to the renewal of that practice by Mozart himself (1784-1791). The spirit of objective record-keeping is hereby invoked.

GIUDITTA

La Betulia liberata is based on the Apocryphal Book of Judith wherein the familiar account of Judith and Holofernes is given. Giuditta,[2] widowed, wealthy, beautiful, and strong of spirit, comes forth from four years of mourning to assist her people in the city of Bethulia, which is under Holofernes's military attack. There is no mistaking that musically she is the *prima donna* of the work, an assignment rarely given to a female alto in the eighteenth century. The entire work centers on her and her actions. What the alto voice lacks in timbral brilliance is more than compensated for in the majesty and dignity of musical character, even when, without mincing words, she describes in gory detail her blood-curdling heroic deed. (Happily, the *recitativo accompagnato* underscoring her narrative tastefully sidesteps any grisly word painting.)

Her solemnity and serene strength pervade the spirit of her first *scena* and its aria (No. 5, "Del pari infeconda"). Metastasio's text is cast as a metaphor: "Equally barren is the bank of the river whether it rises in turbulence or lacks for moisture. Presumption comes from too much hope, faith is lost through too much fear."[3] Through her divinely inspired calm and wisdom Giuditta seeks realism, truth, and moderation. Typical of the musical structures in *La Betulia liberata*, the form of her full-blown *scena* is immediately apparent—an almost textbook example of the modified baroque aria in transition to the newer Viennese classical style. Architecturally, the *scena* is strategically located, to wit, between the chorus with Ozià (prince of Bethulia) (No. 4, "Pietà, se irato sei") and that chorus's exact repetition as No. 6. Equally striking is the musical content of the aria itself; following the pat triadic opening material an extraordinary musical gesture appears, both once in the opening ritornello and thrice after the voice's entrance.[4] (Example 1.)

An obvious reference to this same passage is found in Giuditta's second aria, announcing her departure for the enemy's camp (Aria, No. 8, "Parto, inerme, e non pavento" [I go forth unarmed and unafraid]); now syncopated and *forte*, now both assertive and energetic (see meas. 15-18, in tonic minor; meas. 41-49, in dominant minor; meas. 82-90, back in tonic minor; and the *dal segno* repetition of the last instance), the passage fittingly sets the text "vo per l'ombre, e orror non ho" (I go through the darkness but have no fear).

Not only are these specific operatic circumstances well served but also a more universal musical gesture is confirmed—a gesture which becomes associated with serenity, wisdom, sanctity, realism, and truth in Mozart's musical vocabulary during the remaining two decades of his life. The gesture's harmonies (in progression: tonic, dominant, submediant), when functioning not to conclude a phrase (as in a "deceptive" cadence) but to instigate musical energy, are easily distinguished, for example, in the solemn marches in both *Idomeneo* and *Die Zauberflöte* (example 2)—both by happenstance in the same key as Giuditta's aria. It is as if these sounds had stuck in Mozart's musical and dramatic memory. (The latter example even reuses the mi-sol-do [$\hat{3}$-$\hat{5}$-$\hat{1}$] melodic line of Giuditta's aria.)[5]

GIUNIA

The heroine of *Lucio Silla*, Mozart's last opera written for Italy, is an unhappy one. Giunia, separated by force from her exiled husband, refuses to yield to Lucio Silla's advances. She is ever faithful to her husband, willing to die for him, declining to give in to or to murder the aggressive Silla, and thus rejecting any compromise to her integrity. In the end she wins out; her husband's life, as hers, is spared. But during the process of her victory, her railing against Silla (or Sulla—Lucius Cornelius Sylla [138-78 B.C.]—as we know him), her rage and her distress, are expressed in dramatic coloratura passages worthy of *Die Zauberflöte*'s Queen of Night.[6] At other times, Giunia's grief seems to know no consolation.

Both dimensions of her personality are portrayed in her first appearance (Aria, No. 4, "Dalla sponda tenebrosa") where tempos shift with moods, as the text alternates between its first two sentences in anticipation of the third: "[Addressing first both her father and her husband, *Andante ma Adagio, alla breve*; upon repetition, *Adagio, alla breve*] Come from the gloomy shore, father and beloved husband, to receive my last breath. [Addressing Silla, *Allegro*, common time] Cruel man, you may rage at my disdain, but this is not your greatest punishment. [*Allegro, alla breve*] I shall be satisfied not to have you near me, while you will remain with the remorse in your heart."[7] (Example 3.) The complexity of Giunia's character is not to be compromised by musical convention.

ZAIDE

Zaide, the opera, remains a tantalizing fragment. Zaide, the opera's heroine, whose name we give the untitled *Singspiel*, is the only female and the only soprano in the cast. She is the moving force of the drama. By renouncing her role as the favorite of the Sultan's harem, she defies him. By captivating the heart of Gomatz, a prisoner/slave of the Sultan, she initiates the plot's movement. (Her crucial action comes easily: she simply deposits a miniature portrait of herself beside the sleeping Gomatz.) All this seems normal enough for an operatic plot. Then comes the rub. Judging from the probable source for the unfinished (and lost) libretto, the lovers Zaide and Gomatz apparently turn out to be brother and sister, the children of the overseer of the Sultan's slaves. (Wagnerites here may foresee the likes of Sieglinde and Siegmund.) How librettist Schachtner and composer Mozart would or could have solved the peculiarities of their plot, we do not know. After all, insofar as we are privy to information, neither Zaide nor Gomatz is a god.[8]

Like Giunia's, Zaide's personality is multi-faceted, yet when it comes to love she is single-minded and heroic. She is willing to sacrifice her life for her true love (that is, at least before anyone knows he is her brother). The famous "Ruhe sanft" (Aria, No. 3) — with its graceful tempo, soothing melody, rich *divisi* viola parts, and initial tonic-dominant-submediant harmonies — reveals, however, her gentler side as she places her portrait beside the exhausted Gomatz: "Sleep softly, dear one, till happiness awakens for you...." (Example 4.) On the other hand, and quite separate from "Ruhe sanft," her defiance is unmatched as she hurls her disdain at the Sultan: "Tiger! Wetze nur die Klauen" (Aria, No. 13): "Just sharpen your claws, tiger, look forward to the prey you snatched...." (Example 5.) This aria's broken lines, its *sforzandi*, its agitated accompaniment, chromatic *appoggiature* causing clangorous minor seconds, dissonant melodic tritones and augmented seconds, syncopations, throbbing bass lines, and its concluding spittle-like "Tiger!" combine to show quite another side of her powerful character. Zaide's tears are as genuine as her rage.

ELETTRA

Elettra is not as central to the plot of *Idomeneo* as she wishes she were. Her jealousy of Ilia (and Ilia's of her at the outset) is not a powerful enough force to affect the turn of the plot — a circumstance which is the source of increased frustration and anger for Agamemnon's daughter. Her tainted soul has no capacity to contaminate. Even the ill fortune that has befallen the inhabitants of Crete cannot be blamed on her malevolence, but rather on Idomeneo's pact with Poseidon. Just as Elettra has no hold over the plot, she has no real hold over the audience, for her motives are transparent from the start; and no question about a change of character (for the better) can enter anyone's mind either on stage or in the audience. One's sympathies lie with gentle Ilia against whose goodness Elettra's evil shadow is cast in silhouette.

Inevitably, one compares Elettra with *Die Zauberflöte*'s Queen of Night, those two being Mozart's prizes of perversion.[9] Like the Queen, Elettra revels in self-pity and knows happiness only when she thinks her ambitions are succeeding. Her final aria, No. 29, "D'Oreste, d'Aiace," has justifiably been called "a sustained scream of frustrated rage."[10] At last, her irrationality knows no bounds: "My breast feels the tortures that Orestes and Ajax knew; I am killed by Alecto's burning torch. Snakes, tear out my heart or else I will stab myself." Another translation varies slightly, but the spirit is the same: "... Devour my soul among you ye scorpions and serpents, | Your stings are less deadly than my cruel shame, my cruel shame...."[11] Elettra's venom steadily streams forth musically, first shadowed by dissonant bursts in the violins (example 6a) and eventually cast in a syncopated, serpentine coloratura, slithering to her top *c* (Example 6b).

While Ilia grows in self-confidence in the face of the uncertainties brought on by an earlier jealousy of Elettra, Elettra never sheds her envy of Ilia but instead nurtures that carcinogen into fully consuming vengeance. In the end, Elettra alone finds no resolution. Her aloneness is emphasized in that the final vent of her fury is hurled at the winds, for Mozart directed that no one stay on stage to hear her. In *Die Zauberflöte*, that the Queen of Night is dismissed, sent down to darkness (as, by the way, was Don Giovanni), is perhaps a larger act of mercy than one at first recognizes. But Elettra, defeated and not knowing her fate, must stand to face that fate; she determines to control it though that means enduring unending torture in this life and beyond.[12]

SUSANNA

Susanna emerges from her soubrette prototypes to become the dominating figure in *Le nozze di Figaro*. Nowhere is this more evident than in the second act finale, when confusion is running rampant, at the instant she steps from her hiding place in the Countess's wardrobe. The Count expresses surprise; the Countess expresses surprise; Susanna expresses complete composure, restraint, and authority. The music tells the tale, for Susanna's aristocratic minuet provides the posture of orderliness which she alone possesses within the whirling chaos of the moment. Appropriately, Susanna's minuet is the same dance form, in the same rhythm, provided for the nobility in *Don Giovanni*'s famous ballroom scene, composed a year later.[13] (Example 7.)

Susanna's impact on the opera's structure is far reaching. Her actions trigger responses from other characters — for example, Figaro's determination to keep her, his bride, from the Count or the Count's attempts to claim her on her wedding night. Quick-wittedly, she conjures up schemes. When she is thwarted, her arsenal allows her to be "either malicious and cutting ... or circuitous ... or just impulsive" and to resort "to wit and sensuous duplicity rather than passion," whereby her position of control is maintained.[14] Yet she is not without occasional fear or confusion, deficiencies which persuade us of her humanness. One can speculate how much — if in fact any — of this humanness was inspired by the *prima donna* of the original company and the first Susanna, Mozart's friend Nancy Storace.

It is generally understood that librettist da Ponte made a point of removing from Beaumarchais's original play politically sensitive material, so that the libretto would be acceptable to the Viennese royalty. Yet the music itself, intangibly but unmistakably, conveyed the revolutionary message; the operatic Susanna, a female heroine who does not appear particularly heroic, was capable of fomenting revolutionary ideas without anyone consciously realizing it.

VITELLIA

Vitellia, in sharp contrast to clement Tito, deserves being called "the Lady Macbeth of eighteenth-century opera" and "the horridest female that ever disgraced a libretto."[15] The innocence and charm of Susanna's scheming is turned vile in the hands of Vitellia, whose greed for power is omnipresent as she conspires to have the object of her affection, Tito, murdered (and the entire city of Rome burned) because she is not his first choice, or even his second, as Empress. Without conscience, she involves another in her intrigue; her hold over her accomplice is his love for and loyalty to her, a commitment that overrides even his devotion to Tito. Eventually, the facade of Vitellia's game playing begins to crumble; we are told that the diabolical godlike pose begins to soften. Her remorse, motivated by self-centeredness, is concerned first only for herself (Rondo, No. 23, "Non più di fiori"): "[*Larghetto*] No more shall Hymen descend to weave pretty garlands of flowers," she sings, with an occasional attention-seeking melisma and cadenza; "Bound in sharp cruel chains I see death advancing towards me. [*Allegro*] Unhappy me! How horrible! Oh, what will be said of me? He who could see my suffering, though, would pity me."[16] Her self-indulgent tears of formulaic mourning ("Chi vedesse il mio dolore, pur avria di me pietà") crystallize into an icy coloratura. (Example 8.)

One might well be concerned for the sincerity of the confession of guilt we next hear from her, after sentiments like these! Perhaps Tito is more merciful than he thinks himself to be when he pardons this ambitious woman.

THE QUEEN OF NIGHT

The power, the ferocity, and the shameless evil of all the wicked females heretofore encountered seem to be gathered within the character of *Die Zauberflöte*'s Queen of Night.[17] The opera tells of two prominent women, one who remains so from beginning to end (albeit misguided, deceitful, and stubborn) and the other who emerges, her progress uneven and sometimes uncertain. The former is the mother, the latter the daughter. As the daughter develops, the mother is challenged; and the Queen is her most odious self when confronted with a daughter now clearly unlike the mother. Vitriol spews forth (Aria, No. 14. "Der Hölle Rache"): "The vengeance of Hell boils in my heart; death and despair flame around me! If you do not cause Sarastro a painful death you will be my daughter no more! Outcast forever, abandoned forever, destroyed forever be all ties of nature—if Sarastro does not die through you! Hear me, gods of vengeance! Hear a mother's vow!"[18] The Queen's anger, sent screaming to an f above the staff, twists free of sanity and, at the start of the phrase, perverts Mozart's solemn tonic-dominant-submediant harmonies (Example 9.) The Queen's finish has already been told: she is banished, removed from light and the hope of enlightenment. Her effect, ironically, is contrary to her intentions. It is as if her power only negates those intentions, as if her horrifying demands strip her of her force and serve ultimately to nourish her daughter's quest for truth.[19]

* * *

The array of women in this catalogue offers both variety and stereotype. Most of those glimpsed in the quick summary are royal or at least noble by birth, Susanna being the only real exception. Four of the seven are decidedly good: Giuditta, Giunia, Zaide, and Susanna. The four are characterized by a basic sense of faithfulness and loyalty: to their mates, whether husbands or lovers, or to their nations—and thus to the very moral principles of fidelity and truth. Again Susanna stands apart from her group, not for lack of basic principle but for her inventiveness and apparently impromptu self-sufficiency which have no match among her virtuous and benevolent colleagues. As a result, she seems the least stereotyped and most spontaneous of all; of the seven, she seems to put herself most often in unprotected and precarious situations.

The three evil women (Elettra, Vitellia, and the Queen of Night—clearly the nobility is not exempt from being wicked!) outdo themselves in malice, yet in retrospect they tend to become almost monotonously bad, as if Mozart observed evil uniformly as combining vengeance, greed, envy, and, excepting Elettra, deceit. Each of the three insidiously strives for greater power. In like manner, none of the three triumphs. Elettra meets her match in Ilia; the Queen meets hers, not just in Sarastro, but more significantly in Pamina, whose anguished decision to defy her mother reinforces the younger woman's call for truth and insures the direction of the opera's plot. Only Vitellia, abruptly converted from a Lady Macbeth to the side of the angels, is said to acquire the status she so villainously had sought.

Mozart's women are both ideal and real. They tend to be a courageous lot, but they well know fear, loneliness, sorrow—and self-pity. As unquestionable as is Mozart's attentiveness to women, equally so is his respect for their capacity to be independent. Indeed, Mozart's female roles are equal in dramatic power and function to his male operatic roles; in given circumstances the women are superior to the men. Thus, Mozart treats women not as fragile clinging vines or as mere decorative objects, but as full-blooded and full-bodied humans, sometimes admirable, sometimes demonic, sometimes tender, sometimes vicious, sometimes headstrong, sometimes undecided—but ever a force at times formidable. They can be patient but never passive. Though the situations in which they find themselves may be implausible, never is their behavior completely removed from life. And therein lies the answer: *Così fan tutte. Così fan tutti*!

NOTES

[1] The coincidence between the "*Madamine!*" of the essay's title and the "*Madamina!*" of Leporello's (in)famous "catalogue" aria is not accidental. Nor is the inversion of the title of Mozart's last *opera buffa* to form the essay's subtitle, freely translated: Are all women alike?

[2] Giuditta, like Ilia and Pamina, has a counterpart; Amital (a non-Biblical character inserted by Metastasio) is negative and full of doubt but ultimately worthy of God's forgiveness.

[3] The translation is by Lionel Salter and appears with the brochure notes for Wolfgang Amadeus Mozart, *La Betulia Liberata*, K. 118/(74c), conducted by Vittorio Negri, Philips 6703 087 (1977). All translations cited from K. 118 are taken from Salter's work.

[4] Naïve word painting seems thoroughly denied with (1) the melody's descent for the text "se torbido eccede" ("whether it rises in turbulence") and (2) its conventionalized melisma for "se manca d'umor" ("lacks for moisture"), both in measures 37–42 (and comparable passages later) and in the expected improvised cadenzas.

[5] *La Betulia liberata* foreshadows *Die Zauberflöte* in several ways, not the least of which are (1) the lengthy theological debate, set in recitative, between the not-yet-convinced prince of the Ammonites and the wise prince of Bethulia and (2) Giuditta's analogy of the Ammonite's belief in false gods to "a veil which obscured his mind" and which was "torn away all at once," leaving him "unaccustomed to sustain the rush of so much light" (i.e., faith in the God of Abraham). For comments regarding Mozart's use of the same chant melody both for Giuditta's solos in the finale choral number and for the Requiem, K. 626 (like *Die Zauberflöte*, written in Mozart's last year), see Luigi Ferdinando Tagliavini's foreword to *La Betulia Liberata*, volume I/4/2 of the *Neue Mozart-Ausgabe* (Kassel: Bärenreiter, 1960), p. viii.

[6] "Wolfgang has introduced into her [i.e., Anna De Amicis, the first Giunia, whom, a decade earlier, Mozart at the age of seven had met in Mainz] principal aria [probably No. 11, "Ah se il crudel periglio"] passages which are unusual, quite unique and extremely difficult and which she sings amazingly well." Leopold Mozart's letter of 12 December 1772 to his wife, in Emily Anderson, trans. and ed., *The Letters of Mozart and His Family*, 3d ed., prepared by Stanley Sadie and Fiona Smart (New York: Norton, 1985), p. 220. One such passage from that aria (meas. 56–70, which, unlike her final coloratura passage, does not carry her up to her high *d*) demonstrates Leopold's point (see Example 10).

Aside from the cadenza, roughly one-third of the aria after the opening ritornello consists of such passages. That De Amicis was pleased with the arias written for her tells us of her prowess and courage (see Leopold's letter of 26 December 1776, as well as that of 12 December 1772).

[7] Translation from William Mann, *The Operas of Mozart* (New York: Oxford Univ.

Press, 1977), p. 154. All translations of operatic excerpts are derived from Mann unless specifically indicated otherwise.

[8] Usually in Mozart's operas, unmasking leads to revelation and enlightenment, however far-fetched. If *Zaide* was being directed towards a light-hearted ending, it might have set some records for improbability. However, comments in Mozart's letters to his father (Vienna, 18 April 1781) could imply either that the ending might have been serious (even tragic?) or that the characters themselves, as we ourselves know them, were not comic enough for him to continue work on the "operetta": "As for Schachtner's operetta, there is nothing to be done—for the same reason for which I have often mentioned. . . . [S]ave for the long dialogues, which could easily be altered, the piece [*Zaide*] was very good, but not suitable for Vienna, where people prefer comic pieces." (Anderson, p. 725.) Words written in cyphers are enclosed in angular brackets in the translation.

[9] Interestingly, in the earlier opera, both Idomeneo and Elettra end without partners, as do both Sarastro and the Queen of Night in the later work. Yet one can scarcely imagine more incompatible couples than either of these pairs. Mozart persuades us of that incompatibility in quite different, but equally effective, ways: in *Idomeneo* the Quartet, No. 21, "Andrò ramingo e solo," plays four characters against one another: Idamante, Ilia, Idomeneo, and Elettra, each life at a critical point, each personality reduced to its essence. Not surprisingly, Mozart himself considered this quartet the high point of the opera. (See Mozart's letters of 27 December 1780 and 30 December 1780 in Anderson, pp. 697-99, 701-03.)

In *Die Zauberflöte* the antagonists are separated in time, the Queen of Night's horrifying second act aria immediately preceding Sarastro's becalming one, save for the intervening spoken dialogue between Monostatos (eventually spiritually aligned with the Queen but physically associated within Sarastro's realm) and Pamina (eventually spiritually aligned with Sarastro but physically associated with the Queen's realm).

[10] Charles Osborne, *The Complete Operas of Mozart: A Critical Guide* (New York: Atheneum, 1978; rpt. New York: Da Capo Press, n.d.), p. 165.

[11] English translation by M. and E. Radford, with the brochure notes for Mozart, *Idomeneo*, The Glyndebourne Festival Production, Seraphim SIC-6070.

[12] In Anderson (pp. 703-04) are found Mozart's special instructions that the stage be cleared before this aria (his letter of 3 January 1781 to his father); at the same time, Mozart did not want the staging effect to seem unnatural. Regrettably and reluctantly, the aria was cut at the last minute from the opera's première performance because of the still-unresolved complications in staging and because of concern for the third act's excessive length. (Elettra's aria was not the only one cut; see Mozart's letter of 18 January 1781 [Anderson, pp. 708-09].)

[13] So close is the minuet's association with aristocracy that Hugh Ottoway suggests that the absence of such a dance from Mozart's "Prague" Symphony, K.504, pointedly coincides with that city's "enlightened" status, hence the eschewal of the musical reference to the aristocracy. Ottoway, *Mozart* (Salem, N. H.: Salem House, 1985), p. 128. Wye Jamison Allanbrook's *Rhythmic Gesture in Mozart: Le nozze di Figaro and Don Giovanni* (Chicago: Univ. of Chicago Press, 1983) explores a full range of dance gestures.

[14] Singer, p. 84.

[15] Mann, p. 571; the second epithet is from Donald Francis Tovey and is quoted by Mann.

[16] English translation by Peggie Cochrane, with the brochure notes to Mozart, *La clemenza di Tito*, conducted by Istvan Kertesz, London OSA 1387 (1968).

[17] One feels obliged to recall Mozart's description of his first Queen of Night, his sister-in-law Josepha Hofer (née Weber, 1758?-1819). "The eldest [Josepha] is a lazy, gross perfidious woman, and as cunning as a fox." (Mozart's letter of 15 December 1781 in Anderson, p. 784.) Such a characterization, plus her reputation as a vocalist, well qualified her for the operatic role she premièred.

[18] Translated from the libretto to *Die Zauberflöte*, conducted by Wolfgang Sawallisch, Angel SCL-3807 (1973).

[19] There has been much discussion of the whole matter of Pamina's leadership, its symbolic significance, and the question of male or female superiority in the opera. (Only discussions of *Così fan tutte* might rival those of *Die Zauberflöte* in this last area.) Inextricably involved

in the battle of sexual superiority is discussion of talkativeness; the Priests and Sarastro seem to think that women speak loosely and meaninglessly and therefore are not to be trusted. They overlook Papageno's qualifications for the chatter championship, and instead see his frailty only as limiting his success in true growth. On the other hand, our first inkling of Pamina's strength precedes Sarastro's arrival on stage (during the first act finale) when her succinct response to talkative Papageno's fearful babbling is shaped in a fervent and clarion call for truth (No. 8, Finale to Act 1, meas. 362–70) (see Example 11). Free from sexual bias, Pamina is admitted into the rarefied realm of the enlightened. After all, the comments of Sarastro and the Priest about woman's verbosity are mere words.

MUSICAL EXAMPLES

Example 1. *La Betulia liberata*, K. 118/74c, No. 5, Aria, "Del pari infeconda," meas. 32-36.

Example 2. (a) *Idomeneo*, K. 366, No. 25, Marcia, meas. 1-4; (b) *Die Zauberflöte*, K. 620, No. 9, Marcia, meas. 1-4.

Example 3. *Lucio Silla*, K. 135, No. 4, Aria, "Dalla sponda tenebrosa," (a) *Andante ma Adagio*, meas. 10-18; (b) *Allegro*, meas. 55-63.

Example 4. *Zaide*, K. 344/336b, No. 3, Aria, "Ruhe sanft," meas. 9–16.

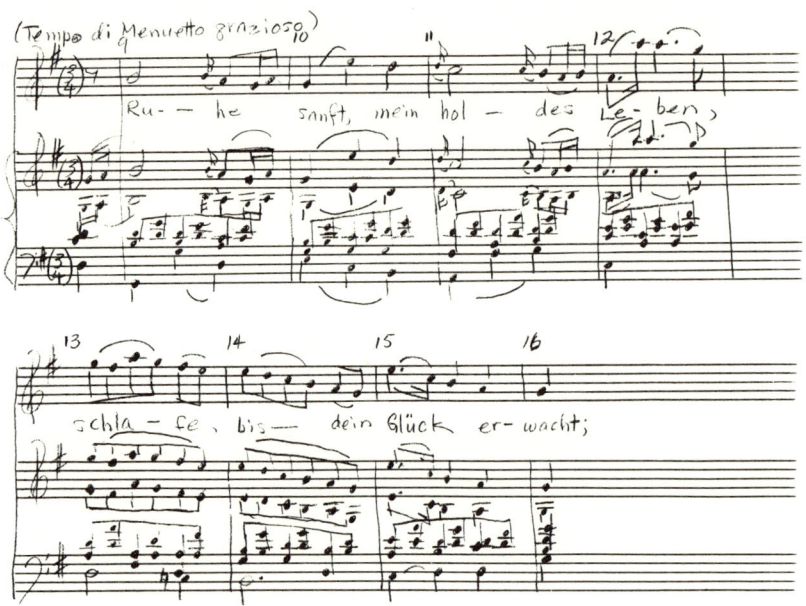

Example 5. *Zaide*, K. 344/336b, No. 13, Aria, "Tiger! wetze nur die Klauen," (a) meas. 1–12; (b) meas. 51–54.

Example 6. *Idomeneo*, K. 366, No. 29, Aria, "D'Oreste, d'Ajace," (a) meas. 4–8; (b) meas. 110–17.

Example 7. (a) *Le nozze di Figaro*, K. 492, No. 16, Finale to Act 2, meas. 122-36; (b) *Don Giovanni*, K. 527, No. 13, Finale to Act 1, meas. 220-27.

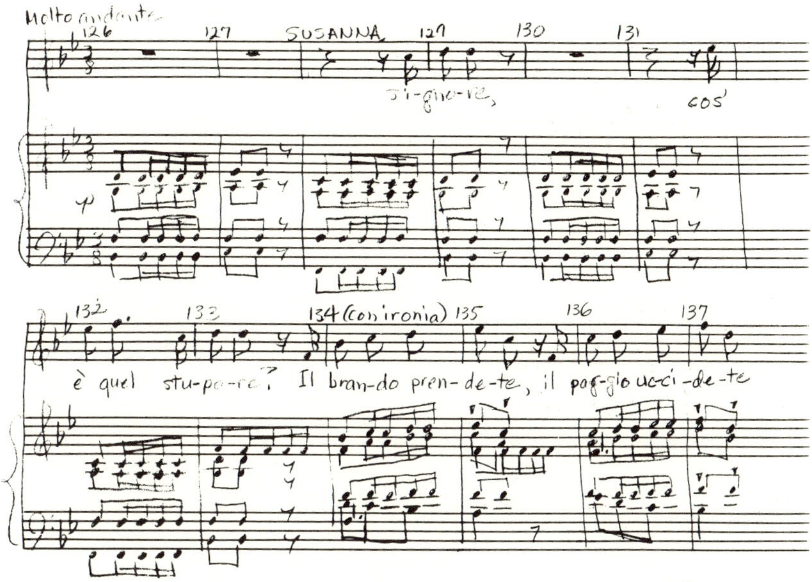

Example 8. *La clemenza di Tito*, K. 621, No. 23, Rondo, "Non più di fiori vaghe catene," (a) meas. 9–12; (b) meas. 25–28; (c) meas. 61–64; (d) meas. 154–68.

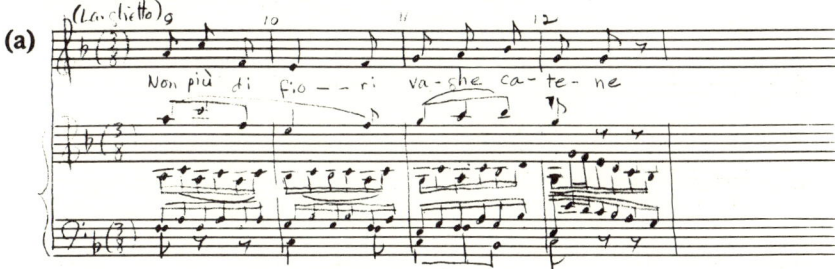

Mozart's Females 103

Example 9. *Die Zauberflöte*, K. 620, No. 14, Aria, "Der Hölle Rache," meas. 36–47.

Example 10. *Lucio Silla*, K. 135, No. 11, Aria, "Ah se il crudel periglio," meas. 56–70.

Example 11. *Die Zauberflöte*, K. 620, No. 8, Finale to Act 1, meas. 362–70.

PARADOX IN PARADISE: NATURE AND ART IN THE EIGHTEENTH-CENTURY LANDSCAPE GARDEN

COLLETTE HALL
PETER PERRETEN
JANE SHINEHOUSE
DERK VISSER

The concept of nature during the Enlightenment is inherently paradoxical, for, despite the statements of poets and philosophers who claimed that they looked at nature to discover its spontaneous beauty, nature was rarely appreciated directly for itself. Rather, it was perceived through the embellishing canons of antique models and eighteenth-century art. These artistic perceptions imposed upon Nature many ideological visions, among which re-creating paradise on Earth was prominent.

This directed viewing of Nature can readily account for the eighteenth-century Englishman's enthusiasm for the American flora and landscape. He was to reproduce in his own backyard the American landscapes which had been described by earlier explorers and settlers as the Garden of Eden. Across the Channel, the French philosopher Diderot epitomized the paradoxical attitude of his contemporaries towards nature. In his *Salons* and discussions of landscape painting, he revealed a dialectic between nature and reality in art. Diderot's dual vision provides a conceptual background against which the development of the English landscape garden can be easily understood.

If, indeed, artistic representation so heavily informed the vision of nature, one may examine the real relationship between the informal garden and the actual landscape. Is the "genius of the place" just another approximation of nature betraying the gardener's inner vision? In truth, the English landscape garden is the result of a unique hybrid of art and nature made up of eclectic impressions, brought together and fused by intertextuality of philosophical speculation, landscape, travel accounts, pictures, and plants.

John Bartram, the first native-born American naturalist, would become the eighteenth century's most important contributor of American plants to European gardens and herbariums. American plant collectors helped to change the face of European gardens. How appropriate that Bartram should have chosen to hew in stone above his greenhouse door a couplet from Pope's *Essay on Man*:

> Slave to no sect, who takes no private road,
> But looks thro' Nature, up to Nature's God.
> (IV,331-32).

Pope, in company with Addison and others, criticized the artificiality of the seventeenth-century formal garden. Pope favored the "amiable Simplicity of unadorned Nature," the simplicity which "was the Taste of Ancients in their Gardens." "How contrary," he said, "to this Simplicity is the modern Practice of Gardening; we seem to make it our Study to recede from Nature ... in monstrous Attempts beyond the reach of the Art itself."[1] Partly because of the contributions of plant hunters like Bartram, the English landscape garden became, by the end of the eighteenth century, a compromise between man and nature.[2] The natural characteristics of the land were to be improved upon by art, made more beautiful by art, so that the garden would look like nature untouched by man.

The intellectual concept for the landscape garden had been suggested earlier in accounts of the sixteenth- and seventeenth-century explorers. John Winthrop described his approach to the New England coast: "We had now fair sunshine weather, and so pleasant a sweet air as did much refresh us, and there came a smell off the shore like the smell of a garden."[3] Many other seventeenth-century explorers reported to their mother countries about the flowers, medicinal plants, and fine woodlands and forests. George Alsop in 1666 wrote about Maryland that "he, who out of curiosity desires to see the Landskip of the Creation drawn to the life, or to read Natures Universal Herbal without book, may ... view Mary-Land drest in her green and fragrant Mantle of Spring ... They need not look for any other Terrestrial Paradice ...while she [Maryland] is extant."[4] Sea Captain Arthur Barlow, in his account for Sir Walter Raleigh, depicted Virginia as a natural garden of unbelievable fertility.[5] In George Percy's observations in 1607, in *Narratives of Early Virginia*, we read that he found "the ground all flowing over with faire flowers of sundry colours and kindes, as though it had been any Garden or Orchard in England ... Wee kept on our way in this Paradise."[6] In the *Natural History of North Carolina*, John Brickell states: "Those that travel through the woods of Carolina—turn your eyes which way you will, you have nothing but pleasing and diverting objects; and the more to be admired being the work of Nature, and not of Art ... Here are in several places large Savannas ... which at certain seasons appear at a distance like so many pleasure Gardens."[7] Many other early visitors and explorers sent back such accounts of the New World, and some also sent back collections of plants and curious wildlife specimens. The European cultivators of all the arts and sciences were looking to the vast unexplored region of the New World for products which would increase the resources of the physicians and the agriculturalists, the profits of the merchants, the enjoyment of the men of leisure, and the knowledge of the naturalists.

John Bannister, a young clergyman of the late seventeenth century, could be considered the New World's first resident naturalist. His major patron was Henry Compton, the Bishop of London, who inherited the bishop's estate at Fulham with "one of the grandest gardens in all England."[8] Bannister joined his many predecessors in describing America as a land of plenty and in feeling all but overcome by this strange new world of plants. In his fourteen years in the province of Virginia, he sent 340 specimens of plants back to Bishop Compton and wrote the most vivid and careful natural history reports received to date from the colonies.

The beginning of the eighteenth century saw its share of superlative descriptions of the New World. A writer from the early part of the century, Robert Beverley of Virginia, in his very lively account *The History and Present State of Virginia*, notes that the name of the colony was selected as a tribute to landscape as well as the queen. "Virginia . . . did still seem to retain the Virgin Purity and Plenty of the first Creation, and the People [the Indians] their primitive Innocence." He goes on to say that "all the countries . . . seated in or near the latitude of Virginia . . . are reckon'd the Gardens of the World."[9] Beverley wanted to reconcile nature and art—to reconcile his admiration for primitive life with what he knew of the needs of the civilized community.

While plant-hunting in the seventeenth century was motivated first by the need to know more of medicine, and then by the desire to find interesting "greens" or flowers for the stylized geometric gardens, in the eighteenth century plants were often collected in a spirit of scientific inquiry.[10] John Bartram, born in 1699, had little formal schooling, but he had an inquiring and independent mind that would lead him "to the frontiers of scientific observations."[11] By his adolescence Bartram had become interested in medicine, and, since medicine then depended heavily on plant drugs, he naturally developed a fascination with "Botanicks."[12] This unlettered farmer was to become what the great Carolus Linnaeus called "the greatest natural botanist in the world."[13]

In 1727 Bartram bought a farm property on the west bank of the Schuylkill River. He started out with local plant hunting excursions, with short trips up the Schuylkill in the fall when the farm harvest was in. Because he was not able to get out and hunt plants in the wilderness as often as he liked, he laid out a garden of about six acres where he planted the specimens and seeds that he gathered. It was the first botanical garden in America. Bartram called it his "garden of delights."

With introductions supplied by James Logan and others, Bartram began to correspond with English gardeners, naturalists, and potential patrons, the most important of whom was Peter Collinson. Collinson was a businessman, a Quaker, and an amateur botanist, who had a wide circle of similarly minded friends in England.

John Bartram the collector and Peter Collinson the disperser worked well together to the benefit of botany and European gardens, and for almost thirty-five years Bartram was to hunt American plants for Collinson.[14] By 1736 Collinson had gathered a group of English gardeners willing to pay an annual fee to share in the shipment of seeds and specimens. He early secured for Bartram the patronage of James Robert, the eighth Baron Lord Petre. Lord Petre, gifted in natural history, grew plants from all over the world in his extensive gardens at Essex. Collinson stated that there were about 10,000 American trees and shrubs mixed with 20,000 European and some Asian specimens in this garden. Walking among them, he said, "one cannot help thinking he is in North American thickets."[15] Lord Petre's gardens and hothouses were probably the most extensive in the kingdom, and he was to order quantities of seeds from time to time.

When Lord Petre died at the age of thirty from smallpox, his nursery plants were sold to the Dukes of Norfolk, Bedford, and Richmond, and to the Earl of Lincoln and others. Thus, plant materials and trees from Bartram helped reforest Essex, Sussex, Surrey, Bedfordshire, and Nottinghamshire.[16] The intrepid colonial plant hunters and naturalists like Bannister and John Bartram, as well as the early writers and explorers who described the American landscape as a garden and a paradise, gave both vision and substance to the late eighteenth-century English landscape garden.

* * * * * * * * *

If the earlier descriptions of the landscape of the American colonies sought to persuade new settlers, those of William Bartram, trained observer though he was, were nonetheless determined by the canons of rhetoric. In this way they are similar to the landscapes painted by their contemporaries as backgrounds to some historical event as in the case of Nicolas Poussin, Claude Lorrain, and their eighteenth-century followers. The dichotomy between representation and its reality, which was accepted as a matter of course by eighteenth-century literati, may occasionally lead to errors in modern appreciation of both their taste and their achievements. Cases in point are the writings of Denis Diderot, the art critic, describing the works exhibited in the *Salons* and that same Diderot, as correspondent of Sophie Volland, describing the landscapes through which he walked. Other cases are posed by such landscape gardens as created by William Kent and Henry Hoare in England, gardens which have been referred to both as Claudean and natural. Each of these cases shall be examined in turn.

A comparison of Diderot's reactions to natural landscapes with his reactions in front of paintings representing landscapes is suggested by the art critic himself. It was not uncommon to hear him exclaim, before a landscape, "What a beautiful painting" and, conversely, looking at a successfully rendered scene to believe he was contemplating nature itself.[17] Substituting nature for art or art for nature to better appreciate the effects of each was a frequent device Diderot used in his *Salons* and in a less obvious manner in his descriptions of real landscapes as they appear in his *Letters to Sophie Volland*.[18] Diderot and his contemporaries were looking at nature itself through distorting lenses, through the vision of a Lorrain or of a Poussin. Thus, when they talk about nature, one may wonder to what reality are they alluding, *"la belle nature des Anciens"* or the actual scenery in front of their eyes.

On the one hand, Diderot advocated naturalness—he liked landscapes unspoiled by men, unmanicured gardens, paintings showing a direct observation of nature. On the other hand, he praised landscape painters such as Joseph Vernet, Jacques-Philippe Loutherbourg, or Hubert Robert whose works, to use Michael Fried's term, strike us by their theatricality and their artificiality.[19] This paradox, far from being an inconsistency on the part of the philosopher, is perfectly in keeping, as we shall see, with the role Diderot assigned to landscape painting and to art in general.

Unlike many of his contemporaries for whom *le retour à la nature* was part of a fashion and an excuse to devote themselves, as the philosopher saw it, "more surely and deliberately in a rustic setting to the boring activities of city life," Diderot seems to have genuinely enjoyed the countryside.[20] He enjoyed landscapes unspoiled by man, which still retained an air of the wilderness. He talked to Sophie about the effects of man's "improving" hand on landscapes, which brings "prettiness but destroys the sublimity of the places planted by nature."[21] He criticized the symmetry of Les Tuileries and the "tedious walks of the Palais Royal" where "all your trees are cut down to cabbage tops and where you still stifle, however hard they have tried to give you some air and space by pruning and cutting and smashing and disfiguring."[22]

Paradise, for the philosopher, must have been Grimm's estate, which he described enthusiastically to Sophie Volland in 1762. Its ponds "with steep banks, full of rushes and marsh weeds," its "old moss-covered bridge over the water," and its "thickets untouched by the gardener's pruning-hook" transported him with delight.[23] This informal landscape epitomizes Diderot's taste, for, if he was affected by the unspoiled quality of some of the sites, he appreciated the blend of art and nature as long as man's influence was not too conspicuous.

If then we compare the simple quality of the natural landscapes Diderot enjoyed and the landscape paintings he held in high esteem, we are struck by their overly dramatic qualities. They represent tormented scenes with rugged hills, awe-inspiring mountains in the manner of Salvator Rosa, cataracts gushing out of precipices or sea storms with raging waters, carrying away pitiful creatures. This taste for what seems today theatrical paintings, a taste Diderot shared with most of the art critics of his generation, fits very well with the philosopher's conceptions of art and with the role he assigned to landscape painting.[24]

In the hierarchy of genres, codified since the end of the seventeenth century by the theoretician André Félibien, history painting was the most elevated genre, and landscape painting was regarded as a lowly one.[25] While Diderot agreed with the Academy that art should not only please but educate the beholder by showing him moral actions (a reason Diderot was so opposed to Boucher's frivolous style and so enthusiastic about Greuze's art), he disagreed with the low status given to landscape painting. He felt that landscapes such as the ones painted by Vernet, Loutherbourg or Hubert Robert, because they could elicit an emotional and imaginative response from the spectator, could rival history painting. In Vernet's sea storms and in Hubert Robert's paintings of ruins, dramatic actions stimulated the beholder's imagination and made him reflect on man's place in the universe or in the frailty of his existence.

In his *Essays on Painting* (1766) Diderot expressed the supremacy of the expressive function of art over its other functions:

> One can, one must sacrifice something to technique. How much? I do not know. But I do not want that sacrifice to cost anything as regards the expression, the effect of the subject. First touch me, astonish me, tear me apart; startle me, make me cry, shudder, arouse my indignation; you will please my eyes afterward, if you can.[26]

This idea, which Diderot had been developing since the 1750s in connection with the author's theater reform, was further reinforced by his reading of Edmund Burke's *Philosophical Enquiry into the Origin of the Sublime and the Beautiful.*[27] Diderot, after Burke, showed the impact that steep mountains, deep rock-bound valleys, or mysterious and dark caverns have on the imagination of the beholder. These scenes, inspiring a terror mixed with pleasure, induce in the beholder a particular "psycho- physical" condition and enhance his power to identify with and enjoy the scene of nature presented by the painting.[28] Likewise, the spectacle of innocent victims in the grip of danger, as in Vernet's sea storm paintings, awakens in the beholder deep feelings of pity and horror which stimulate the aesthetic experience. Diderot, as an advocate of great passions, was acutely aware of this mechanism.[29] For the art critic, though, the aesthetic experience is made up of two opposite elements: one of identification and one of detachment. As Diderot told l'Abbé in his Vernet promenades, "in front of real catastrophes you will despair, whereas in front of a canvas, you will find pleasure in the same scenes. Despite your identification with them, you know in the latter case, that it is an imitation, an illusion of reality."[30] The spectator's emotional responses to art or reality are thus of different natures, as Diderot summarized it with an example from the theatre:

> On stage we prefer to see the righteous man suffering rather than the wicked man punished, and in the theatre of life, on the contrary, we prefer to see the wicked man punished rather than the righteous man suffering.[31]

Similarly, Diderot's experiences in front of natural landscapes and in front of painted ones, even if they bear some resemblances, are of different orders. To better communicate the power and beauty of nature, the work of art has to involve the spectator emotionally; it has to impress his eyes and his soul with its sublimity. And to achieve this goal, art uses a specific language, a pictorial one which does not merely copy nature but re-creates it.

Diderot is the only critic of his time who fully articulated the relationship between the object in nature and its representation, between art and reality. He was aware before anybody else that the "sun of art" is not the "same as the one in nature," for art, through technique, *le faire*, and through the artist's imagination, *l'idéal*, is a restructuring and an interpretation of nature.[32] Paradoxically, the more real a painted object looks, the farther away it is removed from nature, for it is through illusion, *la magie de l'art*, that this mimesis of nature is achieved.[33] The dialogue between nature and art nourished Diderot's thought. It was the works of artists like Vernet or Chardin which Diderot saw as the closest imitation of nature that opened the road to the philosopher's reflection on the nature of art. In the words of Jacques Barzun, "Diderot changed the rather simplistic Neo-Classical idea of painting as skillful illustration and touched-up imitation to the modern idea of painting as, first of all, an inspired construction with internal requirements."[34] Diderot furthermore discovered that painting is a language with its own system of signs; it is a system where everything, as in nature, is linked and, as the encyclopedist saw it, has its own laws. Landscape painting becomes thus the medium through which one can apprehend the natural system. The artist himself, through his "genius" or "intuition," becomes the interpreter of nature, of a nature that Diderot never ceased to contemplate and marvel at whether it be in the countryside or in man's productions.[35]

* * * * * * * *

Diderot's praise of a landscape as approximating art or of a painting as approximating nature sums up the dilemma central to the appreciation of the function of nature in the changing garden design of the eighteenth century. Neither Diderot nor his contemporary British critics Hogarth and Reynolds were much interested in reality. The painters followed the canon of embellishing nature established by these critics. Thus, in the review cited above, Jacques Barzun quotes Quentin de la Tour:

> The more experience and ability one gets, the more one gives up that furious determination to embellish and exaggerate Nature. There comes a time that one finds Nature so beautiful, so unified, so coherent even in its defects, that one prefers rendering it just as one sees it. One is only kept from doing so by old habits and by the extreme difficulty of making that rendering so true as to be still pleasing.

And even this vision of a unified and coherent Nature is an artist's vision of reality.

As classified by Félibien, landscape painting was ranked as the lowest of the painter's art. No doubt such landscape painting comprised the work of a Tillemans rather than a Claude or a Ruysdael. Tillemans, like the much better known Kip, who engraved the drawings of Knyff, produced portraits of gardens much as court painters produced portraits of statesmen.[36] In neither case was the background more than a backdrop. But even in the highest ranked history paintings the landscapes were only settings, the models for which—found in the Romagna—were recognizable mostly because of the classical associations brought out on purpose by painters who painted for educated patrons.

The most significant studies to have appeared in the last decade or so have paid less attention to the relationship between nature and the informal garden than to the literary and artistic expressions of nature which are assumed to have inspired new designs.[37] Or they discuss the ideological signification of the statuary and temples that appeared in these gardens.[38] With a few exceptions, no questions have been raised about the place of the actual English landscape, as opposed to a Claudean rendering of landscape, in the development of the English garden.

The dialectic between the regular (French) garden and the irregular (English) garden is in part accentuated by problems of intertextuality. In discussions on the origins of the English landscape garden another of Pope's dicta—that all gardening is landscape painting—is frequently adduced. He obviously did not refer to the landscape painting by a Tillemans. In view of his approval of Stowe and Rousham, he must have had Claude, Gaspard, and others in mind. Thus, one may wonder whether he actually referred to the English landscape, though he surely did not refer to the garden design of Burlington's Chiswick.³⁹ Similarly, the serpentine lines shown on the plans of Burlington's gardens, which are nevertheless very formal and too small to make the serpentine lines meaningful, are often mentioned together with Hogarth's later advocacy of the serpentine line in painting. One Dutch historian matter-of-factly explains the appearance of the serpentine line in the 1720s as providing more places to put statuary. ⁴⁰

Discussions on the origin of the irregular or landscape garden as developed in England often introduce Sir William Temple, who wrote an essay on the garden of Epicurus — a commonplace of "repose from duty" — and who used the term *sharawaggi*, which scholarly persons have traced to Chinese and Japanese words meaning "disorderly" or "asymmetrical."⁴¹ Although Sir William's use of the term has created quite a stir, he himself made a formal Dutch garden, no doubt in imitation of those he had seen on the estates of his Low Country friends.

If at any time before the eighteenth century a landscape or irregular garden could have been laid out, it should have been Sir William who did so. Here was a man interested in estate development, one who at least twice retired from the court, even in a sort of exile like Cobham's. He was, intellectually at least, interested in varieties of garden design. If Poussin, Claude, and Dutch landscapists were needed as inspiration, Sir William was acquainted with paintings in those styles. For more than a year, during the drawn-out negotiations leading to the peace of Nijmegen of 1679, he sat in halls hung with tapestries in the Poussin style based on Ovid's *Metamorphoses* and Virgil's *Aeneid*.⁴² Sir William's motto was *servare modum, finemque tueri, naturam sequi*, or "observe moderation, strive for the goal, and follow nature." In garden design, as in painting, the goal determined how and to what extent nature was to be followed.⁴³

The various painted or engraved representations of the eighteenth-century garden give us only an approximation of the real garden. Engravings in particular are misleading, for the medium encourages a simplification of lines even if it is the artist himself rather than a printer/illustrator who works the plate.⁴⁴ The collection made by Kip after works by Knyff is a case in point. That the perfection of design influenced the engraving is also demonstrated by the picture of Heemstede, an estate near Utrecht, which is presented as a perfect rectangle, while in fact the angle of the front line ran at sixty degrees.⁴⁵

If the engravers of these French gardens, some of whom reportedly made sketches of the formal gardens in person, presented them more like an architect's project than gardens as they really existed, the engraver of irregular gardens took no less liberty. Bampfylde's presentation of Stourhead can serve as an example.⁴⁶ One of the genial introductions into garden design made at Stourhead is the circuit walk.⁴⁷ The aim of such walks was to surprise the stroller with varying perspectives and new views partly for the purpose of appropriating prospects beyond the estate boundary, thus fictitiously enlarging it. At Stourhead the circuit walk is not along the edge of the estate but around the lake so that one does not look in from any great distance. It was designed to surprise the viewer with perspectives of the architectural embellishments within the estate. Bamfylde's engraving shows the Palladian bridge, the Temple of Flora, and the Pantheon at once from the stationary perspective of the artist's vantage point. Today's Stourhead, much like Stowe, Rousham, and other gardens still mostly preserved, has become "Reptonized" over time, partly because the plantings have been changed. These transitions are well discussed by Edward Hyams.[48]

Essential for the acceptance of Repton and Loudon was the freeing of the mind from conventional intellectual and artistic affectations, from the prescriptions of Le Nôtre no less than those of the early Georgians. The true landscape garden was the creation of the late Georgians. Its origins are primarily sociological and to be found in the emergence of new men whose taste did not run to history paintings by artists such as Wilson. These new men could be portrayed as Gainsborough's Mr. and Mrs. Andrews, in the middle of their farmscape. The taste of such men was perhaps more attracted by the practical commentators of the earlier decades, Stephen Switzer most prominent among them, who dismissed the grandiose garden fit only for kings and courtiers whose income did not depend on the estate turned into garden.[49]

The change of taste reflected in the portrayal of the Andrewses overlooking a working farm rather than either an embroidered terrace or an Elysian grove permits us to observe the estate owner enjoying the "genius of the place" for its own sake. Gainsborough, of course, had been "approved" by Sir Joshua Reynolds, who had dedicated one of his discourses to him. Thus, Reynolds, though in most cases a faithful English counterpart to Diderot, may actually have facilitated the new taste.[50] Among the factors making this change in taste possible was the greater interest in the natural world demonstrated by the Enlightenment's natural scientists and the explorers — among whom the Bartrams stand out — who provided the scientists with their plant specimens and ecological descriptions. It is likely that especially the non-scientists among the Bartram correspondents, such as Lord Petre and Peter Collinson as well as such men as William Byrd II of Virginia — who had estates in England as well as in America and who travelled back and forth across the Atlantic — were significant in bringing about this demonstrable change in taste. What happened in England may perhaps be illustrated by conditions in Virginia where members of the gentry, unaffected by the requirements of conspicuous and imitative consumption in competition with ambitious courtiers, had developed improved landscapes on their working estates as an incidental byproduct of the system of exploitation in the midst of what the earliest explorers already had described in terms of both the best English parks and Eden.

NOTES

[1] *The Prose Works of Alexander Pope*, ed. Norman Ault (New York: Knopf, 1977), p. 40.
[2] Nan Fairbrother, *Men and Gardens* (New York: Knopf, 1956), p. 29.
[3] *Winthrop's Journal, "History of New England,"* ed. James K. Hosmer (New York: Scribner's, 1908), p. 47.
[4] *Narratives of Early Maryland: 1633-1684*, ed. Clayton C. Hall (New York: Scribner's, 1910), p. 344.
[5] "Captain Arthur Barlowe's Narrative of the First Voyage to the Coasts of America," ed. Henry S. Burrage, in *Early English and French Voyages, Chiefly from Hackluyt: 1534-1608* (New York: Scribner's, 1908), pp. 228-29.
[6] "Observations by Master George Percy, 1607," ed. Lyon G. Tyler, in *Narratives of Early Virginia: 1606-1626* (New York: Scribner's, 1907), p. 16.
[7] John Brickell, *The Natural History of North Carolina* (Murfreesboro, N.C.: Johnson, 1968), p. 11.
[8] Joseph Kastner, *A Species of Eternity* (New York: Knopf, 1977), p. 40.
[9] Robert Beverley, *The History and Present State of Virginia*, ed. Louis B. Wright (Chapel Hill: Univ. of North Carolina Press, 1947), p. 17.
[10] Michael S. Tyler-Whittle, *The Plant Hunters* (Philadelphia: Chilton, 1970), p. 45.
[11] Robert Elman, *First in the Field: America's Pioneering Naturalists* (New York: Mason/Charter, 1977), p. 29.
[12] Edmund and Dorothy Berkeley, *The Life and Adventures of John Bartram from Lake Ontario to the River St. John* (Tallahassee: Univ. Presses of Florida, 1982), p. 183.
[13] Nancy Callahan, "The Bartrams, Plantmen Extraordinaire," *DAR Magazine* 114 (1980), 640.
[14] Kastner, p. 49.
[15] Kastner, p. 53.
[16] Berkeley, p. 68.
[17] Diderot, *"Essai sur la peinture,"* in *Oeuvres Complètes de Diderot*, ed. J. Assézat and P. Tourneux (Paris: Garnier, 1873-77), XI, 475. All references to the *Salons* hereafter are taken from this edition.
[18] See in particular the *Salon of 1763* and the famous Vernet promenade in the *Salon of 1767*. In *Lettres à Sophie Volland*, see the letter on 3 Aug. 1759 or the one on 5 Sept. 1767. *Lettres à Sophie Volland: Oeuvres Complètes*, intro. by R. Lewinter (Paris: Le Club Français du livre, 1969-73).
[19] Michael Fried, *Absorption and Theatricality: Painting and Beholder in the Age of Diderot* (Berkeley: Univ. of California Press, 1980).
[20] For a discussion of the feelings of Diderot's contemporaries in front of nature, see Pierre Daniel Mornet, *Le sentiment de la nature en France de J.J. Rousseau à Bernardin de St. Pierre* (Paris: Librairie Hachette, 1907), and Pierre Trahard, *Les maîtres de la sensibilité au XVIIIe siècle: 1715-1789*, I (Paris: Boivin, 1932).
[21] *Diderot's Letters to Sophie Volland: A Selection*, trans. Peter France (London: Univ. Press, 1972), 18 August, 1759.
[22] *Diderot's Letters to Sophie Volland*, 18 Aug. 1759.
[23] *Diderot's Letters to Sophie Volland*, 5 Sept. 1762.
[24] For a thorough discussion of the art critics of Diderot's time see Else Marie Bukdahl,

"Diderot, les salonniers et les esthéticiens de son temps," in *Diderot critique d'art*, II, trans. Jacques Piloz (Copenhague: Rosenkilde et Bagger, 1982).
[25] See Philip Conisbee, *Painting in Eighteenth Century France* (New York: Cornell Univ. Press, 1981). See also Ian J. Lochead, *The Spectator and the Landscape in the Art Criticism of Diderot and his Contemporaries* (Ann Arbor: UMI Research Press, 1981).
[26] "*Essai sur la peinture*," XI, 499.
[27] See Diderot, *Entretiens sur le fils naturel* (1757) and *De la posésie dramatique* (1758) in *Oeuvres Esthétiques*, ed. Paul Vernière (Paris: Garnier, 1968). For a discussion of Burke's influence on Diderot see Gita May, "Diderot and Burke: A Study in Aesthetic Affinity," PMLA 75 (1960), 527-39, and Else Marie Bukdahl, *Diderot critique d'art*, II, passim.
[28] Fried, p. 130.
[29] See *Les Entretiens sur le fils naturel*, pp. 97-98, and *Le Salon de 1767*, XI, 129.
[30] In the *The Paradox of Acting*, Diderot brings forth the same idea, the theater should strive to be more real to move us, but art, at the same time, is unnatural.
[31] *Salon de 1767*, XI, 113.
[32] *Salon de 1767*, XI, 371.
[33] See Marian Hobson, *The Object of Art, The Theory of Illusion in Eighteenth Century France* (Cambridge: Cambridge Univ. Press, 1982) and Jacques Chouillet, *La Formation des idées esthétiques de Diderot: 1745-1763* (Paris: Librairie Armand Colin, 1973). See particularly his chapter on "*Peinture et Magie*."
[34] Jacques Barzun, "Diderot Made Art Reviews into Art," *New York Times*, 28 Aug. 1983.
[35] See Diderot, *De L'interprétation de la nature* (1753) in *Oeuvres Philosophiques*, ed. P. Vernière (Paris: Garnier, 1963).
[36] On Kip, Knyff, Tillemans, and others, see Luke Hermann, *British Landscape Painting of the Eighteenth Century* (New York: Oxford Univ. Press, 1974), pp. 9-19.
[37] For example, Ronald Paulson, *Emblem and Expression: Meaning in English Art of the Eighteenth Century* (Cambridge, Mass.: Harvard Univ. Press, 1975); also below, J. D. Hunt, "The Gardens at Stowe," and George B. Clarke, "Grecian Taste and Gothic Virtue: Lord Cobham's Gardening Programme and its Iconography," in *Apollo* 97 (1973), 558-71.
[38] John Dixon Hunt, *The Figure in the Landscape: Poetry, Painting, and Gardening during the Eighteenth Century* (Baltimore: Johns Hopkins Univ. Press, 1976); Kenneth Woodbridge, "Henry Hoare's Paradise," *Art Bulletin* 47 (1965), 83-116; James Turner, "The Structure of Henry Hoare's Stourhead," *Art Bulletin* 61 (1979), 68-77; John Pinto, "The Landscape of Allusion: Literary Themes in the Gardens of Ancient Rome and Augustan England," *Smith College Studies in History* 48 (1980), 97-113.
[39] Pope wrote in his *Epistle to Burlington*:

Consult the Genius of the Place . . .
. . . . .
Nature shall join you; Time shall make it grow
A work to wonder at—perhaps a STOWE. (lines 57, 69-70)

[40] J. T. P. Bijhouwer, *Nederlandsche Tuinen en Buitenplaatsen* [*Dutch Gardens and Country Places*] (Amsterdam: De Lange, 1943), p. 30.
[41] Edward Hyams, *The English Garden* (New York: Abrams, n.d.), pp. 36-39; *Sir William Temple on the Gardens of Epicurus*, ed. Albert R. Sieveking (London: Chatto and Windus, 1908).
[42] *De Vrede van Nijmegen* [*The Peace of Nijmegen*] (Nijmegen: Nijmegen, 1978). Temple's portraits are on p. 41.
[43] *Het Stadhuis van Nijmegen* [*The Townhall of Nijmegen*] (Nijmegen: Nijmegen, 1982), pp. 130-51.
[44] For example, L. Knyff and J. Kip, *Britannia Illustrata* (London: D. Mortier, et al., 1707); for the Netherlands: Andries de Leth, *De Zegenpralende Vecht* [*The Triumphant River Vecht*] (1719) and M. Brouerius van Nidek, *Het Zegepralend Kennemerland* (1729); for France: Antoine Perelle, *Vues des Belles Maisons de France* (Paris, n.d.).

[45] *De Lusthof Het Loo*, ed. L. R. M. van Everdingen-Meyer, (The Hague, 1974). This is a translation with engravings by his contemporaries of *A Description of the King's Royal Palace and Gardens at Loo* (London, 1699), by William's physician, Dr. Walter Harris.

[46] Bijhouwer, p. 44.

[47] Woodbridge, "Henry Hoare's Paradise"; and Turner, "The Structure."

[48] See *The English Garden*. Also Max F. Schulz, "The Circuit Walk of the Eighteenth-Century Landscape Garden and the Pilgrim's Circuitous Progress," *Eighteenth-Century Studies* 15 (1981), 1-25.

[49] I. W. Case, *Horace Walpole, Gardenist* (Princeton, N. J.: Princeton Univ. Press, 1943), pp. 25-26; George Clarke, "Heresy in Stowe's Elysium," in *Furor Hortensis*, ed. Peter Willis (Edinburgh: Elysium Press, 1974), pp. 46-48; H. F. Clark, "Eighteenth-Century Elysiums," *Journal of the Warburg and Courtauld Institute* 6 (1943), 165-89; also Streatfield and Duckworth, p. 18; Marie Luise Gothein, *A History of Garden Art* (London: J.M. Dent, 1934), II, 278-79.

[50] Sir Joshua Reynolds, *Discourses on Art*, ed. Robert Wark (New Haven, Conn.: Yale Univ. Press, 1975).

III. SOCIETY

"HAD NOT JOSEPH WITHHELD HIM":
THE PORTRAYAL OF THE SOCIAL ELITE IN *JOSEPH ANDREWS*

BRIAN MCCREA

E. P. Thompson concludes his *Whigs and Hunters: The Origin of the Black Act* with a sophisticated and convincing discussion of the relationship between "legal forms" and social conflict in eighteenth-century England.[1] Spurning a simplistic Marxist analysis, Thompson describes how the Whig oligarchy "created new laws and bent old legal forms in order to legitimize its own property and status" (p. 260). He also observes that "the essential precondition for the effectiveness of law, in its function as ideology, is that it shall display an independence from gross manipulation and shall seem to be just. It cannot seem to be so without upholding its own logic and criteria of equity; indeed, on occasion, by actually being just" (p. 263). Consequently, Thompson claims, the law functioned in paradoxical, independent ways. He writes:

> the law can be seen to mediate and legitimate existent class relations. Its forms and procedures may crystallize those relations and mask ulterior injustice. But this mediation, through the forms of law, is something quite distinct from the exercise of unmediated force. The forms and rhetoric of law acquire a distinct identity which may, on occasion, inhibit power and afford some protection to the powerless. Only to the degree that this is seen to be so can the law be of service in its other aspect, as ideology. (p. 266)

Oddly enough, Thompson, who is famous for his studies of working class life, concludes *Whigs and Hunters* by analyzing the motives of the elite. He perhaps leaves open the question of how, apart from physical and emotional coercion, the poor became loyal to legal forms that, by and large, worked to their disadvantage. Eighteenth-century fiction, in its treatment of birth and class, fostered, it can be argued, the mediation Thompson describes. Writers like Fielding and Richardson redirected and, I think, domesticated the rebellious attitudes they initially seemed to encourage. Those members of the servant and lower classes who followed the stories of Pamela and Joseph Andrews were dosed, however gently and subtly, with social conservatism. Thus, while Thompson's general account seems plausible, his claim that "Men whose sensibility had been nourished by *Joseph Andrews* or by Goldsmith found the Black Act less easy to stomach" (p. 254) appears suspect and open to disagreement.

This social conservatism is particularly manifest in Fielding's use of the birth-mystery plot.[2] Having introduced Joseph and Fanny as characters of low birth whose physical charms and Christian virtues far outshine those of their social betters, Fielding turns to a birth-mystery to explain those virtues. We discover that Joseph is, after all, a gentleman and that Fanny is of better birth than we thought; their marriage no longer is the affront to social class that it once (briefly) appeared to be. Of course, one might argue that Fielding's resolution has a literary rather than a social motive; Joseph's acquisition of money and social status perfectly fits Northrop Frye's definition of "New Comedy."[3] But, if Fielding serves literary convention, he also serves the class structure of English society, once seemingly under attack. The elevation of Joseph and Fanny is one part of an ongoing vindication of the social elite—a vindication that Fielding pursues persistently, if sometimes grudgingly, throughout *Joseph Andrews*.

This last claim may seem a bit startling. After all, *Joseph Andrews* offers a group portrait of England's great families that is, on the surface, unflattering. Sir Thomas Booby, Beau Didapper, and the roasting country squire immediately come to mind as aristocrats who are either incompetent, impotent, or cruel. The lone blight upon Mr. Wilson's perfect rural retirement is the squire who is his neighbor—a man who "was as absolute as any Tyrant in the Universe" and "had too great a Fortune to contend with" (p. 228).[4] Lady Booby's passion for Joseph and the equivocations to which it drives her demean notions of aristocratic superiority. Indeed, Fielding seems to delight in counterpointing her passion to that of her waiting maid, Mrs. Slipslop. He claims that he has shown us "the different Operations of this passion Love in the gentle and cultivated Mind of the Lady Booby, from those which it effected in the less polished and coarser Disposition of Mrs. Slipslop." But he actually describes the great lady in "a temper of Mind not greatly different from that of the inflamed Slipslop" (p. 34). He suggests the power of social distinction only to bring it into question. Much the same happens when Adams and Fanny appear before a justice of the peace "who was just returned from the Fox-Chace" and was "in the Height of his Mirth and Cups" (p. 145). The justice has little Latin, less Greek, and views the judicial process as an opportunity to have "good Sport." He releases Adams and Fanny only because of the chance discovery that Adams is a gentleman: "Nobody can say I have committed a Gentleman since I have been in the Commission" (p. 149).

In describing all these members of the elite, Fielding exercises his considerable talent for satire. He also echoes the standard Whig criticism of the fox-hunting, bibulous, Tory country squire. Less obvious, perhaps, is his stimulation and subversion of egalitarian sympathies. Fielding uses these satiric portraits to elicit anger at and criticism of the great; having done so, he then rehabilitates the class and converts anger into submission, criticism into toleration. The shift begins, fittingly enough, at the novel's center. In Book III, Chapter ii—the chapter immediately following Fielding's famous compliment to Ralph Allen as "a Commoner raised higher above the Multitude by superior Talents, than is in the power of his Prince to exalt him" (pp. 190-91)—Fielding describes "several wonderful Adventures" that befall Adams, Joseph, and Fanny. He also announces a development in his narrative technique—a development motivated, finally, by his need to protect the great:

> The Reader must excuse me if I am not particular as to the Way they took; for as we are now drawing near the Seat of the *Boobies*; and as that is a ticklish Name, which malicious Persons may apply according to their evil Inclinations to several worthy Country 'Squires, a Race of Men whom we look upon as entirely inoffensive, and for whom we have an adequate Regard, we shall lend no assistance to any such malicious Purposes (pp. 191-92).

Once again a literary explanation for Fielding's demur offers itself. This passage, one might argue, simply applies the famous formula for general satire that Fielding offers in Book III, Chapter i: "I describe not Men, but Manners; not an Individual, but a Species" (p. 189). That the motivation for the demur is largely social, however, becomes clear if we note two points. First, Fielding's narrative is no less particular after this passage than before it. Second, and most important, the second half of the novel makes amends to the great figures satirized in the first half. Following hard upon the tribute to a great "Commoner," the vindication is not total nor without qualification. Fielding will not claim to love the "Country Squires" but only to find them "inoffensive." His "Regard" for them is "adequate," not great. Satire continues in the novel's second half, sometimes at the expense of the great. But, in conjunction with the birth-mystery plot, Fielding's characterization of the social elite in the novel's second half is conservative. While Thompson believes that *Joseph Andrews* nourished kinder, more democratic sensibilities, the novel finally calls for submission to (and benefit from) one's betters.

Lady Booby, for example, comes off quite well in Book IV, Chapter xiv, Parson Adams's much-discussed "Night Adventures." Amidst all the chaos caused by the characters' mistaking one another's beds, she moves "undauntedly" and "with a bold spirit" (p. 352). She brings light into Slipslop's dark room; while Adams offers supernatural explanations, she finds Didapper's "fine pair of Diamond Buttons" (p. 333) and solves the mystery. She leaves the scene with healthy, hearty laughter, understanding what has happened and enjoying the incongruous sight that Adams and Slipslop present. She is in control, not only of the situation but of herself.

Much the same happens to the incompetent justice of the peace. He reappears in the novel's final chapter to inform Adams that "he had found the Fellow who attempted to swear against him and the young woman the very next day, and had committed him to Salisbury Goal, where he was charged with many Robberies" (p. 341). The justice's appearance has no motivation (he is returning a horse that ran away from the careless, too passionate Adams) other than allowing Fielding to mute his earlier criticism of the law and its officers. This "Gentleman," like Lady Booby, has been satirized, then vindicated. Having earlier used Parson Adams to question legal and social standards, Fielding here achieves a reconciliation. In this same last chapter Adams also finds a place in the Church hierarchy; his other-worldly virtue is placed within the secular community through the good auspices of the new Mr. Booby. Indeed, although Sir Thomas has died, his character is vindicated in that of his nephew, who tirelessly performs good offices, rewarding everyone from Fanny and Adams to the peddler. The reward always comes in the standard coin of the society: a living for Mr. Adams; a civil service position for the peddler; an annuity for Fanny. As Lady Booby finally brings order to the "Night-Adventures," so, in the novel's final chapter, her nephew operates as a social *deus ex machina*.

Fielding's vindication of the elite is not entirely uncritical. Lady Booby returns to the world of London frivolity, apparently uninterested in continuing the service to the village for which Adams praises her (p. 101). The second Mr. Booby is rebuked by Adams for laughing in church and is coupled with a wife who is even more petty and spiteful. The roasting squire, although ducked "twice or thrice" by Adams with near fatal consequences (p. 251), apparently survives unchanged; Wilson's neighbor is unregenerate. Still, loyalty to the existing order is the novel's final, if understated, theme. The earlier satiric episodes are more striking than the quiet and later vindications of the elite. They force the audience to admit egalitarian sympathies which Fielding then can subtly undermine.

Nowhere is this clearer than in Book III, Chapter v, the "tragical Adventure" of Wilson's dog. While Thompson, the greatest authority upon the Black Act, makes no note of this incident, which turns upon the laws that limited poaching, it offers a fine example of Fielding using the law "to mediate . . . existent class relations." The favorite dog of Wilson's daughter is shot and killed by "the young Squire, the son of the Lord of the Manor." Adding insult to injury, the young squire swears that "he would prosecute the Master of him for keeping a Spaniel; for that he had given notice he would not suffer one in the Parish." The young squire's action, of course, is horrible and cruel, but it is also legal. In eighteenth-century England, "By statute a [game] keeper had wide discretionary powers, including the right to destroy dogs disturbing the game."[5] Uninterested in mere legalities, "Adams grasped his Crab-Stick and would have sallied out after the Squire, had not Joseph with-held him." In this exchange I find a synechdoche for Fielding's uneasy social conservatism. The righteousness of Adams, while admirable, is asocial, and must be restrained and directed by the sense of social propriety and submission that Joseph represents. The young squire may be criticized but must not be attacked, at least not until he makes the mistake of violating the law. Adams rightly can hope to "catch him in my Garden." Until that time, the squire, who has "killed all the Dogs, and taken away all the guns in the Neighborhood" (p. 228), is too great "to contend with."

At work in the "tragical Adventure of the Dog," as in *Joseph Andrews* as a whole, is Fielding's conservatism, his loyalty to the social status quo. This loyalty finally masters his satiric, egalitarian, even rebellious sense of social injustice. Joseph must restrain Adams; Adams must be brought to accept a living from a Booby. Motivated by this loyalty, Fielding comes to a grudging admiration for the flawed members of the social elite. Lady Booby must have a good night, and the justice of the peace must get his man. Most fascinating about this quiet conservatism, however, is its efficiency in achieving the mediation that Thompson has described. Fielding's fiction, which opens by seeming to question "existent class relations," closes by vindicating them. The birth-mystery plays a powerful role in that vindication, but so too do the changes in Fielding's portrayal of the boobies and squires. In its conclusion, *Joseph Andrews* suggests that its reader also give to country squires an "adequate Regard." For those readers of the servant and lower classes who were exposed to *Joseph Andrews*, who were charmed and flattered by its opening description of a virtuous and handsome footman, such regard could "mask ulterior injustice" and could lead them, like Adams, to wait for justice rather than question the law.

In this way, *Joseph Andrews*, for all its bright good humor and wealth of classical allusion, becomes as much a social as a literary document; it serves the interests of an elite class. While criticizing the "unmediated force," the excessiveness of the young squire, Fielding vindicates the law—the law controlled by the elite. Fielding's ideology is powerful precisely because it is so quiet. In the midst of all the confusion and laughter, we easily forget Lady Booby's mystery-solving light, her nephew's powerful beneficence, and, most important of all, Joseph's restraining hand. In these and other instances, however, Fielding can be seen "to legitimize . . . property and status" and to merit further analysis in Thompson's terms.

NOTES

¹New York: Pantheon Books, 1975.

²See Brian McCrea, "Rewriting *Pamela*: Social Change and Religious Faith in *Joseph Andrews*," *Studies in the Novel* 16 (1984), 137-49, for an extended discussion of the social applications that Fielding finds for the birth-mystery plot.

³See *The Anatomy of Criticism* (Princeton, N. J.: Princeton Univ. Press, 1957), p. 44 for the definition of "New Comedy" and p. 51 for the discussion of "birth-mystery plots."

⁴Henry Fielding, *Joseph Andrews*, ed. Martin C. Battestin (Middletown, Conn.: Wesleyan Univ. Press, 1967), p. 21. All other citations of *Joseph Andrews* are taken from the Wesleyan edition. Page numbers are given in parentheses.

⁵Douglas Hay, "Poaching and the Game Laws on Cannock Chase," in *Albion's Fatal Tree*, ed. Douglas Hay, Peter Linebaugh, John G. Rule, E. P. Thompson, and Cal Linebaugh (New York: Pantheon Books, 1975), p. 215. Hay is an associate of Thompson, and I cite him because he is so admirably concise. For Thompson's discussion of the statutes concerning dogs, see *Whigs and Hunters*, pp. 63, 65, 104.

SCOTTISH PHILOSOPHY AND POLITICAL ECONOMY

SPENCER DAVIS

In his recent work, *The Economics of David Ricardo*, Samuel Hollander rejects the hallowed distinction between Adam Smith's empirical, inductive economics and David Ricardo's abstract, deductive economics. According to Hollander, Adam Smith was more and Ricardo less a deductive analyst than has been allowed. Smith's important analysis of the corn bounty rested on a rigid deductive model and reached policy conclusions without taking into account the costs of moving from one equilibrium position to another. The highly unrealistic corn model of growth, in which corn is the single input and the single output, was Smith's, not Ricardo's, model. Confronted with the extreme and dogmatic conclusions his friend James Mill asserted in *Elements of Political Economy*, Ricardo reminded Mill of the qualifications that tempered such conclusions. James Mill's dogmatism, Hollander insists, was his own and was not taken over by Ricardo as the method of economic analysis.[1]

Accepting the broad sweep of Hollander's interpretation, I think it worthwhile to seek a source beyond temperamental dogmatism for Mill's claims to completely certain economic knowledge. I have found what I believe to be that source in the Scottish philosophy of common sense, fashioned by Thomas Reid, and taught to Mill at Edinburgh by Dugald Stewart.[2]

It was James Mill who removed the method of Reid and Stewart from its theological setting and coupled it to political economy.[3] Mill was consciously the methodologist.[4] He dismissed the man of so-called practical experience, denying that experience could ever be free of theory. He abhorred the notion that something true in theory "required correction in practice."[5] In *An Essay of the Impolicy of a Bounty on the Exportation of Grain*, Mill distinguished between the argument from experience made by the advocates of the bounty and observed that they had only shown the export bounty and a low price of grain occurring at the same time, which was no proof that the bounty caused the low price.[6]

The need for precise definitions was one of Mill's favorite topics. Their absence in Henry Brougham's *Inquiry into the Colonial Policy of the European Powers* was one of his many criticisms of that work.[7] Mill called the vocabulary of merchants a short-hand, useful to them, but deceptive, because of vagueness and ambiguity as a guide to economic analysis.[8] No one can doubt how large a part of scientific method precise definitions were for Mill after reading John Stuart Mill's account of how his father trained him in the art of dissecting fuzzy definitions.[9]

Mill believed the principles of economics were clearly established. The problem was not the difficulty of the subject but the effort needed to convince the public to believe and act on the principles of economics.[10] And the principles were simple. Mill said, for example, that refuting the argument for the export bounty on grain "requires the examination only of a single principle, a principle very well understood." Mill was consistently able to find things "abundantly certain," "plain," "necessarily and obviously so," "obviously necessary," "incontrovertible," "completely agreed upon by those who had studied the principles of national wealth," "abundantly evident."[11] These expressions are not merely the conventions of early nineteenth-century polemics. We find Mill in his correspondence with Ricardo committed to a science of legislation in spite of Ricardo's (all too polite, we may think) objections.[12]

In *Elements of Political Economy* Mill put the wage fund theory in its starkest form—the average wage was equal to the wage fund divided by the number of workers. As a theory of wages in the short run, the wage fund theory is defensible, but Mill made it true in the long run, everywhere and in all periods.[13] History was a race between the growth of capital (the wage fund) and population. In this contest, Mill claimed, population always increased faster. This astounding proposition Mill proved deductively, dismissing all population statistics as irrelevant. He boldly asserted that all the statistics available were too flawed to rely on. But in any case, the figures proved nothing. Until there were figures on infant mortality and family formation, no one could say why the population of a country was what it was. But Mill did not propose to gather those figures. In fact, what he did was to present figures he thought reasonable. But even as armchair deductive theorizing this was half-hearted, for Mill never bothered to calculate the number of married persons—and how that number might vary—in particular societies. Mill's disdain for statistics and confidence in his own hypothetical estimates, when revision and reworking of available data seemed called for, is a notable feature of his method.[14]

Mill never justified this technique, and his only essay on method never comes to grips with any other problem either. Mill defended the scientific status of political economy for the following reasons. Economic science can be divided into many small propositions, each of which individually can be easily ascertained. Economics was a science since its questions covered the whole field of inquiry. Finally, economics was a science because all those competent in the field concurred on the important doctrines of the science.[15]

We may note some doubts Ricardo had about Mill's simplistic axioms. The most consistent theme in Mill's journalism and in his *History of British India* is the attack on aristocracy. With his typical overstatement, Mill once declared encroaching aristocracy the chief problem throughout history.[16] The rule of an aristocracy not only robbed the people of any role in the nation's political life but had damaging economic consequences as well. In Sicily the nobles had ruined agriculture through their system of price-fixing.[17] The aristocratic devices of primogeniture and entail hindered agricultural improvement.[18] In an essay on Spanish America, Mill lengthened the bill of particulars. Bad government, which is to say aristocratic government, harmed the economy of Spanish America by fastening ignorance and sloth on the people of that region.[19] The *History of British India* divides into three parts: the unsparing portrait of Hindu society, the attack on the East India Company, and the attack on British rule in India. In each of these cases Mill was attacking a privileged order—Brahmins, monopolists, and placeholders.[20]

In attacking aristocracies Mill made them out to be powerful, calculating, and united, as well as grasping to a degree scarcely credible. Ricardo and Mill debated this point in their correspondence. Like Mill, Ricardo had no very high opinion of the Members of Parliament, but he held that the love of ease and thirst for popular acclaim limited the venality of the powerful. Ricardo also inquired of Mill how, given a totally corrupt Parliament, there could ever be the reform Mill desired. Mill responded that "All great changes in society are easily effected, when the time is come," but Ricardo countered this by asking how one knew that the time for reform had arrived and what in the meantime the reformer could accomplish. But these shrewd points by Ricardo had no influence on Mill, and he continued to theorize on the premise of a nearly omnipotent aristocracy.[21]

Now, admitting that James Mill "in a degree once common, but now very unusual, threw his feelings into his opinions," as his son said, it is still of some interest to find the intellectual source of those opinions.[22] Of course, not all Mill's assumptions and procedures can be traced to his predecessors. But to find the source of a number of Mill's opinions on method puts him in a clearer perspective and also clears the way to seeing, or at least entertaining the possibility, that certainty in social science was a common presupposition in late eighteenth- and early nineteenth-century British thought. The source that Mill drew on, and which others may have drawn on, was the Scottish philosophy of common sense.[23]

The philosophy of common sense was designed to refute Hume's arguments against the "religious hypothesis." What Thomas Reid, its founder, proposed to do was to revive under the name of common sense the innate ideas and necessary features of the universe that Hume had banished.[24] According to Reid, all adults share common ideas without which reasoning and life are impossible. These principles were the foundation of science as well as the rules of common sense. "Such principles," said Reid, "when we have occasion to use them in science, are called axioms."[25] The principles of common sense were the principles of mathematics as well as the principles of all the sciences.[26]

Here may be the foundation of the verificationist stress on assumptions. Physics had made such great progress in modern times because Newton had laid down the axioms and thus ended all sterile controversy. For Reid, the solidity of Newton's axioms meant that "there is now no more dispute or controversy among men of knowledge [about physics], than there is about the conclusions of mathematics."[27]

Reid abandoned his definition of common sense in terming the axioms of physical science, which were not common knowledge, principles of common sense. Such principles, he admitted, could be hidden by "vulgar prejudice" and the "enchantment of words" and could not be proven to someone who doubted them. They could, he said, be placed in the proper light, and what was not intuitively obvious would become so.[28]

The principles of common sense Reid adopted were so generous as to eliminate not just skepticism but any problem about knowledge. Reid held that the operations of one's own mind could be known for certain. Memory of recent events was also certain.[29] Perceptions were always perceptions of something and not just mental events.[30] Still, these principles were not enough for Reid. He added the following proviso: "I need hardly say that I shall also take for granted such facts as are attested to by the conviction of all sober and reasonable men, either by our senses, by memory, or by human testimony."[31]

Reid classified knowledge about politics as merely probable since it was based on analogy.[32] But this was a meaningless qualification. Reid insisted that while the senses are fallible, their testimony is not corrupt. Observation and experimentation were for Reid simple and trustworthy processes, since the attributes of an object can be distinguished perfectly easily.[33] In fact, Reid made the seventh principle of common sense that "the natural faculties, by which we distinguish truth from error, are not fallacious."[34] Thus for Reid the inductions performed on the "real facts" gathered by observation and experiment are uncomplicated and trustworthy. I find nothing in Reid to put the knowledge of politics on a less firm basis.

From Reid's perspective, false systems of philosophy and science resulted from human pride and the bewitchment of language. As Reid saw things, a good dose of Christian humility and careful attention to terminology insured accurate results.[35] To this philosophy Dugald Stewart added his rhetorical and persuasive skills and one substantive point. The philosophy of mind was the basis for all social science according to Stewart.[36] And Stewart defined the study of mind as a science itself. All mental operations could be explained as the results of a small number of faculties or principles of action. "These faculties and principles are the general law of our constitution, and hold the same place in the philosophy of mind, that the general laws we investigate in physics, hold in that science" (2:51-52).

Stewart used the mantle of Newton to buttress his opposition to physiological studies of mind. Just as science ultimately reached general facts that could not be explained by science (though, of course, theology could explain them), so the study of mind, once it reached general laws by the inspection of consciousness, could go no further. Stewart thus ruled out anything other than introspection at any stage of the investigation of mind (2:52).

The function of the philosophy of mind was to provide the clear definitions and axioms that the sciences used. Since definitions and axioms were the foundation of science, the philosophy of mind, which provided the definitions and axioms, was the foundation for all science (2:78-87). For Stewart there was no division between physical and social science. Both made predictions using general facts as premises (3:325-32). The facts of human nature yielded predictions just as the astronomer's data, distilled into laws, yielded predictions (2:213-20). With the growth of knowledge and progress of reason, legislation could become a science. "The political history of the world," said Stewart, "will be regulated by steady and uniform causes, and the philosopher will be enabled to form probable conjectures with respect to the future course of human affairs" (2:249).

Stewart argued, with an extremism positively Millian, the inferiority of the man of fact. The man of detail, he said, had "an understanding, minute and circumscribed in its views, timid in its exertions, and formed for servile imitation." There were the men of general views and then there were "the common drudges in business" (2:218). Those who posed as men of detail in politics and statisticians in economics, arguing that experience should be the only guide, received an especially severe rebuke from Stewart as captives of their own unrecognized and self-serving theories (3:333-34).

In attacking the man of detail (and the enemy of reform) Stewart knit together methodology and his belief in progress. The man of detail and enemy of reform, Stewart said, admits nothing to be possible but what already exists and accuses theorists of reasoning mechanically, but those assertions he regarded as fallacious. In the first place, the theorist's knowledge of human nature represents a vaster induction, and so a securer foundation for political reasoning, than the personal experience of the man of detail. Second, with the progress of knowledge, society changes, so the statesman must make policy on the facts of the present and the trend of development, rather than the past alone. And, finally, since society changes and events do not repeat themselves, the repetition that learning from experience requires does not exist. What the advocates of experience pass off as "experience" is nothing but their own theory (2:220-29).

Reid's treatment of method was wholly—and Stewart's was largely—conducted within the confines of the religious controversy with Hume. A passage from Stewart attacking David Hartley demonstrates this point dramatically. Stewart refused to accept Hartley's theory that a hypothesis not contradicted by the facts counted as true. Hartley's view of hypothesis suggested that God had hidden the laws of nature and forced man to guess at them. Stewart would have none of this. He declared that science is

> by the diligent study of facts and analogies legible to all, to discover the key which infinite Wisdom has itself prepared for the interpretation of its own laws. In other words, its object is to concentrate and cast on the unknown parts of the universe, the lights which are reflected from those which are known (3:308-09).

Further on, Stewart returned to this theme, praising Bacon for turning men's attention to the study of nature and thus "laying the foundation of a bulwark against atheism more stable and impregnable than the united labours of the ancients were able to rear" (3:338).

Stewart was in a difficult situation. He had had the bad luck to lecture on political economy while the war against Revolutionary France raged, and he had mentioned Condorcet favorably in *Elements of the Philosophy of Mind*. For these indiscretions he fell from the good graces of Edinburgh's leading reactionaries.[37] The harsher fate others met certainly weighed on Stewart. His device of conjuring up a vast gulf between scientific economic analysis and practical politics by stressing the legislator's need for experience and good judgment is therefore understandable. It is not, however, a tactic likely to deter readers, and especially not a reader like James Mill, from finding Stewart's arguments for certainty in social science.

Mill made a selective use of the elements in Stewart's work. Another of Stewart's students, Francis Horner, reached a position on method very distant from Mill's. While Horner, like Mill, accepted Stewart's arguments that psychology was the basis for social science and that the man of theory was superior to the man of detail, he also learned from Stewart to consider Adam Smith's economics a great but flawed achievement rather than a completed science.[38]

If it is true that Horner was closer than Mill to the general thrust of Stewart's political economy, Mill was drawing on elements easily found in the works of Stewart and Reid. It was from Stewart and Reid that Mill learned that social and physical science were one, that science was the straightforward operation of combining observation with careful definitions, that observation was uncomplicated, that there was a science of legislation, that what was true in theory applied directly to practice. Reid and Stewart argued for certainty in social science less because they believed in it than because refuting Hume required it. Mill, at once cruder and less hypocritical, took their arguments to actually represent method in social science.

NOTES

[1] Samuel Hollander, *The Economics of David Ricardo* (Toronto: Univ. of Toronto Press, 1979), Chs. 1, 2.
[2] That James Mill was Ricardo's teacher on method is argued in T.W. Hutchison, "James Mill and Ricardian Economics," *On Revolutions and Progress in Economic Knowledge* (Cambridge: Cambridge Univ. Press, 1978), Ch. 2.
[3] James Mill, "Politics," *Literary Journal* 1 (6 Jan. 1803), 60.
[4] James Mill, "Sur la Tolération Religieuse," *Edinburgh Review* 32 (Aug. 1810), 413-30; "Liberty of the Press," *Edinburgh Review* 35 (May 1811), 98-123.
[5] John Stuart Mill, *Collected Works*, 21 Vols, 1963-84, eds. John M. Robson and Jack Stillinger (Toronto: Univ. of Toronto Press, 1981), I, 35.
[6] James Mill, "An Essay of the Impolicy of a Bounty on the Exportation of Grain," in *Selected Economic Writings*, ed. Donald Winch (Chicago: Univ. of Chicago Press, 1966), pp. 45-51.
[7] James Mill, "Brougham's 'Inquiry into the Colonial Policy of the European Powers,'" *Literary Journal* 2 (16 Nov. 1803), 513-28.
[8] James Mill, "Paper Currency," *Literary Journal* 3 (1 June 1804), 627-35.
[9] J. S. Mill, *Collected Works*, I, 23-25.
[10] James Mill, *Selected Economic Writings*, p. 42.
[11] James Mill, *Selected Economic Writings*, pp. 55, 60-65, 73.
[12] *Works and Correspondence of David Ricardo*, ed. Piero Sraffa, 10 vols. (Cambridge: Cambridge Univ. Press, 1962), VI, Nos. 109, 114, 134, 135; VII, Nos. 232, 234, 246, 247.
[13] George J. Stigler, *The Economist as Preacher, and Other Essays* (Chicago: Univ. of Chicago Press, 1982), pp. 162-63.
[14] James Mill, *Selected Economic Writings*, pp. 230-35.
[15] James Mill, "Whether Political Economy Is Useful," *Selected Economic Writings*, pp. 377-82.
[16] James Mill, "Voyage aux Indes Orientales," *Edinburgh Review* 33 (Jan. 1810), 378.
[17] James Mill, "Survey of the Foreign Affairs of Great Britain," *Edinburgh Review* 25 (Oct. 1808), 188-97.
[18] James Mill, "Jovellanos on Agriculture and Legislation," *Edinburgh Review* 27 (Apr. 1809), 25-34.
[19] James Mill, "Emancipation of Spanish America," *Edinburgh Review* 26 (Jan. 1809), 281.
[20] James Mill, *History of British India*, 6 vols, 5th ed. (London: James Madden, 1858). On the *History of British India* as a radical document, see Duncan Forbes, "James Mill and India," *Cambridge Journal* 5 (Oct. 1951), 19-23; Eric Stokes, *The English Utilitarians and India* (Oxford: Clarendon Press, 1959), p. 53.
[21] *Works and Correspondence of David Ricardo*, VI, Nos. 109, 114, 134, 135; VII Nos. 232, 234, 246, 247.
[22] J.S. Mill, *Collected Works*, I, 51. In his final estimate of his father, J.S. Mill regret-

ted the "injustice [he did] to his own opinions by the unconscious exaggerations of an intellect emphatically polemical" and admitted that his father "when thinking without an adversary in view, . . . was willing to make room for a great portion of the truths he seemed to deny" (I, 211).

[23] Karl Pearson, *The History of Statistics in the Seventeenth and Eighteenth Centuries*, ed. E. S. Pearson (London: Charles Griffin, 1978), Chs. 9, 10.

[24] Robert H. Hurlbutt, III, *Hume, Newton, and the Design Argument* (Lincoln: Univ. of Nebraska Press, 1965).

[25] Thomas Reid, *Essays on the Intellectual Powers of Man* (Cambridge, Mass.: M.I.T. Press, 1969), p. 31.

[26] Reid, pp. 32-33. Reid called the principles of mathematics self-evident axioms. The principles of other sciences were not self-evident, but they were principles of common sense because unavoidable and universally accepted.

[27] Reid, p. 32. Verificationism has been defined by Mark Blaug as the method of considering positive instances as confirmation of a theory and negative instances as proof not that the theory is wrong but that disturbing causes are at work. Thus, verificationism operates to insulate a theory from disconfirmation. Blaug is particularly harsh on J. S. Mill for using verificationism to protect the exploded Ricardian framework. Mark Blaug, *The Methodology of Economics* (Cambridge: Cambridge Univ. Press, 1980) pp. 55, 59-77, 81.

[28] Reid, p. 33. Transferred to political economy, this is nearly the whole of James Mill's method.

[29] Reid, pp. 34-35.

[30] Reid, p. 37. Reid later went much farther: all perceptions are backed up by God (pp. 82-83, 118, 309).

[31] Reid, p. 40. The list of abilities, concepts, and beliefs we have "by our constitution" is even longer in Norman Daniels's account. See "On Having Concepts 'By Our Constitution,'" *Thomas Reid: Critical Interpretations*, ed. Stephen F. Barker and Tom L. Beauchamp (Philadelphia: Philosophical Monographs, 1976), p. 35.

[32] Reid, *Intellectual Powers*, p. 49.

[33] Reid, p. 480.

[34] Reid, p. 630.

[35] Reid, pp. 485, 707. Cf. Norman Daniels, *Thomas Reid's Inquiry* (New York: Burt Franklin, 1974), p. 29.

[36] John Veitch, "Memoir of Dugald Stewart," *Collected Works of Dugald Stewart*, ed. Sir William Hamilton, 10 vols. plus supp. (Philadelphia: Carey, Lea & Carey, 1827), X, 35. Further references to this work are cited parenthetically by volume and page.

[37] Basic sources on Scotland during the years of the French Revolution are Henry Cockburn, *Memorials of His Time*, New ed. (Edinburgh: Foulis, 1910); Henry W. Meikle, *Scotland and the French Revolution* (Glasgow: James Mackhose, 1912); William Ferguson, *Scotland, 1689 to the Present* (Edinburgh: Oliver and Boyd, 1968); J. B. Morell, "Professors Robison and Playfair, and the *Theophobia Gallica*; Natural philosophy, religion and politics in Edinburgh, 1789-1815," *Notes and Records of the Royal Society of London* 26, 1 (June 1971).

[38] *Memoirs and Correspondence of Francis Horner, M.P.*, 2 vols, ed. Leonard Horner (London: John Murray, 1853), I, 215-16, 237-38; Francis Horner, "Thornton on the paper credit of Great Britain," *Edinburgh Review* 1 (Oct. 1802), 173-74, 180. In a letter to Malthus, Francis Jeffrey noted that, while he would agree with Malthus pamphlets on the corn trade, he thought they would put Horner in "despair" since "Horner is much more Smithish." Lord Cockburn, *Life of Lord Jeffrey*, 2 vols. (Philadelphia: Lippincott, 1856), II, 119-20.

"GOVERNMENT BY CONSENT OF THE GOVERNED" IN EIGHTEENTH-CENTURY CONSTITUTIONAL THEORY

LESLIE FRIEDMAN GOLDSTEIN

Prominent in current scholarship on the U.S. Supreme Court is debate over the question whether the judiciary's power to declare laws void was intended (by the founding generation) to include resort to unwritten natural and customary law, in addition to the letter and spirit of the written Constitution.[1] However, new light can be shed on this debate by attention to the extremely rapid transformation that took place in American constitutional theory during the last quarter of the eighteenth century. The concept of "government by consent of the the governed" was of pivotal importance in this transformation; thus, an examination of this specific evolution, during the period from 1776 to 1803, the date of the U.S. Supreme Court's assertion of its power to declare congressional acts void,[2] illustrates the following: (1) the meaning of government by consent of the governed; (2) the relationship between that concept and the practice of writing and ratifying constitutions; (3) the relationship between that concept and the debate over legislative versus judicial supremacy; and (4) the relationship between that concept and the debate, still current, over textual versus extratextual judicial review.

I. 1776-1786

The galvanizing role of belief in a higher law of natural justice or natural rights as a moral force leading to the American Revolution is widely known.[3] The question to be explored here is the extent to which natural law or natural rights dominated the American view of political life, as contrasted with other possible bases of political/legal obligation such as custom or "the consent of the governed." All three, in fact, played a role, but the dominance of the respective roles changed dramatically over the final quarter of the eighteenth century.

A. Consent of the Governed to Legislation

Although "government by consent of the governed" has been a political shibboleth in America at least since the seventeenth century,[4] its meaning has undergone some twists and turns over the past 300 years. Since the early colonies were settled by groups organized as stockholder companies, often religiously based, their company/colonial charters generally granted voting rights to the adult males who belonged.[5] These voters selected local governing bodies, who were generally left alone by the British authorities.[6]

What began as universal manhood suffrage accompanying home rule in the 1600s became radically transformed by the early 1700s, as more and more people immigrated who belonged to neither the local company nor the local church. By the early eighteenth century property and religious requirements for suffrage were fairly stringent, resulting in an essentially oligarchical system, yet Americans still spoke and wrote of living under "government by consent of the governed."[7]

In the British theory at this time the House of Commons was thought to "re-present" (i.e., to present another version of) the people and to act in their behalf, as distinguished from by their instructions. The people being represented were thought of as having a homogeneous interest and as sending the most virtuous and honorable of their number off to Commons to speak for them. The manner of selection, who participated, what size election districts, etc., was not particularly important, except that all who participated in the selection needed to have an independent will and a stake in the community, both of which were viewed in the eighteenth century as requiring property. The sense in which "the people" were thought to give consent to public policy was that they shared in the lawmaking process: Commons had to consent in the name of the people, as did Lords in the name of the nobility or property, and the monarch in the name of the whole nation.[8]

The American colonies, of course, had no house of aristocrats, and, until the crises of the 1760s, the King had left them pretty much to be ruled by their own assemblies. These assemblies did generally have an upper house, appointed by the crown, and also had to work with a governor appointed by the crown, but these colonial upper houses were not really second legislative chambers in the full sense; although they had some legislative responsibilities, they functioned largely as advisers to the governor.[9] Thus, the legislative house elected by the people had a much more dominant role over policy than it had in England.

Moreover, the degree of popular consent entailed in the voting for members of those American legislatures had yet again transformed itself by the 1770s. Because religious exclusion was largely unenforced and because property was readily available, the oligarchical system of the earlier eighteenth century had given way to one in which, at least in the northern colonies, very substantial majorities of the adult male population now constituted the electorate, despite property qualifications similar to those in England. One recent survey of the literature estimates that the standard voter turnout rates, for the adult male population in the northern colonies in the 1770s, were actually slightly higher than they are currently in the U.S.[10]

The Revolution then intensified these already large differences from the British pattern. The prevailing assumption of the homogeneity of the community and of its "common good" had in turn supported the idea that non-voters could be "virtually" represented as the voters were "actually" represented.[11] During the heated 1760s the colonists began to challenge the British notion of virtual representation, and, although the idea did survive the Revolution, it had come under enough of a shadow that suffrage restrictions were substantially eased in the early post-Revolution constitutions. Vermont formally instituted universal manhood suffrage. New Hampshire did the same, and Delaware, Georgia, and North Carolina instituted the practical equivalent of manhood suffrage for non-slaves. Moreover, Pennsylvania changed its rules to the point that 90% of adult males qualified.[12] Significantly, after the Revolution the size of state legislative bodies was greatly expanded, sometimes doubled or tripled. The logic here was to put the people in closer touch with their representative, and the expansion apparently had the effect, probably fostered also by changes in popular attitudes brought about by the Revolution,[13] of bringing a much larger portion of the socially "common" element into state legislatures.[14] Also, the legislatures themselves were radically democratized by making the upper chamber elective and by generally allowing the same people to vote for its members who voted for the lower house members.[15]

One additional change greatly enhanced the role of popular consent in the legislative process. Accustomed to thinking of the crown as peculiarly "the ruler" and the judges as his lackeys, the early post-Revolution state constitutions radically weakened both the executive and judicial branches, and tended to place them under the thumb of the legislatures.[16] With an independent executive veto out of the picture, legislation really could be viewed as the will of the people, at least if one considers "people" in the sense of the majority of males.

Thus, by the late 1700s the colonial maxim of "government by consent of the governed" referred to a dramatically new reality, produced by America's peculiar history and revolutionary experience.

B. POPULAR CONSENT TO THE CONSTITUTION OF GOVERNMENT

The Pilgrim Code of 1636 stated:

> We . . . freeborn subjects of the state of England. . . do ordain constitute and enact that no act imposition law or ordinance be . . . imposed upon us . . . but such as shall be imposed by consent of the body of associates or their representatives legally assembled.[17]

This is an assertion of a right of popular consent to legislation, or to government policy, not of a right in the people to determine the structure of government and the limits of its power. The notion of the latter evolved more slowly in America, stimulated by the social contract theories of Hobbes, Locke, Puffendorf, and Vattel, by the tradition of corporate charters—originally granted by the crown, but later written by the colonists, often for their own consumption.[18] Its development was slowed, however, by the higher law tradition of natural and common law exemplified by Sir Edward Coke and by the eighteenth-century theory that viewed the legislature as embodying the people.

The sixteenth- and early seventeenth-century colonial charters somehow evolved from authorization for commercial and religious enterprises to frames of local government.[19] Also, the distance from England and the absence of a professional American bar in the seventeenth century made it useful to compile in writing—in approximately the same Charter format—the basic legal rights and privileges of Englishmen (i.e., of the common law), which were in turn understood to be derived from the principles of human nature and/or from the Judaeo-Christian moral code.[20] Thus, the seventeenth century had familiarized Americans with the practice of having their elected representatives draw up charters of the people's liberties; these were understood to be declarations of the common understanding rather than grants as such.

The Lockean principles embodied in the Declaration of Independence put forth as self-evident truth the idea that individuals are by nature equally free and freely choose to empower government to secure their natural rights.[21] Moreover, they retain an indefeasible right to "alter or abolish" their "form" of government if they decide that it has become destructive of their rights. With this pronouncement, it became the acknowledged birthright of all Americans to live under a "form" of government to which they had given consent.

It may then come as a surprise that the first six constitutions adopted by the American states were adopted not by any extraordinary act of the people but by the state legislatures.[22] Even after Delaware (1776), North Carolina (1776), and New York (1777) established a precedent by having constitutions drawn up by conventions specially elected for the purpose, four additional states for a while continued the pattern of having the legislative body write the constitution, although after 1780 all the states did employ specially elected conventions. Not until the Massachusetts Constitution of 1780 was the additional step of ratification directly by the people included in the process. The popularity of this step did not spread quickly: New Hampshire used it in 1784, Pennsylvania in 1790, New Hampshire in 1792, and the U.S. Constitution through the indirect mechanism of elected ratifying conventions. But this is only five using the technique out of a total of ten constitutions adopted between 1780 and 1800.[23] During the late 1770s and early 1780s, state legislatures amended constitutions, claimed power authoritatively to interpret them, and—in a number of cases—flagrantly violated them.[24]

Apart from the legislature's power over the writing of the constitution, which power did decrease after 1780, the very meaning of a constitution as a restraint on government was quite different in the late 1770s from what it became in the nineteenth century. While scholars continue to debate the question whether more Americans sided with Coke or with Blackstone as to the issue of Parliament's supremacy against the courts as final interpreter of the British constitution, understood as an amalgam of fundamental charters, common law, and natural law,[25] the way that America's state constitutions were worded before 1787 made that very issue close to meaningless. The constitutions of those years contained Declarations of Rights that were often worded in the form of moral admonitions; some of their clauses called upon government to adhere firmly "to justice, moderation, temperance, frugality, and virtue" (e.g., Virginia, 1776). Where the 1787 U.S. Constitution has imperative commands, "shall" or "shall not," these earlier state documents would have "ought" or "would" or "recommend," as in "freedom of the press ought not to be restrained"—1776, Pennsylvania. And probably most telling, almost all the early state constitutions suggested circumstances where the legislature would be permitted to violate what were being declared to be "rights"; for example, the 1784 New Hampshire Constitution states: "But no part of a man's property shall be taken from him ... without his own consent, *or that of the legislative body of the people*" (Art. XII).[26]

This legislative power over constitutions stemmed from the prevailing assumption in 1776 that the legislature re-presented the people. That "ruler" whose arbitrary power the revolutionaries wanted to curtail had been eliminated from the picture. Thus, it was to take time for the idea to dawn on Americans that they might have use for constitutions which could check themselves qua rulers. It seemed in 1776 that constitutions could be used instead for expressing the public consensus on how government would be arranged and what it should be doing.

The old idea of a higher law that limited government had not disappeared; in fact, writing down that law was one way that Americans believed they were improving upon the British system. Although some, like James Otis in 1765[27] and Ellsworth and James Wilson opposing the *ex post facto* laws clauses at the Constitutional Convention,[28] argued that it would be a mistake to try to codify the basic privileges available to all Anglo-Americans as a matter of "right reason," most were persuaded that explicit confirmation of those rights in a visible, concrete document would be beneficial.[29] But the prevailing idea in 1776 was not that we had these rights because the written constitutions embodied them; rather the idea was that we had them because right reason, as applied to human nature and as evolved through the Anglo-American tradition, told us they were true. The state constitutions' declarations of rights were just that: they were announcements of rights that would exist with or without the announcement; they were not viewed as withholdings of powers from the government, because powers over those rights were not viewed as transferable, or alienable.[30]

As one of the more striking examples of this outlook one can cite the 1786 Rhode Island Supreme Court case of *Trevett v. Weeden*. Trial by jury had been denied to certain defendants, and the state constitution, adapted from the colonial charter by the legislature, had no explicit guarantee of trial by jury. The attorney, James Varnum, argued that the right was nonetheless "a fundamental, a constitutional right," implied in the charter clause that assured the privileges of Englishmen, and he buttressed this argument by maintaining that trial by jury was fundamental because it provided the best practical security for the natural rights of life and liberty. His reasoning explicitly presupposed even more public consensus on the idea that judges could not allow legislatures to violate natural or divine law than on the idea that written constitutions limited the government.[31]

C. CHANGES IN THE 1780s

That the mid-1780s were years of genuine political crisis in the United States is by now well documented. Abuses of legislative power were legion: paper money schemes, tender laws, suspension of debt collection, legislative interferences with trial by jury, bills of attainder, grants of exemption from the standing laws, etc.[32] In the course of this crisis, the dominant American political ideology underwent a profound shift.

The first and crucial element of the shift was that the people developed a sense of themselves as separate from the legislative body. This gradually led to a number of important changes after 1780. (1) Authors of state constitutions, actually beginning in 1777, realizing that the legislature did have the power of "rulers" and that such power could usefully be checked, strengthened the executive and judicial branches.[33] (2) Beginning with the Massachusetts Constitution of 1780, states began, albeit somewhat haltingly, to combine the writing of constitutions by specially elected bodies with the ratification of them by the people.[34] Once the constitution really did emerge out of popular consent, the institutional groundwork was laid for a popular-sovereignty-based theory of higher law and of judicial review. Just such a theory emerged in the mid-1780s. (3) As popular sovereignty was working its way into the authoritative structuring of constitutions, it was also working its way into legislative activities; the American tradition of petitioning legislators evolved into a custom of delivering insistent and binding "instructions." The power to give such instructions was enshrined in constitutions, and legislators took these instructions quite seriously.[35] Thus, in a truly paradoxical development, the 1780s was a period of an increase in the direct power of the people to legislate through instructions and an increase in the power of the people to check legislation through their role as authors of binding constitutions.

The first American version of a full-blown theory of popular control over government through a written constitution appears to have been written by Thomas Tudor Tucker in 1784.[36] After outlining the flaws of Britain's *ad hoc* constitutional system, Tudor reasoned that "all authority is derived from the people at large, held only during their pleasure ... No man has any privilege above his fellow-citizens, except ... what they have thought proper to vest in him." Thus, a constitution should be based "on the firm and proper foundation of the *express consent of the people, unalterable by the legislature*, or any other authority but that by which it is to be framed."[37] Once this outlook became widespread, as it eventually did, the legislature could be viewed as neither the "rulers" nor the "people" but as the deputies of the people, an idea implicit in Locke and in the Declaration but one for which the institutional expression of constitutional conventions and ratifications was just beginning to be developed.

The earliest experiments with judicial review also occurred in the 1780s, and, as with the theory of consent to the constitution, a role for popular sovereignty emerged only gradually.[38] As noted above, it was not unusual for arguments and court opinions for these cases to allude to unwritten "constitutional" rights, as well as to the written text.

Also during this period, and continuing into the decade of the nineties, judicial review was extremely controversial. Its exercise was debated rather than assumed by both attorneys and judges, and perceptions that it had been exercised, even when it sometimes had not, evoked popular protests and legislative efforts to discipline the judges involved.[39]

II. 1787-1803: THE MERGER OF MAJORITY WILL AND WISDOM

Popular sovereignty was very much in the air in 1787, but whether it could be saved from itself was an open question. Leading statesmen were in despair over the lack of republican virtue that our republics had produced; what had been thought a contradiction in terms in 1776, "democratic despotism," seemed to be on our doorstep.[40]

The ingenious Federalist solution to the problem was to turn the people against themselves. The people *qua* nation would be used to limit the people *qua* states. Within the nation majority rule would prevail, so that there still was "popular government," but the majority would be counted in three ways, once for the House, once for the Senate, and once for the President. Similarly, for ascertaining the voice of "the people" to amend the Constitution, extraordinary majorities would be apportioned three ways: ⅔ in the House, ⅔ in the Senate, and ¾ of the state legislatures. Any of these three embodiments of "the people" would be given the power to block action by the parallel other versions of "the people." Thus, by making the sense of the community very deliberate indeed, the Federalists hoped to make it more likely that majority will would approximate civic wisdom, thereby bringing about (at the level of public policy if not in the individual soul) at least an analogue for republican virtue.

True to the essence of this solution, the Federalist scheme for adoption of the Constitution utilized popular approval through ratifying conventions. At the national level, then, this enhanced the potential acceptability of theories of judicial review that were based on popular sovereignty. As it happened, in 1786 in preparation for a state supreme court case, *Bayard v. Singleton*,[41] the attorney, James Iredell, elaborated just such a theory in a North Carolina newspaper; moreover, he outlined the same arguments in a letter in August 1787 to Richard Spaight, a delegate then attending the Constitutional Convention. Sylvia Snowiss makes a convincing case that Iredell's arguments provided the inspirations both for Hamilton's explanation of judicial review in *Federalist 78* and for James Wilson's explanations of it in his lectures in law, delivered in 1790–91 but published in 1793.[42] Both of these were enormously influential in shaping the American understanding of judicial review and its relation to popular sovereignty. Iredell's argument was as follows:

> . . . the power of the Assembly is limited and defined by the Constitution. It is a creature of the Constitution . . . The people have chosen to be governed under such and such principles. They have not chosen to be governed, not promised to submit upon any other; and the Assembly have no . . . right to obedience on other terms. . . .
> The [Judicial] duty . . . I conceive, in all cases, is to decide according to the laws of the State. It will not be denied, I suppose, that the constitution is a law of the State, as well as an act of Assembly. For this reason, the latter act is to be obeyed, and not the former. An act of Assembly cannot repeal the constitution, or any part of it. For that reason, an act of Assembly, inconsistent with the constitution, is void, and cannot be obeyed, without disobeying the superior law to which we were previously and irrevocably bound.

> The judges, therefore, must take care at their peril, that every act of Assembly they presume to enforce is warranted by the constitution, since if it is not, they act without lawful authority. This is not a usurped or a discretionary power, but one inevitably resulting from the constitution of their office, they being judges for the benefit of the whole people, not mere servants of the Assembly.[43]

This description of judicial review requires that judges "take notice of" any direct clash between a statute and a constitution, of which, as we have seen, there were many in the 1780s, and consider the latter as a law of superior obligation, because it comes from "the whole people."[44] Hamilton's famous version of the argument, from *Federalist 78*, is:

> ... [E]very act of a delegated authority, contrary to the tenor of the commission under which it is exercised, is void. No legislative act, therefore, contrary to the Constitution, can be valid. To deny this would be to affirm that the deputy is greater than his principal; that the servant is above his master; that the representatives of the people are superior to the people themselves ... If there should happen to be an irreconcilable variance between [a statute and the Constitution], that which has the superior obligation and validity ought, of course, to be preferred ...

Wilson's was:

> From the constitution, the legislative department, as well as every other part of government derives its power: by the constitution, the legislative, as well as every other department, must be directed; of the constitution, no alteration by the legislature can be made or authorized ... The constitution is the supreme law of the land: to that supreme law every other power must be inferior and subordinate. Now, let us suppose, that the legislature should pass an act, manifestly repugnant to some part of the constitution; and that the operation and validity of both should come regularly in question before a court, forming a part of the judicial department. In that department, the "judicial power of the United States is vested" by the "people," who "ordained and established" the constitution ... [T]wo contradictory rules ... cannot possibly be administered ... The supreme power of the United States has given one rule: a subordinate power ... a contradictory rule: the former is the law of the land: as a necessary consequence, the latter is void ... In this manner ... it is the duty of a court of justice, under the constitution of the United States, to decide.[45]

In subsequent court cases that employed judicial review in the 1790–1802 period, the rationale developed by Iredell, Hamilton, and Wilson is unmistakably prominent. During this same period judicial review overcame its intensely controversial status. Judges and lawyers began to assume its legitimacy and state legislatures honored its exercise.

During the 1790s judicial review not only gained a mighty ally in the Iredell-Hamilton-Wilson argument concerning popular consent to the rules of the Constitution, it also gained renewed strength from tougher wording in the state constitutions. Following the example of the U.S. Constitution, the six eighteenth-century constitutions adopted after it moved toward the use of *shall* in place of the formerly preferred *ought*. In sum, the 1790s in America witnessed a change in the very concept of written constitutions. Now they were written in a language meant to be binding, and they were viewed as binding at least in part because they expressed "the consent of the governed." To a nation which took its bearings from the Declaration of Independence, this was no small addition to the argument.

NOTES

[1] Compare Thomas Grey's pro-unwritten law argument "Do We Have an Unwritten Constitution?" 27 *Stanford Law Review* 843 (1978) with Ralph K. Winter, "The Growth of Judicial Power," in Leonard Theberge, ed., *The Judiciary in a Democratic Society* (Lexington, Mass.: Heath, 1979), pp. 29–66. Winter argues that the decision in the Constitutional Convention to reject a Council of Revision amounted to a rejection of an unwritten law veto power for the federal courts. This is one of many examples.

[2] *Marbury v. Madison*, 1 Cranch 138.

[3] James Otis's much celebrated protest against the Writs of Assistance that "an act against the Constitution is void: an act against natural equity is void" was described by John Adams as causing all who heard it to leave the meeting "ready to take arms. . . . then and there the child Independence was born." C. F. Adams, ed. *The Works of John Adams*, (Boston: Little, Brown, 1856), II, 521, and X, 247–48.

[4] Donald Lutz, *Popular Consent and Popular Control* (Baton Rouge: Louisiana State Univ. Press, 1980), pp. 24–31, discusses and provides excerpts from colonial charters that established government "by consent."

[5] The earliest extended discussions I can find of the exclusion of females from political rights are in John Adams, *Works* (1776), IX, 375–78, and James Wilson, *Works* (1790–91), ed. Robert G. McCloskey, 2 vols. (Cambridge, Mass.: Harvard Univ. Press, 1967) I, 85–89. Jefferson was more terse in his Letter to Samuel Kercheval, Sept. 1816: "Were our state a pure democracy in which all its inhabitants should meet together to transact all their business, there would yet be excluded. . . women, who, to prevent depravation of morals and ambiguity of issue, could not mix promiscuously in the public meetings of men." *Letters of Thomas Jefferson*, selected and ed. Frank Irwin, Tilton, N.H.: Hillside Press, 1975.

[6] Lutz, pp. 24–26, 100–01.

[7] Lutz, pp. 101–02.

[8] Bernard Bailyn, *The Ideological Origins of the American Revolution* (Cambridge, Mass.: Harvard Univ. Press, 1967), pp. 161–75; Lutz, pp. 12–13; Gordon S. Wood, *The Creation of the American Republic 1776–1787* (Chapel Hill: Univ. of North Carolina Press, 1969), pp. 173–81.

[9] Lutz, p. 102.

[10] Lutz, pp. 24–26, 87–88, 100–05, and Wood, p. 167. More precisely, Lutz likens turnout of that period to the 1950s, when it was 60–65%, but turnout (in presidential races) is now only in the 50–55% range. Eighteenth-century American suffrage estimates remain a matter of controversy among historians.

[11] See citations in n. 8 above.

[12] Lutz, pp. 105-08. Because Tories were simultaneously disfranchised, the impact of these changes is hard to measure. The virtual guarantee came from a rule that adult male taxpayers could vote.

[13] Elisha P. Douglass, *Rebels and Democrats* (Chapel Hill: Univ. of North Carolina Press, 1955).

[14] Lutz, pp. 106-10; Wood, pp. 167-68; Jackson Turner Main, "Government by the People: The American Revolution and the Democratization of the Legislatures," *William and Mary Quarterly* 3rd Ser., 23 (1966), 391-407.

[15] Gestures were made in the direction of having an upper house that would represent "property" in accordance with traditional Anglo-American Whig theories of "balanced" government (i.e., balanced between the principles of human numbers and property), by imposing much stiffer property requirements on *candidates* for the upper house than on candidates for the lower house. These gestures proved futile, because the groups of *voters* were the same, and the resulting state senates proved indistinguishable in behavior from the state assemblies. Lutz, pp. 88-89, 108-09, 207-08; Wood, pp. 206-14. See also Jackson T. Main, *The Upper House in Revolutionary America* (Madison: Univ. of Wisconsin Press, 1967).

[16] Wood, pp. 135-50, 160-73; Lutz, p. 44.

[17] Quoted in Lutz, p. 29.

[18] For a list of these charters, see Lutz, pp. 27-29.

[19] Bailyn, pp. 189-93.

[20] Bailyn, pp. 193-98. See also pp. 187-89 and n. 4 above.

[21] In Locke's *Second Treatise* (c. 1688-1690), these are rights to life, liberty, and property. In our Declaration, of course, they are life, liberty, and the pursuit of happiness. In many of the discussions of these rights, for instance in eighteenth-century American court cases, the trilogy is again life, liberty, and property.

[22] Lutz, p. 45.

[23] Lutz, pp. 45, 65-69, 81-84, n. 30 at p. 83.

[24] Lutz, pp. 62-65 and 121; Wood, pp. 274-75; Corwin, "The Progress of Constitutional Theory Between the Declaration of Independence and the Meeting of the Philadelphia Convention," *American Historical Review* 30 (April 1925), 511-36, esp. 511-20; and Sylvia Snowiss, "From Fundamental Law to the Supreme Law of the Land...," unpublished paper delivered at 1981 Annual Meeting of the American Political Science Association, pp. 13-14.

[25] Compare Grey, "Origins," with Bailyn, *Ideological Origins*, Chapter 5. See also statements from the 1780s about the power of courts to enforce unwritten natural rights in Herbert J. Storing, "The Constitution and the Bill of Rights," in *The American Founding*, ed. Ralph Rossum and Gary McDowell (Port Washington, N.Y.: Kennikat Press, 1981), pp. 29-45, esp. p. 37.

[26] Lutz, pp. 61-68, 49, 35; and Wood, pp. 271-73.

[27] Bailyn, *Ideological Origins*, p. 189; and Wood, p. 277.

[28] Max Farrand, ed., *The Records of the Federal Convention of 1787* (New Haven: Yale Univ. Press, 1911), II, 376.

[29] Bailyn, pp. 189-90, 192; Wood, pp. 266-68; Snowiss, p. 16; Gary Jacobsohn, "E.T.: The Extra-textual in Constitutional Interpretation," *Constitutional Commentary* I (1984), 21-42; see particularly Judge Tucker's opinion in *Kamper v. Hawkins* 1 Va. Cases 20, 77-78 (1793), cited in Charles Haines, *The American Doctrine of Judicial Supremacy* (Berkeley: Univ. of California Press, 1932), p. 156.

[30] See Grey, "Origins," for the latest treatment, but much evidence of this is in the older work of scholars such as Edward S. Corwin, Clinton Rossiter, and Andrew C. McLaughlin. See also Wood, pp. 456-57.

[31] James Varnum, *The Case, Trevett against Weeden* ... (Providence, 1787), pp. 21-33.

[32] Corwin "The Progress," pp. 511-20; Wood, pp. 403-25; Lutz, 116-22. See also James Madison, "Vices of the Political Systems of the United States," (1787) in *Writings*, ed. Gaillard Hunt (New York: Putnam's, 1901), II, 361 ff.

[33] Lutz, p. 45; Wood, pp. 161, 447-63.

[34] Lutz, pp. 62–65. See Wood, Chapter 8, for a brilliant discussion of how the American extra-legislative and sub-legislative tradition of political activities by people "out-of-doors" became transubstantiated in the 1780s into a supra-legislative authority.

[35] Lutz, pp. 115–18; Wood, pp. 363–89.

[36] Wood, pp. 280–82.

[37] Wood, p. 281. See also Haines, p. 95, for remark in 1785 by Gouvernor Morris that if the Constitution can be changed by the legislature, it is no more.

[38] These cases are canvassed in Haines, chs. 4–7; in Julius Goebel, Jr., *Antecedents and Beginnings to 1801*, Vol I, History of the Supreme Court of the U.S., 19 vols. (New York: Macmillan, 1971), pp. 124–42; and in William Winslow Crosskey, *Politics and the Constitution in the History of the U.S.* (Chicago: Univ. of Chicago Press, 1953), II, 943–75.

[39] Haines; Goebel; Crosskey.

[40] Wood, p. 404, paraphrasing John Adams.

[41] Martin 42 (1787).

[42] Snowiss, p. 16.

[43] *Life and Correspondence of James Iredell*, ed. Griffith J. McRee (New York: Peter Smith, 1949) II, "To the Public," 145–49.

[44] The "take notice of" phrase is from Iredell's letter to Spaight (McRee, II, p. 173), and it was also used by the deciding judge in the case.

[45] Wilson, *Works*, I, 329–31.

IV. RELIGION,

MORALITY,

AND LITERATURE

EARLY EIGHTEENTH-CENTURY PARAPHRASES OF THE BOOK OF JOB

JAMES E. MAY

Although the Book of Job had long been valued in England as the oldest poem in the Bible, it received increased attention after John Dennis championed the Bible for sublimity.[1] The superiority of its figures and images over those of classical literature was argued by Isaac Watts (1709) and in *The Guardian* (1713), and William Smith's notes to his translation of Longinus (1739) refer so often to Job that they nearly contain a commentary on its sublimity.[2] But, although poets found its materials and intent invited sublime treatment, the vogue for sublime poetry only partly explains their handling of the biblical work. Some turned to it as an occasion for pathos, others for the picturesque. Many tried to clarify the wisdom of the obscure but ancient book within an edifying poem. As Matthew Henry wrote, "There are many passages in it dark, and hard to understand."[3] Like the commentators, especially Simon Patrick,[4] who influenced them, the poets aimed at celebrating, elucidating, applying, expanding, and embellishing the original. There are theological as well as poetic motives for the alterations. As can be seen in the poets' development of four justifications of God within the theophany, the paraphrases reveal much about eighteenth-century notions of God, nature, the Bible, and imitation.

The only early eighteenth-century versifications of the whole book were those of Sir Richard Blackmore (1700) and Daniel Baker (1706), who followed Bishop Patrick's interpretation of God's justification and incorporated many of his comments, phrases, and images.[5] Although a few poets loosely paraphrased several chapters, most closely followed single chapters.[6] Paraphrases of some chapters, as of the frequently paraphrased Third, form a tradition such that topics introduced into the original were repeated by later versifiers. Biblical paraphrase was a kind of poetic exercise, as the pastoral had been, wherein previous performances were both materials for invention and rivals to excel. Although the reputation of Blackmore's version was ruined by Pope's *Peri Bathos* (1728), none was so thoroughly mined for phrases and images, by Baker, Henry, Edward Young, William Thompson, William

Broome, Christopher Pitt, John Husbands, and Thomas Warton.[7] The age also produced loose adaptations of Job, including collections of hymns as well as narrative retellings of Job's story, two of which present a Christianized Job who checks his anger with a vision of the last day.[8] Of all these paraphrases, those by Young (1719), Thompson (1726), and Broome (before 1727), which treat God's answer to Job, are decidedly the best.

Much of this poetic interest is due to the Book of Job's preeminence among Old Testament books for reasons somewhat peculiar to the period. It was valued above all as a great theodicy, a poetic kind much in vogue then, and as *"a monument of primitive theology"* (Henry, p. 514). Most would have agreed that its principal design was to show that God rules the world and rules it well, so submit. For Blackmore, who questioned its historicity (sigs. b2^r-c2^r), but especially for Henry, who valued it as "a true history, not a romance" (p. 514), the book's antiquity ensured a more accurate account of God's attributes and of his creation and maintenance of the world.

The Book of Job was also valued for presenting moral instruction through a Christian mythos. Henry, who refers to Patrick's quoting St. Jerome to this effect, called Job himself "an illustrious type of Christ": "Job was a great sufferer, was emptied and humbled, but in order to his greater glory. So Christ abased himself, that we might be exalted" (p. 514). Baker thought Job "a most proper Subject for a Christian poem" (sig. A2^r), for, unlike the classical epics which illustrate active virtues, Job illustrates "gentle passive Virtues" of Christianity: "We have learnt that Humility, Patience, Self-denial, and Resignation . . . are Virtues of First Rank" (sig. A3^r). Moreover, Job's story could be applied to the sufferings of the entire nation, as Patrick implied, writing that it was needed in 1679 "when the State of our affairs is so dangerously perplexed," for it showed that God is "wont many times to bring the greatest good out of the greatest evil" (sig. A3^v) and that he will care for our church and state and "hath no mind to cast us off" (sig. A4^r).

Of all the Old Testament books, Job had a special appeal to an age that looked askance at the Mosaic Law and the Old Covenant yet still believed the oldest works partook of the excellence of primitive man. Isaac Watts, while paraphrasing the Psalms, complained that "Some of 'em are almost opposite to the spirit of the gospel."[9] In this context, it is interesting that Patrick and Henry repeated Eusebius' judgment that Job lived before Moses and was not a Jew. For Patrick, as later for Blackmore (sig. h2^r) and Henry (p. 514), the work evinces that there is "a Law written into our hearts" that informs us "what are the true natural dictates of human reason" (sig. A8^r). Patrick introduced Christian apologetics when he wrote that Eusebius, noting parallels between the Book of Job and Christian teaching, had held that Christ taught the "ancient manner of Godlines . . . so that the New Covenant is no other than the old godly polity, which was before the time of Moses" (sig. A8^v).

Around 1700, one of the most appealing features of the Book of Job, particularly to poets, was the centrality of natural descriptions to the work's theodicy. Although the paraphrasers found other arguments for God's justice and love than those from nature,[10] the work's primary justifications of God involved arguments touching on the design of nature. This suited the poem to an age when, as Basil Willey claimed, "even the orthodox, who retained the supernatural basis, felt that faith must be grounded firmly upon Nature before one had recourse to super-nature," and thus sought in nature the "principal evidences of religion."[11] Eighteenth-century writers developed four answers to Job's complaint, which they found within God's survey of creation. These justifications involve God's sovereign power, man's ignorance, God's providential care for his creatures, and the faith-inducing sublimity of creation.

The first justification is the toughest and most prominent in the Old Testament text: God is all-powerful, and the created universe, including man, is his property. Thus, as king and possessor, he may do with it what he pleases and may not be questioned. Blackmore's summary of the poem indicates that this was God's primary defense: God "insists on no other Justification of his proceedings with Man, than his Dominion and Property, his absolute Transcendent Greatness, that render him unaccountable to his Creatures" (sig. g2ʳ). Young's practice of beginning his verse paragraphs treating Chapter 38 with "who" questions of agency (as at lines 103, 125, and 133) expands God's defense through sovereignty evident in the King James version, as at 38:4–6.[12]

The theme of God's greatness and man's smallness, which implied God's sovereignty, was perceived as predominant in the behemoth and leviathan portraits. Patrick had supposed that God introduced them that Job "might learn more Humility; when he saw how he was unable to stand before one of his Creatures. That use He himself teaches Job to make of his description, v. 10, 11" (p. 193). Similarly, Blackmore (p. 177) and Baker added transitions to the behemoth passage wherein God describes these creatures as a "Lecture in Humility" (Baker, p. 124). In the first verse Patrick cited, God argues by degrees: "None is so fierce that dare stir him up: who then is able to stand before me?" (41:10). That comparison recurs in all the poets discussed here. The following verse humbles man with reference to God's sovereign domain: "Who hath prevented me, that I should repay him? Whatsoever is under the whole heaven is mine." Curiously, this topic of ownership, used by Blackmore, Baker, and Young, was neglected by Thompson and by John Wesley when he edited Young's paraphrase in 1744,[13] perhaps as inappropriate to their conceptions of the deity.

Since the behemoth is called "the chief of the ways of God" (40:19), the poets could use the beast to symbolically refer to God's sovereignty or, as another justification, his benevolence. Consider, for instance, their rendering of the "Surely the mountains bring him forth food, where all the beasts of the field play" (40:20). Patrick's and Baker's versions imply benevolence: "harmless Creatures round him play" (Baker, p. 125). But Blackmore had him "a Monarch reign" (p. 178), and Young developed an image of sovereignty suited to his overall depiction of God, wherein the behemoth gives:

> ... the Mountain Law;
> The Mountains feed Him; there the Beasts admire
> The mighty Stranger, and in Dread retire;
> At length his Greatness nearer They survey,
> Graze in his Shadow, and his Eye obey. (lines 310–14)

The second justification, that Job simply does not know enough to question God, is more evident in some paraphrases than in the King James version, though God's opening accusation is that Job "darkeneth counsel by words without knowledge" (38:2). Henry thought the original first emphasized Job's ignorance (up to 38:24), then his impotence (p. 570). For Patrick, God would deter Job from questioning his goodness "by showing him how little he understood of the most obvious things in the World" (p. 176). Young did not develop this knowledge theme: his God accuses Job of rebelliously telling the "World's Creator what is Just" (line 46). But Thompson stressed it:

> ... Presumptuous Man, prepare,
> To own thy Ignorance of Counsels high,
> My secret Purposes and deep Decrees
> From utmost Reach of Men and Angels Sight. (lines 3–6)

Although the original insists on Job's ignorance through questions like "Knowest thou the ordinances of heaven?" (38:33), Blackmore, through expansions and additions, further stressed man's blindness to natural processes, paradoxically introducing scientific explanations in the work. For "Who hath divided . . . a way for the lightning" (38:25), Blackmore asked "Canst thou declare" how sulphur and other metals are fanned by winds to produce lightning (p. 169). He also added an account of how hail and snow are made and then had God (who Himself would stumble on it) ask Job if he understood it (p. 168). Patrick had already turned the original verse on snow (38:22) into a process question (p. 179), but Blackmore throughout infused a special concern for understanding natural phenomena. When Broome added a Newtonian account of the rainbow,[14] he followed Blackmore's lead. James Thomson's scientific descriptions in *The Seasons* are somewhat anticipated by paraphrasers of Job, especially Blackmore.[15]

In Blackmore the desire to argue man's ignorance is undercut by his delight in what is known about the universe. The Book of Job was valued for its observations on nature. As Anthony Blackwell remarked, it excelled Aristotle's and Pliny's works "in the truth of philosophy."[16] Patrick digressed from theological concerns to explain its natural imagery, noting, for instance, that the leviathan's portrait accurately describes the crocodile, which has been seen "twenty, nay forty foot long; and in some places a hundred" (p. 193). Young, except for adopting Patrick's names for the creatures, did not introduce scientific lore into his poem, but he did add six pages of notes, most of which argue that Moses, as an Egyptian, was the likely author and a "Naturalist" besides. The notes document from sources like Pliny that the imagery is neither fanciful nor hyperbolic, as that hippos could virtually drink a stream dry (sig. E4^r). Thus, though Young's text remains primitive, his notes show the historical and scientific interests that led others to modernize and rationalize the King James version. Young wrote, "My author accurately understood the Nature of the Creatures he describes, and seems to have been a Naturalist as well as a poet" (sig. E3^v). In the second edition (1719), Young omitted reiteration that Moses was a naturalist, perhaps fearing to identify himself with the advocates of natural revelation. The Book of Job was an ideal opportunity to direct imaginative reverence toward both scripture and nature; it allowed a via media between two polarizing positions,[17] wherein poets could securely praise nature without suggesting a heretical reverence for it. Yet not all paraphrasers were as sensitive to the work's natural imagery as Young and Broome. Baker, by contrast, neglected many vivid biblical images and stressed the utility of nature, as in his character of the ostrich: "Beauty without, but Folly dwells within / That Bird, the Emblem of deceitful Sin" (p. 119).

Not surprisingly, in view of their interest in nature, the poets greatly expanded a third justification rarely evident in the original: that the harmonious ordering of the universe and, especially, the provisions made for specific creatures imply God's loving care for man. This justification called for a close analysis of the universe. Through this argument from providential design, Job and its paraphrases influenced later poems with physico-theological arguments. Like the deists proposing an orderly world, the Job paraphrasers responded to the Lucretian conception of nature as an imperfect accident. When, in the preface to *Winter*, Thomson identified his poem with Job, he hinted at more than its debt to Job and paraphrases of it for sublime imagery and intent.[18]

The framing logic in *Winter*'s conclusion resembles the biblical works and alludes to the situation and complaint of Job himself: "Ye vainly wise! ye blind presumptuous! now, / Confounded in the dust, adore that Power / And Wisdom—oft arraigned" (lines 1050-52). *Winter*, like Job's theophany, has shown "the cause . . . why the good man's share / In life was gall" (lines 1052; 1054–55). Later, in 1758, Amyas Bushe would echo God's interrogatory reproof of Job when his Socrates proves to a pupil "God's peculiar care of human kind."[19]

The original theophany presents the world, not as beautiful, benevolent, and man-centered but as a place with profound seas, vengeful hail, oceans turned to stone, and rain for land unoccupied by man (38:12–38). Yet even those poets desiring the original's horrific and expansive imagery for sublimity mitigated its presentation of nature as austere and indifferent to man. The image of the dayspring, which the original emphasizes as hid from the wicked (38:15), becomes a beautiful dawn landscape in William Thompson (lines 34–37) and Broome (lines 30–36). Thompson turns the unmodified reference to the "east wind" (38:24) into a breeze cooling the midday sun and wafting mariners over the seas (lines 72–75). Following Patrick, Blackmore (p. 170) and Thompson (lines 92–101) expand the question "Canst thou bind the sweet influences of Pleiades, or loose the bands of Orion?" (38:31) to include pastoral and agrarian imagery.

God's love for his creation is mostly developed within his catalogue of the creatures. With logic ridiculous to a skeptic, the paraphrasers found the existence of food and shelter for a creature to be proof of God's love; thus, Henry comments on 38:39–41, "See the bounty of the divine Providence, that, wherever it has given life, it will give livelihood" (p. 570). Where the Bible notes the hardships of animals, these authors added compensatory gifts or interpreted descriptive details in the Bible as God's statement of such compensations. For example, the hind's labor pains (39:1–3) could be seen as testifying to God's indifference, but to the passage most added that thunder induces labor.[20] Similarly, the ostrich's abandonment of her young could be used to deny providential care, for it is God who "hath deprived her of wisdom" (39:17). But Thompson, like Young before him, added the idea that the "genial Warmth" of the sun cherishes the eggs (line 173). Also, he noted the chicks are taught by "early Instinct" to "recompence the loss" of their mother (lines 178–79). Patrick, Blackmore, and Baker, those most anxious to argue God's beneficence, all added a declaration of God's love for man. Patrick preceded his rephrasing of 40:8 with the addition: "Is there any reason to suspect my Care of Mankind, who have shewn it so much about other Creatures?" (p. 190). Blackmore's addition is similar (p. 176), as is Baker's: "Wilt thou suspect my Care of Humankind, / Whom all the World does so indulgent find?" (p. 123). Blackmore (p. 185) and Baker (pp. 129–30) also have Job affirm God's "Paternal Love" in his last speech.

A fourth justification of God, prominent in only the poetical paraphrases of the theophany, involves the effect of wonderment. Some wonder is created by the other three strategies, but, whereas those are rational appeals, the fourth is supra-rational and enthusiastic. This poetic assault forces Job and the reader to transcend grief and self-interest through rapture over creation and astonishment at its creator. The same intention is evident in psalms of adoration with natural description, also commonly paraphrased after 1700. Both paraphrases of the theophany and of these psalms were attempts to produce sublime effects. They contain phrasing and imagery borrowed from *Paradise Lost*, and from each other, and from the other's original.[21] Both groups occasionally approach the reverential and aesthetic response to all nature in Shaftesbury's *The Moralists* (1709), but redirect this reverence from nature to God. There are two versions of this poetic appeal in paraphrases of Job: Broome's, which stresses natural beauty in elegant language; and Young's and Thompson's, more akin to the original yet more innovative as English nature poetry, which stress the terrific dimensions of God and the austerity of nature in sublime language.

Broome's version of Chapters 38-39, like his paraphrase of Ecclesiasticus, Chapter 43 (1727), is a nature poem which freely adds and omits materials. Softening the biblical tone, Broome makes little attempt to render God fearsomely great or to humble man. God and his interrogative syntax often disappear. There is no withholding light from the wicked, no freezing wind or vengeful snow, and Broome expanded descriptions of the dawn and added others of the rainbow, plant life, and the night. For the hemistich "as for darkness, where is the place thereof . . . ?" (38:19), Broome substitutes a fourteen-line nightpiece with lines like:

> No air of breath disturbs the drowzy wood,
> No whispers murmur from the silent floods!
> The Moon sheds down a silver-streaming light,
> And glads the melancholic face of night:
> Now clouds swift-skimming veil her sullied ray,
> Now bright she blazes with a fuller day. (p. 529)

His treatment is so strikingly at variance with the others' that Broome may have deliberately departed from tradition, perhaps thinking that a more amiable nature was a better mirror of God and a spur to transcendence.

Insofar as Young and Thompson succeed in conveying the sublimity of God's speech, they suggest the mystical answer that God imparts to Job's spirit, wherein the medium is the message. The creation God asks Job to see, God's manner of address, and the effect on Job need all be sublime. Thompson noted in his preface that the materials of God's speech were sublime: "nothing does with greater Force produce this strong and agreeable Emotion in us, than the delightful Scenes and Paintings of Nature, which every where occur throughout this whole Speech."[22] Although Young and Thompson added details on God's providence and the world's beauty, most of what they added raises sublimity through grandeur or terror. More than Thompson, Young fully exploited the terrifying dimensions of both creation and the dramatic encounter of man with "Majesty incens'd" (sig. E2^r). Thompson omitted their exchanges after the first speech and at the close, and Blackmore and Baker extended both until they lose their intensity. Taking hints from Patrick and Milton, Young depicted God as grimly ironic and proud, and ultimately inscrutable, hence more terrifying. Also, he retained every reference to divine retribution but that on light withheld from the wicked, and added an image of the comet hung out in resentment (lines 133-36).

Moreover, as Young (sig. E3^r) and William Smith (pp. 130 and 154) observed, the style of the original was sublime; so, poets would fall back on the King James version. Unlike Young and Thompson, Blackmore and Baker failed to exploit the diction and imagery of the King James. For example, they followed Patrick in correcting the line "Hast thou clothed his neck with thunder" (39:19) to read "with such a Stately Main." Blackmore and Baker tried to make the Bible rational and easy for a broad audience, but Young and Thompson, not so handicapped, employed more of its primitive boldness. Accordingly, Young's ocean is chained with God's word (line 67); whereas, Baker's is chained with "Banks of Sand" (p. 115) and Blackmore's with "Sandy Chains" (p. 166).

To inspire awe for God and creation, Young, in particular, employed the resources critics had prescribed for sublimity. For instance, he fulfilled Dennis' advice for *enargeia*, that sublime emotions are best raised by "lively Pictures of the Thing which they represent, set ... as it were, before our Eyes," and drawn "in Motion; especially if the Motion is violent" (I, 218). All Young's creatures, even the peacock, are in motion. Young reorganized and added details to create narrative scenes of the horse, lion, behemoth, and leviathan. We see the lion hunting in the moonlight, and, through the eyes of a horrified shepherd, we see in the dust his bloody tracks (lines 277-96). In contrast the other paraphrases contain the original's depiction of the lion crouched for ambush in his den. Although the original is full of great thoughts and animating figures, as Longinus advocated (Section 8), Young complemented it in both respects. He added images of vastness akin to those in Longinus (Section 9), as of the mountain casting "its Shadow into distant Lands" (line 62) and of walking the ocean floor with "Whole Worlds of Waters rolling o'er thy Head" (line 76). He added catalogues that amplify number for sublimity (as lines 343-46) and images that juxtapose the great and the small, the abstract and the concrete, to figure forth what Dennis called "exalted Notions of the Power of an Infinite Being" (I, 271). Chief among these are the images of the hand of God, as in "Put forth thy Hand, and shade the World with Night" (line 102). The miraculous, which Dennis praised in classical poetry (I, 231), is also intensified, as when, drawing upon *Paradise Lost* (VII.242), Young's God asks concerning the earth, "What Hand, declare, / Hung it on Nought, and fastened it in Air. . .?" (lines 54-55).

Defining the fourth answer to Job's complaint, the appeal through aesthetic transport, I have had to touch on the poetic quality of Broome's, Thompson's, and Young's paraphrases since that justification implies some poetical success. There is a tendency, evident in David Morris's *The Religious Sublime*,[23] to minimize the merit of biblical paraphrases, but I think that Broome's and Thompson's poems are interesting and, on the whole, successful. They reflect the powerful yet puzzling light of the original, and they reveal a broad spectrum of attitudes to God, nature, and man.

NOTES

[1]See John Dennis, *The Advancement and Reformation of Modern Poetry* (1701) and *The Grounds of Criticism in Poetry* (1704); rpt. *The Critical Works of John Dennis*, ed. E. N. Hooker (Baltimore: Johns Hopkins Univ. Press, 1939). See I, 266 ff. and I, 363 ff. on the Bible's providing material for great poetry.

[2]See Watts, *The Poetical Works of Isaac Watts and Henry K. White* (Boston: Houghton, Mifflin, n.d.), pp. lxxxv-lxxxviii; *The Guardian*, No. 86 (19 June 1713); rpt. *The British Essayists*, ed. A. Chalmers (Boston: Little, Brown, 1856), XIV, 179; and Smith, *Dionysius Longinus on the Sublime* (1739; facs. rpt. Delmar, N.Y.: Scholars' Facsimiles and Reprints, 1975), especially pp. 127, 151, 154, and 171f.

[3]*Commentary on the Whole Bible* (Grand Rapids, Michigan: Zondervan, 1961), p. 514. This compendium contains a slightly abridged but otherwise unaltered reprinting of Henry's commentary on Job, first published in *An Exposition of the Five Poetical Books of the Old Testament* (n.d.; 2nd ed., publ. J. Lawrence, is dated 1712). Parenthetic references are to the Zondervan edition.

[4]*The Book of Job Paraphrased* (1679; rpt. London: L. Meredith, 1697); all references to Patrick are to the 1697 edition.

[5]Blackmore, *A Paraphrase on the Book of Job* (London: A. and J. Churchill, 1700); Baker, *The History of Job in Five Books* (London: R. Clavel, 1706). Parenthetic references to both poems are to these editions. Cf. Blackmore's phrase "seat of strength" at p. 182 with Patrick's comment on 41:22, and cf. Baker's "Deeds of Darkness" on p. 115 with Patrick on verse 38:13. Other influences are noted later in the text.

[6]Of importance to my discussion are the freer paraphrases of the theophany chapters: Edward Young's *A Paraphrase on a Part of the Book of Job* (London: Tonson, 1719); William Thompson's *A Poetical Paraphrase on Part of the Book of Job: In Imitation of the Style of Milton* (Dublin, 1726; rpt. London: Worral, 1726); and William Broome's "Part of the 38th and 39th Chapters of Job" (1727; rev. 1739; rpt. in *Minor English Poets 1660-1800*, ed. A. Chalmers, comp. David French [New York: Blom, 1967], III, 529-30). A manuscript version of Broome's poem, with fewer lines than the 1727 version, is at the Winchester College Library. Close paraphrases of single chapters include that of Job 39 by the younger Thomas Warton (1750; rpt. *The Poetical Works of the Late Thomas Warton*, ed. Richard Mant [London: Rivington, 1802], pp. 109-11); and of Job 3 by John Husbands, *A Miscellany of Poems by Several Hands* (1731; facs. rpt. New York: Garland, 1970), pp. 184-89; and by Christopher Pitt (rpt. in *Minor English Poets 1660-1800* [cited above], III, 596-97; see p. 567 for his paraphrase of Job 25). Future references are to reprint editions wherever cited.

[7]For example, cf. Baker on the behemoth's diet (p. 125) with Blackmore, p. 177; Henry on angling for leviathan (p. 573) with p. 179; Young on "sluces" for rain (line 112) with p. 171, lines 16 and 21; Thompson's "Harvest Home" (line 160) and "Populous Town" (line 154) with p. 173, line 10 and p. 172, line 20; Pitt's "Like a full stream o'er-charg'd, my sorrows flow" with Blackmore's "as a roaring Flood my raging Sorrow flows," p. 14; Broome's lines 1-2 & 13 with p. 164, lines 16-22; Husbands' "let all the Sons of Mourning Curse" (p. 185) and the image of arms embracing death (p. 188) with pp. 12, line 1, and p. 13, line 19, respectively; and Warton's images of the ostrich running (lines 37-38) with p. 175, lines 5-6.

[8]Of note are Thomas Gent's homiletic abridgement, *The Pattern of Piety* (Scarborough: Gent, 1734) and two anonymous monologues alluding to the resurrection: *The Complaint of Job* (London: Wellington, 1734) and *Age in Distress: or Job's Lamentation for his Children*, ded. to Young (London: Fuller, 1750).

[9]Quoted in Arthur P. Davis's *Isaac Watts: His Life and Works* (New York: Dryden, 1943), p. 199.

[10]For instance, Patrick found in Elihu's speech evidence that dreams and the chastening discipline of sickness showed "the care of God over man" (p. 148).

[11]*The Eighteenth Century Background* (1940; rpt.. Boston: Beacon Press, 1961), p. 3. On the Christian rationalists' regard for nature as "a faithful record of the Creator's power and beneficence," see Cecil A. Moore's discussion, which discriminates between orthodox and heretical ("The Return to Nature in English Poetry of the Eighteenth Century," *Studies in Philology* 14 [1917], 251 ff.).

[12]Throughout this essay, all quotations from and references to the Book of Job are to *The Holy Bible containing the Old and New Testaments in the King James Version* (Camden, N.J.: Thomas Nelson, 1970). Bishop Patrick's paraphrase is, typically, of this version. I consider this the original which the poets paraphrased.

[13]Wesley omitted from *A Collection of Moral and Sacred Poems* (Bristol: Farley, 1744), at II, 68, the following couplet (whose opening sentence had been used by Patrick): "Am I a Debtor? hast Thou ever heard / Whence come Gifts which are on Me conferr'd?" (lines 341-42).

[14]Broome says of the rainbow's origin that the sun "pours forth his golden streams, / And humid clouds imbibe the glittering beams" (III, 530).

[15]For instance, in *Spring*, Thomson described lightning as "sulphureous glooms" (line 327) and offered a Newtonian explanation of rainbows (lines 203-9); see *The Seasons*, ed. James Sambrook (Oxford: Clarendon Press, 1981, pp. 18 and 12). Further references to *The Seasons* are to this edition.

[16]*The Sacred Classics Defended and Illustrated* (1727; facs. rpt. New York: Garland, 1970), pp. 13-14.

[17]See Moore's "The Return to Nature" on the Church's response to natural revelation (pp. 251 ff.) and *The Moralists* (1709) on Shaftesbury's nearly being prosecuted for overly revering nature (pp. 257 f.).

[18]*The Seasons*, p. 305. Thomson identified the Book of Job, like Virgil's *Georgics*, as part of a tradition describing "the grand works of Nature" to which his poem belonged. Ralph Cohen remarked that Thomson's "reliance upon Job is more in sublime intent than in actual borrowing" (*The Art of Discrimination* [Berkeley: Univ. of California Press, 1964], p. 21). However, the recurrence of topics and imagery from Job in *The Seasons* shows that he closely perused it. Moreover, Thomson's debt to Job is also to paraphrases of it. When Thomson asks the winds, "Where are your Stores . . . Where your aerial Magazines reserved / To swell . . . the Storm," he takes a hint from Job 38:22-23, on the treasures of the snows "reserved against the time of trouble." But he may owe more to Blackmore (p. 168), Baker (p. 116), or Young (line 120), whose paraphrases of these verses use the word "Magazine." Or, later, when Thomson describes the effect of snow ("Low the woods / Bow their hoar head," lines 235-36), though there is nothing resembling this image in the King James version, there is in Blackmore's paraphrase of the verse on frost ("Oppress the Trees, and bend their hoary Heads," p. 170). Thomson's image of the winter landscape which follows ("Earth's universal Face, deep-hid and chill, / Is one wild dazzling Waste," lines 238-39) recalls Young's version of Job 38:30: "A sudden Desart spreads o'er Realms defac'd, / And lays one half of the Creation waste" (lines 95-96).

[19] In *Socrates. A Dramatic Poem* (London: R. & J. Dodsley, 1758), Bushe echoed questions about the weather in Job 38:16, 28-30:

> ... know'st thou, what rounds the hail,
> Or points the flaming dart? how the hoar frost
> Is form'd of pearly dew? how icy chains
> Restrain the fluid mass, and stay the course
> of limpid streams. (p. 8)

As elsewhere, Bushe's treatment of the borrowing recalls Blackmore: "the Icy chain / Which do's the fluid Element restrain" (p. 170).

[20] Patrick noted, citing Psalm 29:9, that God "is wont to help and promote" the hind's delivery by a clap of thunder (p. 182). To emphasize God's care, Baker also spoke of a "Midwife-Thunder" (p. 118), as did Thompson (p. 140). Young repeated this information in his notes and added Pliny's observation that "a certain Herb call'd *Seselis*... facilitates birth" (sig. E3^v).

[21] Borrowings from Milton are ubiquitous in early eighteenth-century paraphrases of *Job* and the Psalms. For instance, Milton's image "Earth self-balanc't on her Centre hung" (VIII.242) reappears in paraphrases of Job 38:6 by Young ("What Hand, declare, / Hung it on Nought," ll. 54-55) and Broome (the celestial orbs "hung self-balanc'd in the fluid air," l. 25) and in the paraphrase of Psalm 104 in Husbands' *Miscellany* ("he fix'd this Globe, / Self-balanc'd, Pendent in the Fluid space," p. 13). Raymond D. Havens did not record these borrowings in his list appended to *The Influence of Milton on English Poetry* (1922; rpt. New York: Russell & Russell, 1961), but he does record others within the Husbands' *Miscellany* (pp. 639-40) and the Thompson paraphrase of *Job* (p. 112). To the last may be added ll. 17-19, drawing on *Paradise Lost*, VII.256-59 and 364, and ll. 27-28, borrowing a line from VII.289-90. Curiously, Havens errored in attributing two phrases in Thompson to Milton, the "Eye-lids" image on p. 16 and the "soft Influence" phrase on p. 2--like much else, Milton took these from *Job* (see 41:18 and 38:31). As for the influence of paraphrases of *Job* and the Psalms on each other, cf. Broome's "Till, as a giant strong, a bridegroom gay, / The sun springs dancing" (III, 529) with Psalm 19.5 on the sun, "as a bridegroom coming out of his chamber, and rejoiceth as a strong man to run a race." Or, cf. the idea in Job 38:10-11 of God's calling the ocean to stillness with Christopher Pitt's rendering of Psalm 29.3 and William Hamilton's of Psalm 65.7. (*Minor English Poets 1660-1800*, cited in n. 11, III, 593 and IV, 155). Hamilton's image of clouds as "cloudy cisterns," added to Psalm 65:9-10, recalls Blackmore's "floating Cisterns" (p. 171). One important influence of Psalm 148, probably through Milton's loose paraphrase in *Paradise Lost* (V. 153-208), is the chain-of-being structure Young imposed on materials in *Job* 38-39, reorganizing the items not only to omit redundancy but to pass from small birds to larger birds and then from small to larger mammals.

[22] Sig. A2^r. Whether or not William Thompson knew Dennis' remarks on the sources of sublimity, Dennis' claim "That the Wonders of the Universe afford... a more admirable Spirit, the more they show the Attributes of the Creator" explains much of Young's and Thompson's interest in the theophany (I, 350).

[23] *The Religious Sublime* (Lexington: Univ. Press of Kentucky, 1972), pp. 110-14.

MAN AND GOD IN RICHARDSON'S *SIR CHARLES GRANDISON*

SYLVIA KASEY MARKS

Samuel Richardson did not lack advice during the composition of his last work, *Sir Charles Grandison*. Lady Dorothy Bradshaigh, Richardson's favorite correspondent, speculated about the mien of the good man:

> I am willing to think Miss Byron happened to see him first at the church, and was struck with his behaviour. Who would not? To see a man, in person like Lovelace, in an act of sincere devotion: only think of that![1]

Another correspondent, Philip Skelton, advised:

> As to your *good man*, I need not bid you christen him; but I would willingly see him as good a Christian, as a fine gentleman can be. I don't mean that the two characters are in the least inconsistent, for I am sure the latter is impossible without the former; but I mean that he should appear on all occasions to act, and suffer, upon Christian principles; that he should fast and pray, but not fast every day, nor pray every hour. The devotional part of Pamela's character was a little too much charged, that of Clarissa somewhat too little, till towards her death. I wish to see the present warm in that respect, but duly tempered; that he may be rather a Christian hero than a saint.

In attempting to come to terms with the theme of man and God in Richardson's *Sir Charles Grandison*, it is evident that these bits of advice were not ignored. The obvious religious significance of the work appears in its very intriguing story depicting the conflict of an ideal hero whose affections are torn between a good English Protestant, Harriet Byron, and an equally good Italian Catholic, Clementina della Porretta. Other fascinating conflicts complement this story. Yet they are dilemmas that prompt the response of a very practical kind of Christianity.

That Richardson wrote a work like *Sir Charles Grandison* should not be surprising. He wanted to be a clergyman, but limited finances prevented him from acquiring the proper education. He became a printer, he said, to satisfy his thirst for reading. Sermons, devotional manuals, and conduct books, as well as works by Defoe, Elizabeth Carter, Edward Young, and James Thomson, illustrate the range of his publishing activities. His personal charity extended from friends and relatives to the venerable Dr. Johnson and the infamous Laetitia Pilkington. Mrs. Pilkington's account of Richardson's behavior squares exactly with the character of a Grandison. Of Richardson's religious practices, we know little. He wrote to Lady Bradshaigh that he was collecting sayings from the Bible, and he argued against deism in his conduct manual, the *Apprentice's Vade Mecum* (1733). In general, however, there seemed to be no place for theological fine points in his thinking. He followed Lady Bradshaigh's suggestion that he read Swift's sermon on the Trinity but declared that, "All that concerns us to know for the conduct of life, in order to fill us with a blessed hope, is plain and easy." For Richardson, religion was "the cheerfulest thing in the world."[2]

Richardson's view of other religions appears to have been exceedingly tolerant. Writing to Benjamin Kennicott, he remarks that Joseph Swinton, author of the *Universal History*, which Richardson published, should not have attacked the Moslems so strongly; while a Christian must be zealous in the cause of his faith, he must not allow his passions to rule. In his preface to his edition of *Aesop's Fables*, Richardson asks readers to make allowances for Roger L'Estrange, an early editor of the *Fables* and a papist, because he lived in difficult times. Richardson once wrote that he himself had almost married a "violent Roman Catholic lady . . . a zealous professor." This may partially account for his sympathy toward Catholics. It is intriguing to recall that Richardson's country home in Hammersmith was close to one of the few Catholic strongholds in England. Lady Bradshaigh lived in Lancashire, another area with a large Catholic population, although, with the exception of Richardson's autobiographical note, both are silent in their correspondence about contacts with English Catholics.[3]

Richardson's last work appears to be an attempt to moderate or correct the anti-Catholic sentiment of his time. Many authors had written about the corrupting influence of Italy on young men making the Grand Tour, and one well-known work, Daniel Defoe's *New Family Instructor*, which Richardson printed, dealt with the fears and terrors of parents whose son actually did convert to Catholicism in Italy. Some of Richardson's readers thought he had gone too far and complained about the kind of example Grandison was setting in even entertaining the idea of marrying a Catholic; others accused Richardson of being more Catholic than Protestant. In fact, while there is some eavesdropping on the part of the Italians, the novel contains no sneaking Jesuits or odd abbesses. If Clementina is an ardent Catholic, she is not superstitious, and Harriet fairmindedly notes that her "glorious Enthusiasm, . . . rightly directed, has heretofore given the palm of martyrdom to Saints."

Throughout all the difficulties the Italians create for him, Sir Charles maintains that he respects good people of every persuasion, and after returning from the Grand Tour, his friends include members of the College of Cardinals.

Tolerance of other Protestant denominations seems to be a hallmark of the novel as well. Sir Charles is solicitous of the needs of his tenants regardless of religious conviction, while Grandmother Shirley has reconciled two clergymen of different faiths. The eccentric Aunt Nell and the reformed alcoholic Mrs. O-Hara have turned Methodist; this is not appealing to Grandison's lively sister Charlotte, but she nevertheless admires the zeal of this sect and its missionary effort to reach "subterranean colliers, tinners, and the most profligate of men." Our final view of the Italian Catholics and English Protestants gathered at Grandison Hall leaves the impression of great harmony. Harriet writes to Grandmother Shirley:

> Except at certain devotional hours of retirement, we know not, but that we are all of one faith. Nothing of religious subjects is ever mentioned among us, but in those points in which all good Christians are agreed.[4]

If Richardson was not formally ordained, he put his instincts as a preacher to work in other ways. Like Dr. Johnson, in *Rambler 4*, he worried about the effect of romances on youth. His clergyman friend Edward Young wrote that "When the pulpit fails, other expedients are necessary. I look on you as a peculiar instrument of Providence, adjusted to the peculiar exigence of the times; in which all would be *fine gentlemen*, and only are at a loss to know what he means." Richardson himself had once observed to Aaron Hill:

> The Spectators did some Good, as to prescribing to the Tastes of the Many—But that Work has been published some time: And a Son of Thunder is wanted to rouse the Public out of its Stupidity, and tell it what it should, and what it should not, approve of.

Without exaggeration, one may say that Richardson's whole literary career, beginning with the *Apprentice's Vade Mecum*, is one sustained effort to perfect his writing of the conduct book. The preface to his letter-writing manual states that it is designed to

> inculcate the principles of virtue and benevolence; to describe properly, and recommend strongly, the social and relative duties; and to place them in such practical lights, that the letters may serve for rules to think and act by, as well as forms to write after.

Whatever one may think of *Pamela*, its express purpose was to "promote the cause of religion and virtue," clearly the purpose of its sequel as well.

Of *Clarissa*, Richardson hoped Lady Bradshaigh would place it on the same shelf with her copies of "Taylor's Living and Dying, with your Practice of Piety, and Nelson's Fasts and Festivals." He might have said the same thing of *Grandison*.[5]

The readers of *Grandison*, as of all Richardson's works, fell into two groups, those who read only for the story and those who, while not viewing it as an old-fashioned devotional manual, nevertheless thought of it as a guide to right conduct. Richardson felt he was following "the Christian system." Christian Gellert, one of Richardson's translators, records that one morning he read *Sir Charles Grandison* instead of his usual Tillotson sermon— something that would certainly have warmed Richardson's heart! At the same time, Richardson's brand of Christianity was a practical one. His last novel was commended for being "a living system of manners," "y^e. most complete System of life & manners & y^e. best calculated for y^e. amendment of head & heart, that ever has been exhibited in Prophane writing." One writer claimed that the work might "supply the place of a Tutor, and boarding school: Young persons may learn how to act in all the important conjunctures, and how to behave Gracefully, properly, and Politly in all Common Occurrences of life." This, of course, was the task undertaken by conduct books.[6]

The courtesy or conduct book was especially influential in the seventeenth and eighteenth centuries. Its subject matter ranged from the education of a young man to the secrets of angling, and the authors included kings and the fathers of apprentice sons. But the main purpose of these books, regardless of author or period, was the formation of a good and virtuous person by emphasizing his duties. As Samuel Clarke observed, "every person, in every station of life whatsoever, wherein the Providence of God thinks fit to place him, has always some *plain* and *certain Duty*, which 'tis his present proper Business to attend to." James I's *Basilikon Doron* (1599) begins with a description of the young prince's duties to God, while at the other end of the social spectrum William Gouge's *Of Domesticall Duties* (1622) delineates mutual duties of husbands and wives as well as the the duties of children, parents, servants, and masters. Even Lord Chesterfield discusses what he calls religious and moral duties, the first consisting in an observance of the commandments and the second in following the Golden Rule. George Whitefield, whose emphasis was different from the established church, nevertheless acknowledged that, while one could not depend on salvation by good works, there "is no Doubt but you are to do your Duty." Finally, Richard Allestree, author of *The Whole Duty of Man* (1658), spoke in terms of our duty to God, ourselves, and our neighbor.[7]

When viewed as a conduct book, however, *Grandison* is much more complicated and fascinating than the conventional conduct book. Its story contains a full spectrum of characters and situations. Children, for example, are to be dutiful, but what if parents are unreasonable, as in the case of the Grandison sisters' father, or irresponsible and inebriated, as Mrs. 0-Hara is. What if they have left a female ward to her own discretion in choosing a husband? Great demands are made upon the filial duty of the hero, since his father, Sir Thomas, has had a long affair with the housekeeper and is about to begin another liaison at the time of his death. Sir Charles, in this instance, is compared to the two good sons of Noah who covered their father's nakedness. After Sir Thomas' death, he refuses to dwell on his faults. The material and spiritual welfare of the mistress and her offspring are attended to, while his father's prospective paramour is furnished with a suitable dowry and admonitions to conduct herself respectably in the future.[8]

One conduct writer, Isaac Barrow, wrote that because a gentleman was born to more benefits, he also incurred more obligations, and therefore, in addition to giving financial help to his neighbor, he had a duty to

> direct and advise the ignorant, to comfort the afflicted, to reclaim the wicked, and encourage the good by his wisedom. It is his business to protect the weak, to rescue the oppressed, to ease those who grone under heavy burthens. . .[9]

Grandison is not remiss in this regard. He aids families in difficult straits from his own funds as well as through his attempts to mediate legal entanglements and family disputes. Charlotte, his charming but willful sister, is rescued from the clutches of an illiterate soldier owing to Grandison's efforts. Many others benefit from Sir Charles' rescues and reproofs, and needless to say, such tasks are delicate ones. Archbishop John Tillotson cautions, "It requires a great deal of address and gentle application so to manage the business of reproof, as not to irritate and exasperate the person whom we reprove, insted of curing him."[10] Grandison's manner is graceful and his methods are quietly forceful. He can associate with rakes without demeaning himself. In the course of the story he deflects several dueling challenges, a practice the conduct books unanimously abhor, and invariably he makes friends of his enemies, much to their amazement. Harriet Byron sums it up accurately when she observes:

> See him so delicate in his behaviour and address to Miss Mansfield, and carry in your thoughts his gaiety and adroit management to Lady Beauchamp . . . and you will hardly think him the same man. . . Yet *this* may be said in his behalf; — He but accommodates himself to the persons he has to deal with: — . . . and, that virtue, for its own sake, is his choice; since had he been a free-liver, he would have been a dangerous man.[11]

Are we then to conclude, as some readers did, that Richardson's hero is a *"faultless monster"*? Hester Mulso, one of Richardson's correspondents, wrote, "The only objection I have to his book is, that I apprehend it will occasion the kingdom's being overrun with old maids. It will give the women an idea of perfection in a man which they never had before." Such an example would cause women to be more particular, the consequence of which "will be a single life to ninety-nine out of a hundred."[12] Lady Bradshaigh did not see a faultless monster in Grandison, but she wrote to one of her friends that Richardson was setting a standard of "not what we *are*, but what we *ought* to be . . . there is nothing recom̄ended . . . but what is preach'd by our most Eminent devines, and what is Com̄anded in Scripture as *duties*, by our *Saviour* himself."[13] Any criticism of Richardson's good man that depicts him as an inimitable paragon is likely to overlook the fact that Grandison himself admits to having faults, particularly a passionate temperament coupled with pride in his family name. He does not lack human warmth and emotion; anger, exasperation, and momentary loss of composure are experienced by Sir Charles. He is subject to temptations and is also prey to adversity and great distress in his encounters with the Porretta family. His sisters attribute his difficulties to a "compassionate nature."[14]

It must be added that no character could be further removed from a religious zealot than Grandison. As an Anglican, he follows the required external observances. He opposes a chamber marriage for Charlotte and insists on having his nephew christened at church. Sir Charles will not travel on the Sabbath. The Sunday following his wedding he appears according to form at parish services and later takes communion. However, pomp and parade play no part here; a "chearful piety" is evident in his demeanor when he worships. In each instance, Sir Charles is concerned with setting a good example "to the lower orders of people." Dr. Bartlett, his chaplain, looks after the spiritual welfare of the servants at Grandison Hall and leads them in regular prayers, a practice highly recommended by the conduct-book writers. The servants also have available to them a library containing spiritual books. All in all, Sir Charles, "without making an ostentatious pretension to religion, is the very Christian in practice, that these doctrines teach a man to be."[15]

In Italy, Grandison continues his confidently discreet behavior. He declines debating religious questions and refuses the Porretta request that he change his religion for appearance's sake. As part of the contract being considered for his marriage to Clementina, he allows Clementina her own confessor and agrees to employ Catholic servants in his household. He will not, however, permit those servants to come between him and his wife; should that happen, he reserves the power of dismissal. Eventually Clementina argues her superior duty to God as a reason for not marrying Grandison. Concerned that she may lose her faith if she is married to so good a man as Sir Charles, she begs to be allowed to retire to a convent. Grandison counters that if

Clementina cloisters herself, she will limit her potential to do good — a characteristically Protestant, Latitudinarian argument![16]

In spite of its highly practical approach to religion, *Grandison* is not entirely without references to the hereafter. When Clementina's jealous and vindictive cousin Laurana commits suicide, Sir Charles is disturbed by such self-destruction and reflects "how ill was such a soul as Laurana's prepared to rush into Eternity." Conduct books frequently warned against the expectations of a deathbed repentance, and Richardson presents us with contrasting deathbed scenes. Lady Grandison's last moments afford an example of an individual properly disposed for her final hour. On the other hand, young Lorimer, Sir Charles' first tutor, dies "in horror not to be described; begging for longer life, and promising reformation on that condition." Sir Hargrave finds repentance nearly impossible, while Sir Thomas Grandison intends to repent but "lived not to begin the promised *alteration*." Sir Charles, who has warned Jeronymo, Clementina's brother, about the inability of a guilty life to soften "the agonies of the inevitable hour," does not himself fear death. Harriet remarks, "He can pity a dying friend, without saddening his own heart; for he lives the life of duty as he goes along, and fears not the inevitable lot!" Moreover, his notions of an earthly life as preparation for an eternal one are expressed in private meditations he has composed.[17] Yet Grandison derives his greatest satisfaction from the sheer delight in doing good. Tillotson explains that to "do good, is to be like God," and in another sermon he observes that "they that are advanced to a great height above others, may, like the heavenly bodies, dispense a general light and influence, and scatter happiness and blessings among all that are below them." It is with just such an idea in mind that Sir Charles is referred to as an imitator of the Almighty and an instrument of Providence. He and the other characters often remark that "goodness and beneficence brought with them their own rewards." And here again, Tillotson is a useful guide:

> So that the benefits we do to others are not more welcome to them that receive them, than they are delightful to us that do them . . . But the pleasure of doing good remains after a thing is done, the thoughts of it lie easy in our minds, and the reflection upon it afterwards does for ever minister joy and delight to us.[18]

This aspect of Grandison's character prompts Clementina to conclude that no reward, including her own hand in marriage, would be adequate to thank Grandison for rescuing her brother Jeronymo from assassins: "Who, that knows him, knows not that he can enjoy the reward in the action?" As we recall Richardson's three major works, we begin to see a pattern: Pamela's virtue is repaid with earthly benefits, Clarissa's goodness is recognized in heaven, and Sir Charles Grandison's benevolence is its own reward.[19]

Harriet Byron, in a discussion with Sir Hargrave Pollexfen, her abductor, says that the afterlife "is a very material consideration with me, tho' I am not fond of talking upon it, except on proper occasions, and to *proper* persons." It would appear that Richardson himself did not feel *Sir Charles Grandison* was the proper vehicle for a discussion of eternal life. Rather, he concentrates on the effect of one's actions here and now. Thus, the assessment in the Preface is accurate: Grandison is "the Example of a Man acting uniformly well thro' a Variety of trying Scenes." Or, as Harriet reflects:

> After the Anderson, the Danby, the Lord W. affairs, he appeared to me in a much more shining light than an hero would have done, returning in a triumphal car covered with laurels, and dragging captive princes at its wheels. How much more glorious a character is that of *The Friend of Mankind*, than that of *The Conqueror of Nations!*[20]

NOTES

[1] Lady Bradshaigh to Richardson, 16 April 1751, in Samuel Richardson, *The Correspondence of Samuel Richardson*, ed. Anna Laetitia Barbauld, 6 vols. (1804; rpt., New York: AMS Press, 1966, VI,114–15. Hereafter, *Corr.* designates Mrs. Barbauld's edition. Philip Skelton to Richardson, 10 May 1751, *Corr.*, V, 209.

[2] Richardson to Johannes Stinstra, 2 June 1753, in Samuel Richardson, *Selected Letters of Samuel Richardson*, ed. John Carroll (Oxford: Clarendon Press, 1964, 229. Hereafter, *Selected Letters* designates the Carroll edition. For a complete record of Richardson's publishing ventures, see William M. Sale, Jr., *Samuel Richardson: Master Printer* (1950: rpt. Westport, Conn.: Greenwood Press, 1978); on Mrs. Pilkington see T.C. Duncan Eaves and Ben D. Kimpel, *Samuel Richardson* (Oxford: Clarendon Press, 1971), 337, and *Corr.*, II, 113–57; Richardson to Lady Bradshaigh, 24 February 1753, *Selected Letters*, 235; Richardson to Lady Bradshaigh, [late November 1749?], *Selected Letters*, 135. Doubtful dates follow Eaves, *Richardson*, 620–704.

[3] Richardson to Benjamin Kennicott, [November?] 1754, Osborn Collection, Yale, ff. 1-2; [Samuel Richardson], *Aesop's Fables* (London: J.F. and C. Rivington et al., n.d.), vi; Richardson to Lady Bradshaigh, [c. 1 October 1755], *Selected Letters*, 323.

[4] Richardson to [Cox Macro?], 22 March 1754, British Library 32557, f. 176 and 176b; Richardson to Alexis Claude Clairaut, 5 July 1753, British Library C.44.g. facing p. 396, sheet number 68; for Harriet on Clementina see Samuel Richardson, *The History of Sir Charles Grandison*, ed. Jocelyn Harris, 3 vols. (London: Oxford Univ. Press, 1972), III, 351. Hereafter, *SCG* refers to the Harris edition. On Sir Charles see *SCG*, III, 140; for Charlotte's views see *SCG*, III, 22; for Harriet's observations see *SCG* III, 410.

[5] Edward Young to Richardson, 14 March 1754, *Corr.*, II, 32–33; Richardson to Aaron Hill, 7 November 1748, *Selected Letters*, 100. In quotations, a word preceded and followed by a short dash has been deleted by Richardson; crosses denote his additions. Samuel Richardson, *Familiar Letters on Important Occasions*, ed. Brian W. Downs (London: George Routledge and Sons, 1928), xxvii; Richardson to Aaron Hill, [1 February 1741?], *Selected Letters*, 41; Richardson to Lady Bradshaigh, 15 December 1748, *Corr.*, IV, 237–38.

[6] Richardson to Thomas Edwards, [August 1755?], Forster Collection, Victoria and Albert Museum, XII, 1, f. 145v. Hereafter, FC refers to the Forster Collection. Richardson to Lady Bradshaigh, 15 December 1748, *Corr.*, IV, 225; Christian F. Gellert to Count Hans Moritz de Buhl of Martinskinker, 3 April 1755, Yale Speck Collection G24b.B755.4:3, typescript trans. of German original; Philocalus to the reader, n.d., FC XV, 4, f. 45; Frances Grainger to Richard-

son, 23 May 1754, FC XV, 3, f. 49; Anonymous to Richardson, n.d., FC XV, 3, f. 61, 2v.

[7]Sermon III, "Every Man is principally to regard his own proper Duty," Samuel Clarke, *Sermons*, 7th ed., 2 vols. (London: J. and P. Knapton, 1749), VII, 35; Philip Dormer Stanhope, Fourth Earl of Chesterfield, *Letters of Philip Dormer Fourth Earl of Chesterfield to His Godson and Successor*, ed. The Earl of Carnarvon (Oxford: Clarendon Press, 1890), CVIII, 142, and CXXIX, No. 1, 31 October 1765, 165; "The Necessity of the Righteousness of Christ, A Farewell Sermon Presented at Morefields June 3, 1739," George Whitefield, *Discourses* (London: Charles Whitefield, 1739), p. 14; [Richard Allestree], *The Whole Duty of Man* (London: John Eyre, 1741), p. 1.

[8]Sir Charles and the sons of Noah, *SCG* I, 317.

[9]Isaac Barrow, *Of Industry* (London: Brab. Aylmer, 1712), 135-37.

[10]Sermon XLII, "Against evil-speaking," John Tillotson, *The Works of the Most Reverend John Tillotson, Lord Archbishop of Canterbury*, 12 vols. (London: C. Hitch et al., 1757), III, 192.

[11]Harriet on Sir Charles, *SCG* II, 272.

[12]Richardson to Hester Mulso, 11 July 1751, *Corr.*, II, 168; Mulso Chapone to Elizabeth Carter, 11 February [?], R. Brimley Johnson, ed., *Bluestocking Letters* (London: John Lane, The Bodley Head Ltd., 1926), 175.

[13]Lady Bradshaigh to Richardson, 11 December 1753, FC XI, f. 57.

[14]On Sir Charles' faults see *SCG* II, 113; on his passionate nature *SCG* I, 206 and II, 63; on pride in family name, *SCG* I, 378, I, 384, and II, 223; on temptations, *SCG* II, 492; on compassionate nature, *SCG* III, 68.

[15]On chamber marriage, *SCG* II, 327-28; on christening, *SCG* III, 265-66; on Sabbath, *SCG* II, 379; on Sir Charles's demeanor, *SCG* III, 84; on example, *SCG* III, 266; on servants' library, *SCG* III, 286; on Sir Charles as a Christian, *SCG* I, 440.

[16]On religious debates, *SCG* II, 155; on changing religion, *SCG* II, 528 and 530; on Catholic servants, *SCG* II, 531-32; Sir Charles's arguments, *SCG* II, 619-21 and III, 431.

[17]On Laurana's suicide, *SCG* III, 448; on Lady Grandison's death, *SCG* I, 315-18; on Lorimer's death, *SCG* I, 461; on Pollexfen, *SCG* III, 142-44 and III, 461-62; on Sir Thomas's temporary resolution, *SCG* I, 323; Sir Charles's comment, *SCG* II, 140; Harriet on Sir Charles, *SCG* III, 266; Sir Charles's meditations, *SCG* III, 292-93.

[18]Sermon CLVIII, "Of doing good," Tillotson, *Works*, IX, 20; Sermon CCXII, "Of diligence in our general and particular calling," Tillotson, *Works*, XI, 95; on self-rewarding goodness, *SCG* II, 665 and 667; Sermon XVIII, "The example of Jesus in doing good," Tillotson, *Works*, I, 427-28.

[19]Clementina's comment, *SCG* II, 566.

[20]Harriet on afterlife, *SCG* I, 96; Preface, *SCG* I, 4; Harriet's comment, *SCG* II, 70.

THE PATHETIC AND THE SUBLIME:
THE TRAGIC FORMULA OF JOHN HOME'S *DOUGLAS*

DAVID WHEELER

Despite the lofty position accorded it in traditional eighteenth-century hierarchies of genres, tragic drama does not fare well during the period. The most frequently anthologized specimens of eighteenth-century tragedy are undoubtedly *Cato* (1713) and *The London Merchant* (1731), both works whose stage lives have long ago expired and whose literary reputations have been justly eclipsed by their contemporary comic counterparts—plays by Wycherley, Congreve, Goldsmith, and Sheridan—which still enjoy constant revival and acclaim. However, though *Cato* and *The London Merchant* are not good plays, we cannot ignore their eighteenth-century success nor the elaborate tragic theories—which, for convenience, we may label the Aristotelian and the sentimental—that justified and explained them. Less known than either of these, John Home's *Douglas*, first produced in 1756, closely follows neither example, yet it too is surrounded by a body of criticism and critical theory that so clearly accounts for its composition as to render the play almost formulaic. Furthermore, the preeminence of this criticism as a mid-century poetic earned the play a theatrical life of more than half a century and its author the title of the "Scots Shakespeare." Discrepancy between contemporary reception and lasting reputation is common and is perhaps even to be expected. But the phenomenon suggests that, as well as texts, literary historians need to analyze audiences, particularly the literary values and expectations possessed by those audiences.

The mid-eighteenth century marks a transition in English literary history, though not, as is sometimes still argued, a transition from neoclassicism to romanticism. Rather, the transition involves a shift of emphasis within the neoclassical critical apparatus, a shift made necessary by a greater appreciation of the older literature of the medieval and Elizabethan periods and made possible by the death of Pope and the ascendancy of new poetic models, particularly Thomson and Gray.

This kind of poetry, contrasting so sharply with the ordered and witty couplets of the Augustans, for whom the lyric was demoted on the scale of genres and for whom description was subordinated to an ornamental role, emerged collaterally with a body of criticism and theory that also departed somewhat radically in both emphasis and methodology from the formalist criticism which preceded it. The 1750s and 1760s were rich with major critical statements: Thomas Warton's *Observations on the Fairy Queen of Spenser* (1754), Joseph Warton's first volume of his *Essay on the Genius and Writings of Pope* (1756), Burke's *Philosophical Enquiry into the Origin of Our Ideas of the Sublime and the Beautiful* (1757), Hume's *Four Dissertations* (1757), Young's *Conjectures on Original Composition* (1759), Gerard's *Essay on Taste* (1759), Hurd's *Letters on Chivalry and Romance* (1762), Kames's *Elements of Criticism* (1762), and Blair's *Critical Dissertation on the Poems of Ossian* (1763). Although different from each other, these works all examine something that does not particularly concern Dryden in his *Essay on Dramatic Poesy* nor Addison in his analysis of *Paradise Lost* nor Pope in his preface to the *Iliad*: they all address the emotional response of the reader as he confronts the literary work. Their critical methodology changed from a systematized analysis of parts to a Longinian search for individual, emotionally-charged passages that could sublimely transport a reader. Thus, the lyric, particularly the ode as practiced by Gray, rose in esteem as a form capable of affecting the passions.

R. S. Crane notes that this focus characterizes a "species of criticism of which few models, in the form of extended works, at any rate, are found earlier."[1] It marks a distinct shift in emphasis from poem to reader in the author-poem-reader relationship. As an instrument to generate emotional response, tragedy is particularly powerful, but concomitant to this shift in poetics occurred a modification of tragic theory as well. Since Aristotle's primary discussion of the tragedy concerned a proper plot, Restoration and early eighteenth-century critics also often concerned themselves (though not as earnestly as was once assumed) with plot—singleness of action and maintenance of the other unities of time and place. As an illustration of this concern, we need only recall the structural regularity of Dryden's *All for Love*, especially in contrast with its Shakespearean model, *Antony and Cleopatra*. Aristotle's pity and fear, though emotional responses, were perceived as producing an essentially moral effect: pity over the fall of great and virtuous personages, fear that similar calamities may befall us all. This traditional notion of the tragic hero as moral exemplar may be seen in the Prologue that Pope wrote for *Cato*, where he says of Addison:

> Virtue confessed in human shape he draws,
> What Plato thought, and godlike Cato was:
> No common object to your sight displays,
> But—what with pleasure heav'n itself surveys—

A brave man struggling in the storms of fate,
And greatly falling with a falling state! (lines 17-22)

As in nearly all Augustan literature, the moral issue is a great public one, not just the fall of a man, but the fall of a republic. Even in Johnson's *Irene*, the moral issue, apostasy, is public and the moral lessons universal:

Our daring Bard with Spirits unconfin'd,
Spreads wide the mighty Moral for Mankind.
Learn here how Heav'n supports the virtuous Mind,
Daring, tho' calm; and vigorous tho' resign'd.
Learn here what Anguish racks the guilty Breast,
In Pow'r dependent, in Success deprest.
Learn here that Peace from Innocence must flow;
All else is empty Sound, and idle Show.

(Prologue, lines 7-14)

While retaining a classical structure, Lillo, in *The London Merchant* (1731), had replaced the tragic hero of Cato's dimension with the simpler George Barnwell, a reformed sinner who learns too late (too late to save his life, if not his soul) the value of virtue and the exemplary Thorowgood, whose virtue seems inherent. In addition to moving tragedy into a middle-class, domestic sphere, Lillo amplifies the emotional level of his drama; indeed, the entire fifth act, where Barnwell as a death row inmate says his farewells to a succession of weeping friends, seems designed to jerk tears from Lillo's audience. Nevertheless, despite its heightened emotionalism, *The London Merchant*'s ultimate purpose, like that of all sentimental literature (and Richardson's novels provide the best-known examples), is moral instruction. And the critical and intellectual heritage for such literature has long since been documented by Crane and applied specifically to drama by Arthur Sherbo.[2] Home's play, however, bears little relation to the latitudinarian divines or the theories of benevolence; his interest in pathos comes from elsewhere.

The central figure in *Douglas*, Lady Matilda Randolph, is never forced to test her moral principles. Rather than her morally exemplary behavior, Home stresses her essential humanity; her situation involves not a moral dilemma (requisite for sentimental drama), but a simple and powerful sense of loss. As the play opens, we witness her private lament for the loss of her secret husband, the great warrior Douglas (of Shakespearean fame) and their infant son, who had been sent away at birth and never heard of again. Predictably, the son, young Douglas, returns, only to become a victim of the jealousies of Lord Randolph, whom Matilda had married for convenience, and of the power-play machinations of the villainous Glenalvon. Almanzorlike in his spirit and courage, young Douglas finds it impossible to heed his mother's cautions and falls easily into Glenalvon's trap. While Douglas fights Randolph, Glenalvon ambushes the young hero:

> *Douglas*: It was Glenalvon,
> Just as my arm had master'd Randolph's sword,
> The villian came behind me: but I slew him.

Lady Randolph succumbs to a suicidal despair, and Randolph, after learning about the stranger's true identity and his wife's death, wanders the stage in confusion, finally resolving to purge himself in battle against the Danes.

Void of the moral dilemma found in sentimental tragedy, *Douglas* also lacks the grand scale of the Greek or Shakespearean tragedy. The characters are never developed into the heroic stature that a Shakespeare would have given them. Nor is there any full treatment of Glenalvon's schemings or the backdrop war between Denmark and Scotland. Rather, the focus is on Lady Randolph's emotional state as she rises from long suffering grief to renewed hope, enjoys brief happiness, and then falls quickly into fatal despair. In this first play Home was testing the tragic waters, and the measure of his success was to be not the reviews of critics nor the quality of the moral lesson to be learned from a character's example; rather, it was simply to bring tears to the eyes of his audience. Home states his affective purpose clearly in the play's prologue:

> Listen attentive to the various tale,
> Mark if the author's kindred feelings fail;
> Sway'd by alternate hopes, alternate fears,
> He waits the test of your congenial tears.
>
> (Edinburgh, lines 30-33)[3]

Presumably Home perceives different requirements for the genre than the ones assumed by Addison, Pope, and Johnson. A grand scale and public issues may be necessary for the presentation of moral exemplars and universal truths, but in this case their emphasis would detract from Lady Randolph's personal anguish and therefore diminish Home's desired effect. Though, in this transitional work, vestiges of heroic tragedy remain—a kingdom is at stake, the characters are of noble blood, Douglas possesses an hereditary courage that leads to his downfall—they are downplayed in favor of close scrutiny of the heroine's emotions.

Home seems to be subscribing to a set of literary values held commonly at mid-century but expressed perhaps most simply by Joseph Warton in his dedication to the *Essay on the Genius and Writings of Pope* (1756), a popular and widely-discussed work, the first volume of which was published the same year as *Douglas*'s first performance: "The sublime and the pathetick are the two chief nerves of all poetry."[4] The poetic sublime for Warton is accomplished through pictorial description of the kind found in Young's *Night Thoughts* (1742-45) and in the odes of Collins, Gray, and Warton himself. The effect produced on the reader is not so much terror (as it is in the Burkean sublime), though it could be, as it is a state of contemplative reflection of things essentially supernatural and ultimately divine.

The opening lines of *Douglas* sound familiar echoes to anyone experienced with mid-century lyric poetry and signal the play's literary heritage:

> *L. Randolph.* Ye woods and wilds, whose melancholy gloom
> Accords with my soul's sadness, and draws forth
> The voice of sorrow from my bursting heart,
> Farewel a while: I will not leave you long;
> For in your shades I deem some spirit dwells,
> Who from the chiding stream, or groaning oak,
> Still hears, and answers to MATILDA'S moan.
> O DOUGLAS! DOUGLAS! if departed ghosts
> Are e'er permitted to review this world,
> Within the circle of that wood thou art,
> And with the passion of immortals, hear'st
> My lamentation: hear'st thy wretched wife
> Weep for her husband slain, her infant lost. (I, 1-14)

This melancholy world where hearts burst and oaks groan, where streams chide and spirits dwell, is a world Lady Matilda Randolph shares with the poetic personae of Collins and Gray, of the Wartons, of Akenside and Young. If *Douglas* has a medieval setting, it also has a heroine with a mid-eighteenth-century sensibility, one who clearly derives the pleasures of melancholy and of solitary contemplation from her gloomy and ghostly surroundings. And the lone figure, the antiquated diction, and the gothic description are the trademarks of the graveyard poets and the formula for the poetic sublime. Home makes use of such passages throughout *Douglas*, especially at crucial moments such as in the establishment of the setting for the fatal confrontation between young Douglas, Randolph, and Glenalvon:

> *Douglas.* THIS is the place, the centre of the grove.
> Here stands the oak, the monarch of the wood.
> How sweet and solemn is this mid-night scene!
> The livry moon, unclouded, holds her way
> Thro' skies where I could count each little star.

> The fanning west wind scarcely stirs the leaves;
> The river, rushing o'er its pebbled bed,
> Imposes silence with a stilly sound.
> In such a place as this, at such an hour,
> If ancestry can be in ought believ'd,
> Descending spirits have convers'd with man,
> And told the secrets of the world unknown. (V, 1-12)

Using the accepted formula, Home is striving for the poetic sublime to create in his audience a receptive mood for the pathos they are about to witness.

The example Warton furnishes as the most pathetic in all of literature is telling, for it too is a depiction of parental loss. The passage is found in Canto 33 of Dante's *Inferno*, where Count Ugolin, imprisoned with his four children, watches helplessly as they succumb one by one to starvation. Though none would deny *The Divine Comedy*'s essential morality, the pathos in this episode, while provoking a brief political attack on Pisa, is pure, uninterrupted by the kind of moral commentary found in *The London Merchant*.

Douglas's pathetic episodes are of a similar kind. In the first act Lady Randolph's story of her lost husband and child, told in confidence to her maid, elicits Anna's response: "My dearest Lady! Many a tale of tears / I've listen'd to; but never did I hear / A tale so sad as this" (I, 226-28). Lady Randolph's tale gets sadder, however, and her final speech carries portrayal of human suffering to its extreme:

> ... My son! my son!
> My beautiful! my brave! how proud was I
> Of thee, and of thy valour; My fond heart
> O'er flow'd this day with transport, when I thought
> Of growing old amidst a race of thine,
> Who might make up to me their father's childhood,
> And bear my brother's and my husband's name:
> Now all my hopes are dead! A little while
> Was I a wife! a mother not so long! (V, 282-93)

Most of us, whose experience with tragedy is drawn from the Greeks, from Shakespeare, even from Ibsen, expect in a final speech heroic dignity rather than such a melodramatic rendering of grief. But as with Home's depictions of the sublime, these portraits of the pathetic are not isolated aberrations, but part of an emerging, elaborate tragic aesthetic.

In his Dedication to *Four Dissertations*, which contained the influential "Of Tragedy" and was published in 1757, the same year as *Douglas*, David Hume said of his friend Home: "You possess the true theatric genius of

Shakespear and *Otway*, refined from the unhappy barbarism of the one, and licentiousness of the other." Though such praise from a fellow Scot and a close friend may be suspect, an examination of Hume's essay on tragedy suggests the elements in *Douglas* that Hume deemed worthy of praise. In the essay Hume follows the custom of many eighteenth-century tragic theorists in searching for the cause of the seemingly paradoxical pleasure derived from viewing tragedy and begins the piece by stating the paradox:

> The whole art of the poet is employed in rousing and supporting the compassion and indignation, the anxiety and resentment, of his audience. They are pleased in proportion as they are afflicted, and never are so happy as when they employ tears, sobs, and cries to give vent to their sorrow and relieve their heart, swollen with the tenderest sympathy and compassion.[5]

Hume goes on to distinguish on artistic ground the anguish we feel when observing an actual tragic event from the pleasure gained by viewing a stage representation of tragic action, i.e., the audience derives pleasure from successful imitation, eloquent language, and the force of oratory. Nevertheless, in departing from a standard explanation of the phenomenon expressed by Fontenelle and by Samuel Johnson that we are relieved of any possible anguish by a knowledge of the play's essential fiction, Hume lays the groundwork for a theory of tragedy based on sympathy.

The theory of sympathy is expressed more fully and forcefully the same year by Edmund Burke: "Most of the ideas which are capable of making a powerful impression on the mind . . . may be reduced very nearly to these two heads, of self-preservation and society."[6] Self-preservation, for Burke, is the principle behind sublime terror. Society is a natural impulse to sympathize with fellow humans in distress and the principle behind the literary effectiveness of pathos. Burke continues to explain that

> it is by this principle sympathy chiefly that poetry, painting, and other affecting arts, transfuse their passions from one breast to another, and are often capable of grafting a delight on wretchedness, misery, and death itself.[7]

A few years later, Lord Kames invents the notion of an "ideal presence" (as opposed to being actually present) and, finding the drama most powerful in producing such an ideal presence, even explains drama's moral function in terms of sympathy: "the extensive influence which language hath over the heart . . . strengthens the bond of society, and attracts individuals from their private system to perform acts of generosity and benevolence."[8] Kames brings the theory of sympathy back in line with the moral purpose of art and is actually closer to describing how sentimental literature works. Hume,

Burke, and Kames are followed by a succession of critics to create a sympathetic theory of tragedy which has been summed up nicely by Earl Wasserman: "The end of tragedy becomes then, not the purgation of pity and fear, nor the inculcation of specific moral and ethical doctrines through pity and fear, but rather the exercise and strengthening of the spectator's general faculty for sympathy."[9]

If one were to study the literary criticism of the late 1750s and early 1760s and then sit down and write a tragedy, it is likely that a play like *Douglas* is the kind of composition that would emerge. John Home was no critical theorist, but his first play is so much the product of the theoretical milieu in which he was writing that its main value now is in exploring the relationship between theory and practice. His sublime poetical description is of the sort advanced theoretically by Warton and composed by Gray and Collins (who had dedicated his "Ode on the Popular Superstitions of Scotland" to Home); his notion of how tragedy works conforms to the tragic theory emerging around him. More popular as the century wore on, *Douglas* even provided the passionate tragic actress Mrs. Siddons with her final role in 1819.[10] Clearly she saw the role of Lady Randolph as one that would allow her the full range of her talents.

That *Douglas* has since sunk into oblivion is hardly surprising; pathos is a word or experience we associate with melodrama, with Douglas Jerrold and Dion Boucicault, with made-for-television films about talented children or athletes stricken with cancer, films that offer an abundance of pathos and excite our emotions but seldom earn the label of successful tragedy or even of art. We have discarded pathos as a legitimate literary value, ranking the pathetic considerably below the tragic on our scale of aesthetic experience. That they were once so closely identified raises some interesting questions; indeed, changing literary values have always presented problems in evaluation for the critic. We recall the more rigid neoclassical critics struggling over the formally irregular works of Tasso, Spenser, and Shakespeare and romantic critics trivializing Pope for his lack of sincerity. Not that in relegating *Douglas* to a dark corner of a scholar's library we are guilty of the same blindness to literary quality. However, because of our high regard for psychologically complex characters, richly ambiguous language, and universally tragic experience, factors which contribute to our primary critical endeavor of interpreting meaning, we are able to praise the Greeks, Shakespeare, and many modern dramatists but must omit most of the tragedy composed in the eighteenth and nineteenth centuries. Such tragedy was composed according to a different set of values which had little to do with meaning, a term that almost never enters into eighteenth-century formalist or affective criticism. We appreciate these centuries for other modes—the satire, the romantic lyric, the novel—but I would argue that the literary values for these modes have remained more static than those for tragedy. Likewise, I would suggest that the lasting appeal of Restoration comedy is attributable not to the obvious fact that Wycherley and Congreve wrote good plays (a simplification) but that we perceive the plays as good because we share a system of comic values that includes rapid exchange of witty dialogue, social satire, and even exaggerated, stereotypical characters. After all, these ingredients provided the formula for our own long-running *All in the Family* and *M*A*S*H*.

But what do we do with *Douglas*? To call it a bad tragedy says as much about our literary values, our generic expectations and requirements, as it does about the play itself. Though it would be a travesty to judge it favorably by applying Home's own standards, how can we be confident that our own standards are any more proper? We are left with the same kind of dilemma confronting any critic whose approach is essentially a generic one. Perhaps that is why, when confronted with an author whose works were too large for eighteenth-century evaluative tools, Samuel Johnson, the most sensible of critics, appealed not to any set of standards but to the "length of duration and continuance of esteem"—to the test of time: "What mankind have long possessed, they have often examined and compared, and if they persist to value the possession, it is because frequent comparisons have confirmed opinion in its favor."[11] Johnson suggests that greatness produces a popular esteem that can transcend transformations of genres and changes in literary values. If, after over two hundred years, John Home has not shared Shakespeare's fate, it is probably not the fault of the critics, and we are back where we started: regarding *Douglas* as a historical rather than literary phenomenon.

NOTES

[1] R. S. Crane, "English Neoclassical Criticism," in *Dictionary of World Literature: Criticism—Forms—Technique*, ed. Joseph T. Shipley (New York: Philosophical Library, 1943), p. 194.

[2] See R. S. Crane, "Suggestions Toward a Genealogy of the 'Man of Feeling,'" *ELH* 1 (1934), 205-30, and Arthur Sherbo, *English Sentimental Drama* (East Lansing: Michigan State Univ. Press, 1957).

[3] *Douglas* opened in Edinburgh on 14 December 1756 and at Covent Garden on 14 March 1757. This prologue (in places quite nationalistic) was spoken at the Edinburgh productions. The text I have used is based on the first Edinburgh edition (1757) and has been edited by Gerald D. Parker (Edinburgh: Oliver and Boyd, 1972).

[4] Joseph Warton, *An Essay on the Genius and Writings of Pope* (London, 1756).

[5] David Hume, "Of Tragedy," in *Eighteenth-Century Critical Essays*, ed. Scott Elledge (Ithaca, N.Y.: Cornell Univ. Press, 1961), II, 804.

[6] Edmund Burke, *A Philosophical Enquiry into the Origin of Our Ideas of the Sublime and the Beautiful*, ed. James T. Boulton (Notre Dame, Ind: Univ. of Notre Dame Press, 1968), p. 38.

[7] Burke, p. 44.
[8] Scott Elledge, *Eighteenth-Century Critical Essays*, 2 vols. (Ithaca: Cornell Univ. Press, 1961), II, 843–45.
[9] Earl Wasserman, "The Pleasures of Tragedy," *ELH* 14 (1947), 305.
[10] Thomas Campbell, *Life of Mrs. Siddons* (1839; rpt. New York: Benjamin Blom, 1972), p. 361.
[11] Samuel Johnson, "Preface to Shakespeare," in *Eighteenth-Century Essays on Shakespeare*, ed. David Nichol Smith (1903; rpt. New York: Russell and Russell, 1962), p. 113.

THE FEAR OF FICTION

ROBERT W. UPHAUS

Speaking of the French Realists, Ian Watt comments that they drew "attention to an issue which the novel raises more sharply than any other literary form—the problem of the correspondence between the literary work and the reality which it imitates. This is essentially an epistemological problem, and it therefore seems likely that the nature of the novel's realism, *whether in the early eighteenth century or later*, can best be clarified by the help of those professionally concerned with the analysis of concepts, the philosophers."[1] I have selected this quotation from Watt's influential book for two reasons: first, because he has correctly stated a central issue of the rise of the novel—namely the relation between the mimetic novel and the reality that it purports to imitate; and second, because from this statement Watt deduces the wrong conclusion, namely, that this is "essentially an epistemological problem." In the early eighteenth century it was not an epistemological problem, but a moral problem. The emergence and influence of the novel raised a number of moral questions that I have collected under the heading of "the fear of fiction." Basically, the fear was that the novel, or what was more commonly called the comedy of romance or familiar history, would serve as an influence and instrument of moral education and therefore become a rival to, and possibly supersede, such traditional avenues of moral education as conduct books, moral tracts, the sermon, and perhaps scripture itself.

First, let me briefly examine the question of whether the correspondence between the literary work and the reality which it imitates was essentially an epistemological problem. For reasons of convenience and accessibility, I shall use two books that offer a broadly representative, sometimes overlapping collection of what eighteenth-century authors thought about their own fiction and the rise of the novel. The two books are George L. Barnett's edition, *Eighteenth-Century British Novelists on the Novel* and Ioan Williams's edition, *Novel and Romance 1700–1800*. In neither volume is the novel's imitation of reality treated as an epistemological problem. Rather, as Jerry Beasley has recently observed, "Only two imperatives, . . . the ethical and the mimetic, are constants in most commentary by early eighteenth-century fiction writers on their own work."[2] In the former, generic case sample comments range from Roger Boyle's familiar remark that "romances tell us what may be, whereas true histories tell us what is,"[3] to Congreve's observation that "novels are of a more familiar nature, come near us and represent to us intrigues in practice . . . but not such as are wholly unusual or unprecedented . . . Romances give more of wonder, novels more delight" (*ECBN*, p. 18), to Smollett's more sophisticated definition of a novel as:

> A large diffused picture, comprehending the characters of life, disposed in different groups, and exhibited in various attitudes for the purposes of an uniform plan, and general occurrence, to which every individual figure is subservient. But this plan cannot be executed with propriety, probablility or success, without a principal personage to attract the attention, unite the incidents, unwind the clue of the labyrinth, and at last close the scene by virtue of his own importance. (*ECBN*, p. 65)

In the latter moral case, the principal concern is with what the novelist chooses to imitate and what that imitation teaches. Speaking of his own prose romance, Robert Boyle expresses the familiar desire "to propose patterns of virtue than models of skill or eloquence" (*ECBN*, p. 16). The somewhat notorious Mrs. Mary Manley suggests that the historical novelist "ought with great care to observe the probability of truth, which consists in saying nothing but what may be morally believed." (*ECBN*, p. 23), a comment later echoed by John Hawkesworth when he speaks of the "moral probability preserved" in the oriental apologue (*ECBN*, p. 100). Though one could quote at length from Richardson and Johnson, for now it is more surprising and illuminating to hear from Henry Mackenzie, well known as an author of sentimental novels, who provides a remarkable insider's estimate of the dangers of sentimental fiction.

Writing in 1785, Mackenzie initially denies that he is "disposed to carry the idea of the dangerous tendency of all novels quite so far as some rigid moralists have done." Still, he goes on to argue that:

> The principal danger of novels, as forming a mistaken and pernicious system of morality, seems to me to arise from that contrast between one virtue or excellence and another, that war of duties which is to be found in many of them, particularly in that species called the *Sentimental*. . . . In this rivalship of virtue and of duties, those are always likely to be preferred which in truth and reason are subordinate, and those to be degraded which ought to be paramount. . . . In the enthusiasm of sentiment there is much the same danger as in the enthusiasm of religion, of substituting certain impulses and feelings of what may be called a visionary kind, in the place of real practical duties, which in morals, as in theology, we might not improperly denominate good works.[4]

Lest we think Mackenizie is simply attacking minor prose fiction, he cautions us — without naming names — that he does not have in mind "that common herd of novels (the wretched offspring of circulating libraries)," but rather the "admired ones" which youth read "for imitation as well as amusement" (*N & R*, p. 331). Mackenzie accuses these admired novels, including possibly some of his own, of separating "conscience from virtue," of eluding "the strongest obligation to rectitude," and of blunting "the strongest incitement to virtue" (*N & R*, p. 330).

At this point a modern reader may be tempted to exclaim: Who is Henry Mackenzie anyway? How old-fashioned can you get? Doesn't he know how to read fiction? What's virtue got to do with art? Well, the truth is Mackenzie represents the mainstream of eighteenth-century thinking about fiction. As a novelist and critic, he is fully aware of and responsive to the problematical moral status of the novel. As Ioan Williams has commented, there was "such an enormous increase in the production of fiction that many observers felt that the novel was a threat to cultural and moral standards" (*N & R*, p. 1). And in his comprehensive study of the novel in the eighteenth-century magazines, Robert Mayo confirms that "for most of the eighteenth century the novel was under intermittent attack in the magazines. . . . The objections raised were both aesthetic and ethical, but the latter were more urgently voiced. The novel was a literary form of doubtful origin and dubious associations."[5]

The question naturally arises: Why was the novel under attack during the eighteenth century? What was there to fear? Why were romances regarded as "dangerous recreation" (*N & R*, p. 327)? Were these fears being voiced by cranks, eighteenth-century forerunners of the Moral Majority? To attempt an answer to these questions, one might as well turn to Johnson's *Rambler 4*, an essay perfectly situated historically. Published in 1750, this essay is written late enough that Johnson had examples from the fiction of Defoe, Richardson, Fielding, and Smollett, but it is also written early enough that he could recommend how this developing form — which, in Maximillian Novak's words, did not so much rise "as it lurched in various directions"[6] — might be used and what responsibilities, artistic and ethical, it entailed. Treated most often as a piece of literary criticism, *Rambler 4* can also be read as the statement of an author who practiced fiction (the oriental apologue). *Rambler 4* could easily serve as the preface to *Rasselas*.

The customary reading of *Rambler 4* has been concisely summarized by Robert Mayo:

> It can be read . . . as a defense of *Clarissa* against its detractors, and a conscious or unconscious rejoinder to Fielding's theory of the novel as expressed in the initial chapters of *Tom Jones*. . . . without naming him, Johnson seems to be attacking the 'mixed charac-

ter' of Tom Jones, and his paper further supports Richardson's canons of criticism . . . by emphasizing ethical rather than technical questions. . . . In according the novel recognition as a genuine literary genre, Johnson performed a service to the new fiction of his day, but in seeming to reduce it to a mere arm of pedagogy, he was a force for reaction and prejudice.[7]

Regrettably, Mayo's summary involves a good deal of hedging: that is, *Rambler 4* is a "conscious or unconscious" rejoinder to Fielding, Johnson "seems" to be attacking Fielding's "mixed" characters, Johnson "seems" to reduce the novel to pedagogy. Such a reading, which evidently dates back to Alexander Chalmers,[8] ought to arouse suspicion; for when Johnson means to attack a writer—say James Macpherson or Soame Jenyns—he does so overtly.

The fact is *Rambler 4* is not an attack on Fielding nor a defense of Richardson. How such a reading developed is a matter worth examining, but not at this time. For now let me suggest that *Rambler 4* is a meditation on the rise of the novel, one more flexible and far-reaching than many modern critical approaches. In the essay Johnson briefly examines the origin of the novel, its modern design, its intended audience and likely effects, and the author's responsibility. In doing so, Johnson coherently summarizes the principal grounds for the eighteenth-century fear of fiction, a fear which grew out of the view that the novel, in its preoccupation with imitating ordinary experience, would break away from the classical assumption that "the chief means of moral education is the telling of stories."[9] If this were to occur, as Johnson feared, art and life would become opposed to one another, and the artist—in this case the novelist—might claim exemption from his traditional moral tasks.

Like so many of his predecessors, Johnson initially distinguished the novel, or what he calls the comedy of romance, from the heroic romance. He associates the novel with the exhibition of "life in its true state, diversified only by accidents that daily happen in the world, and influenced by passions and qualities which are really to be found in conversing with mankind."[10] The province of the novel, unlike that of the heroic romance, is "to bring about natural events by easy means, and to keep up curiosity without the help of wonder" (3.19). Johnson would surely agree with Ian Watt that the novel is distinguished by its "truth to individual experience" and by its desire to "present a full and authentic report of human experience." But he would not accept, as we shall see, Watt's contention that such truth to experience is the novel's "primary criterion."[11] Because of the novel's appeal to ordinary experience, it requires of its authors not simply the learning gained from books, which is sufficient for heroic romance, but also, as Johnson says, "that experience which can never be attained by solitary diligence, but must arise from general converse, and accurate observation of the living world" (3.20).

There is a danger, however. As Johnson notices: "Other writings are safe, except from the malice of learning, but these are in danger from every common reader" (3.20). Novels, or novelists, are in "danger" in the sense that their claim to realistic accuracy invites the most common, as distinguished from learned, assessment. No common reader mistook a heroic romance for truth; but many common readers were encouraged to think of the novel as true. This is why they were presented as memoirs, biographies, and histories. The danger arose because the truths of fiction laid claim to the truths of experience.

Herein lay the grounds for the fear of fiction. Appealing to common readers, many novelists understandably shared "the fear of not being approved as just copyers of human manners" (3.20). But what Johnson and others, like Mackenzie, feared was that the novelists would be content with merely being "just copyers" who, in Johnson's memorable phrase, would settle for "promiscuously describing" the world (3.22). Writing novels was not simply an art but a responsibility. Johnson feared that many novelists would sacrifice the latter to the former.

There are two key assumptions behind Johnson's fear of fiction: First, he assumes that these novels "are written chiefly for the young, the ignorant, and the idle, to whom they serve as lectures of conduct, and introductions into life" (3.21). Second, he assumes that "what we cannot credit we shall never imitate," which is to say that the great power of realistic or mimetic fiction is that it so successfully imitates human experience that it has the seductive power of commanding belief, if not assent. It is, as he implies, a rival to traditional lectures of conduct and introductions into life. Listen to how clearly Johnson understands the potential moral impact (and consequent problems) of mimetic fiction:

> But when an adventurer is levelled with the rest of the world, and acts in such scenes of the universal drama, as may be the lot of any other man; young spectators fix their eyes upon him with closer attention, and hope by observing his behaviour and success to regulate their own practices. . . . For this reason these familiar histories may perhaps be made of greater use than the solemnities of professed morality, and convey the knowledge of vice and virtue with more efficacy than axioms and definitions. . . . It is justly considered as the greatest excellency of art, to imitate nature; but it is necessary to distinguish those parts of nature, which are most proper for imitation. (3.21-22)

Johnson refuses to exempt art from its traditional moral responsibility. He clearly anticipates, and therefore fears, that this is precisely what will occur in mimetic fiction. In fact, this is Johnson's fundamental fear of mimetic literature generally. Years later he would accuse Shakespeare, whose realistic tragi-comedies he often praised, of sacrificing virtue to artistic convenience. Johnson obviously believed that there could be moral fiction—a kind of fiction that would, at one and the same time, satisfy the desire to imitate nature and still preserve the traditional obligation of sustaining moral distinctions. Where these two needs frequently conflict in mimetic fiction is in the choice and representation of character—a concept crucial to the eighteenth-century fear of fiction. The main line of defense against this fear of fiction, as Johnson recognized, would be the development of a moral fiction whose primary vehicle would be the use of a realistic representation of character as an instrument of virtue.

Despite powerful examples from the fiction of Richardson, Fielding, Defoe, Smollett, and Austen, some modern-day critics continue to confirm the eighteenth century's worst fears of fiction by attempting to drive a destructive wedge between so-called moral (or didactic) fiction and mimetic fiction. For example, Sheldon Sacks concedes that neither Richardson nor Fielding "seemed to have any notion of freeing himself from the constraint of a moral aim imposed by a critical tradition; on the contrary, there is explicit evidence that the moral effect of their works was a primary consideration."[12] Yet Sacks persists in separating "authorial intention from artistic end," probably because he mistakenly believes that "the ethical beliefs, opinions, and prejudices of novelists do not shape their novels." Where this kind of reasoning leads can be seen in Ian Watt's attempt to credit Richardson with great "psychological penetration" in *Clarissa*, at the same time that, in order to congratulate Richardson for his wonderful insight, Watt must argue that this "shows how, if the need arises, Richardson the novelist can silence Richardson the writer of conduct books."[13] In other words, to invent a Richardson who is modern, relevant, and psychological, Watt—and he is by no means alone in this enterprise—must first sap Richardson of his moral strength. This is exactly what Johnson and some of his contemporaries feared—that there would develop an arbitrary division between moral and mimetic fiction, a recent example of which can be seen in William Beatty Warner's book, *Reading Clarissa* (New Haven & London: Yale Univ. Press, 1979).

Recently, one modern novelist and critic has revived the line of argument Johnson initiated in *Rambler 4*. Like Johnson, John Gardner defends the "traditional view . . . that true art is moral."[14] Like Johnson, as we shall see, Gardner argues that "moral art in its highest form holds up models of virtue, whether they be heroic models like Homer's Achilles or models of quiet endurance." Gardner understands that "discursive thought is not [moral] fiction's most efficient tool; the interaction of charcters is everything." Furthermore, Gardner realizes that you can have mimetic fiction that is moral because, as he says, "a simulation of real experience is morally educational."

For Johnson, the concept of character embodies both the potential moral strength of mimetic fiction and the grounds for fearing such fiction. Arguing that "the power of example is so great, as to take possession of the memory by a kind of violence, and produce effects almost without the intervention of the will" (3.22), Johnson reasons that it is "not a sufficient vindication of a character, that it is drawn as it appears, for many characters ought never to be drawn" (3.22). Johnson's principal objection against "mixed" characters is that "many writers, for the sake of following nature, so mingle good and bad qualities in their principal personages, that they are both equally conspicuous" (3.23).

How, then, can the representation of character be simultaneously moral and mimetic, without succumbing either to pompous didacticism or to promiscuous description? Johnson's answer is quick but complicated. In one elaborate sentence he pulls together his views of mimesis and morality:

> In narratives, where historical veracity has no place, I cannot discover why there should not be exhibited the most perfect idea of virtue; of virtue not angelical, nor above probability, for what we cannot credit we shall never imitate, but the highest and purest that humanity can reach, which, exercised in such trials as the various revolutions of things shall bring upon it, may, by conquering some calamities, and enduring others, teach us what we may hope, and what we can perform. (3.24)

The stages of Johnson's sentence trace his concern with the generic characteristics of the novel, its intended audience and likely effects, and the author's responsibility. Johnson is careful to distinguish the novel from narratives (history, in particular) which do require "historical veracity." Because the novel is based on probability, it can select its version of truth. Such a selection must be based on plausibility because, as Johnson realizes, "what we cannot credit we shall never imitate." The novelist is answerable to the audience's expectation of probability and verisimilitude; but the novelist is also answerable for what he or she chooses to represent.

This is where the central idea of virtue emerges as an antidote to the potentially dangerous effects of a mimetic fiction that would opt for "promiscuous description." The idea of virtue provides the moral center of mimetic fiction. For Johnson, virtue is not simply a theme, as it has been traced by R. F. Brissenden, for example.[15] Rather, virtue is the context within which a moral action occurs. Virtue is "exercised in such trials as the various revolutions of things shall bring upon it." Johnson does not understand virtue melodramatically, as an opportunity for distinguishing victors and victims. The action of virtue will show characters "conquering some calamities, and enduring others," and it will "teach us what we may hope, and what we can perform." To the question of whether such a formulation could actually work in eighteenth-century fiction, I can only answer: read or reread *Roxana, Clarissa, Tom Jones* (if you believe it is "an exercise in the fictive definition of Virtue"),[16] *Humphry Clinker*, and anything by Jane Austen.

To sum up: the idea of virtue in mimetic fiction does not presuppose some simple formula of poetic justice. Expressed through characters who are not "angelical, nor above probability," the action of virtue provides the morally educational experience of mimetic fiction and thereby counters the fear that such fiction would undermine traditional avenues of moral and religious education. There need not be a rivalry between mimesis and morality, even though modern practice seems to insist on it.

NOTES

[1] Ian Watt, *The Rise of the Novel* (Berkeley: Univ. of California Press, 1974), p. 11 (italics added).

[2] Jerry C. Beasley, *Novels of the 1740s* (Athens: Univ. of Georgia Press, 1982), p. 8.

[3] George L. Barnett, ed., *Eighteenth-Century British Novelists on the Novel* (New York: Appleton-Century-Crofts, 1968), p. 4. Hereafter referred to as *ECBN*. All further references are cited within the text.

[4] *Novel and Romance 1700-1800*, ed. Ioan Williams (London: Routledge and Kegan Paul, 1970), pp. 329-30. Hereafter referred to as *N&R*. All further references are cited within the text.

[5] Robert D. Mayo, *The English Novel in the Magazines 1740-1815*. (Evanston, Ill.: Northwestern Univ. Press, 1962), pp. 13-14.

[6] Maximillian E. Novak, *Realism, Myth, and History in Defoe's Fiction* (Lincoln and London: Univ. of Nebraska Press, 1983), p. 7.

[7] Mayo, pp. 99-100.

[8] See Williams's headnote to "Rambler 4" in *Novel and Romance*, p. 142.

[9] Alasdair MacIntyre, *After Virtue* (Notre Dame, Ind.: Univ. of Notre Dame Press, 1981), p. 114; see also p. 211. I am greatly indebted to MacIntyre's book.

[10] The Yale Edition of the Works of Samuel Johnson: *The Rambler*, 3 vols., ed. W. J. Bate and Albrecht B. Strauss (New Haven & London: Yale Univ. Press, 1969), III, 19. All further references are cited within the text.

[11] Watt, pp. 13, 32.

[12] Sheldon Sacks, *Fiction and the Shape of Belief* (Berkeley and Los Angeles: Univ. of California Press, 1967), p. 246. The subsequent quotations are on pages 247 and 69.

[13] Watt, p. 213.

[14] John Gardner, *On Moral Fiction* (New York: Basic Books, 1978), p. 5. The subsequent quotations are on pages 82, 92, 114.

[15] See R. F. Brissenden, *Virtue in Distress* (London: Macmillan, 1974).

[16] Martin C. Battestin, *The Providence of Wit* (Oxford: Clarendon Press, 1974), p. 165.

V. SCIENCE

THE SCIENTIST IN SHIRT-SLEEVES: CHARLES BONNET'S LETTERS ON PARTHENOGENESIS

VIRGINIA P. DAWSON

One of the problems of interpreting the eighteenth-century scientific text is the sheer mass of empirical detail which every scientist of the period felt obliged to present, interpreting Newton's famous dictum, "*Hypotheses non fingo*," as a command to let bare facts speak for themselves.[1] For the eighteenth-century reader, empirically derived facts, presented as though no theory were necessary, were sufficient, since presumably all shared a common background of ideas. Now it is more difficult to see their significance. A microbiologist might take a certain antiquarian pleasure in picking up an old book related to his field, but it is doubtful that he would expect to be enlightened by its factual content. Moreover, unlike great works of art or literature which continue to be universally enjoyed, a scientific text generally has little lasting aesthetic appeal. Especially in works of natural history, while the dry recounting of particulars with a meticulous thoroughness certainly did appeal to most eighteenth-century tastes, these hard lumps of empirical detail at first seem impervious to interpretation, devoid of historical content. Yet it is precisely the historical content of these old scientific works which makes them valuable as cultural documents. If they are to have significance, the historian must assay the elusive metal of ideas from the dross of empirical detail.

One of the reasons why the scientific writers of the eighteenth century felt compelled to present facts, not theory, was their revulsion against the excessive Cartesian rationalism of the preceding century. Though early eighteenth-century French science retained a Cartesian emphasis on clear thinking and rational demonstration of facts, which to an extent it has never lost, the Cartesian philosophy in its totality—the belief in a world machine created by God according to immutable laws of matter in motion—lost ground as emphasis on observation and experiment increased.

Particularly in the study of the living "organized body" (*le corps organisé*), the concept of the Cartesian animal machine came under scrutiny. Could the complex internal structure of an animal be comprehended merely as a system of levers, pulleys, gears, and hydraulic pumps? The machine analogy was increasingly called into question as careful observation revealed new facts. The historian Jacques Roger has eloquently described the limitations of Cartesian biology: "Born of an imperious need for clarity, very satisfying for the intelligence who sees things from above, a mechanical conception of life is destined to be buffeted at every moment by facts revealed by observation for which it cannot account."[2] Roger has pointed out that the discovery of the microscope at the beginning of the seventeenth century and its skillful use by early practitioners such as Anton van Leeuwenhoek, Marcello Malpighi, and Jan Swammerdam greatly assisted the empirical cause at the expense of the internal consistency of the Cartesian system. The extraordinary vogue of the new instrument on a popular as well as a scholarly level succeeded in turning the dominant emphasis of biological study away from human anatomy towards a preoccupation with the serious study of insects.

The miscroscope revealed the complexity of the internal anatomy of insects; the reviled caterpillar had a heart (or, more correctly, a string of hearts), viscera, and reproductive organs analogous to those of higher animals. Maggots and flies reproduced, not spontaneously, as the ancients had thought, but according to natural law, and the microscope made it possible to distinguish between male and female in some of nature's most diminutive species. However, with the unveiling of the complex structures in insects, not every special mechanism which insects possessed was found to have an analogy in the structure of the higher animals. Were insects, perhaps, even more admirable than larger animals because of their complexity, their minuteness, the skillful artistry which their study revealed? "Insects," Roger has written, "threw the scholars out of their ruts, refused to be placed in traditional frames of reference, ruined the most solid analogies and the most accepted laws."[3]

Charles Bonnet's study of the reproductive behavior of the female plant louse (aphid) presented naturalists with just such an anomaly. Bonnet was the first to prove that the reproduction of plant lice presented an exception to what had been presumed a natural law: that to reproduce, all animals required the joining of male and female. Bonnet regarded his discovery as the product of observation, unaided by any kind of theoretical framework, and he wrote that, if his work had any value, it was to put naturalists "on guard against general rules." To emphasize this point, he continued, "all that has passed previously in our minds as a general law must only be regarded now as the result of experiments which have not been carried far enough."[4]

The zeal with which Bonnet presented facts and his avoidance of theoretical discussion in his published work present a methodological problem for the historian. Since we must assume that all observation is selective, seen through a filter which prevents the so-called bare facts from ever presenting themselves free of ideological bias, how are we to assess these facts? Here, the usefulness of letters as sources in the history of science becomes apparent. While the eighteenth-century scientist refused to present any hypothesis, pretended or not, in published work, he was not as reticent in his correspondence. Letters that chronicle the history of a discovery do not conceal musings and dead ends, inappropriate in the finished version. They situate a particular discovery in time and often provide unexpected insights deriving from ideas which have no place in the structure of the science of the present. For example, through letters to his compatriot, Abraham Trembley (famous for his discovery of the polyp), and the French academician René-Antoine Réaumur, Bonnet's study of plant lice can be seen within the context of eighteenth-century ideas. Viewed as indelicate by his Jesuit critics of the *Journal de Trévoux*,[5] Bonnet's early observations of insects nevertheless laid the groundwork for his future career in metaphysics. In a letter to Réaumur, author of the most comprehensive work on insects of the period, *Mémoires pour servir à l'histoire des insectes* (1734–42), Bonnet described his devotion to one female plant louse which he had kept carefully within view for over a month, filling a journal of over a hundred pages. "I noted there its precise movements and least trifle. Not only did I observe day by day and hour by hour, but always with a glass to render the observations more exact. But if I have expended great effort, nevertheless, I have reason to believe that it has not been without profit."[6]

The profit that he reaped was the discovery which earned him his early reputation in science: that plant lice are capable of reproducing without male fertilization—the phenomenon known today as parthenogenesis. However, though Bonnet is glibly referred to as the first to discover parthenogenesis, the use of this term is an anachronism. Bonnet believed that he had discovered the ability of lice to reproduce *"sans accouplement"*—that is, without coupling or mating. Since biologists now think nothing of "tricking" a nucleus into reproducing itself and the idea of a clone is popularly accepted, it is easy to be misled into thinking that Bonnet actually visualized the self-replication of the egg cell. In fact, cell theory did not exist until the early nineteenth century, and parthenogenesis did not enter the scientific vocabulary until after the middle of that century.[7]

If we were to rely merely on Bonnet's rather tiresome descriptions in his published work on the subject, *Traité d'insectologie* (1745), it would be difficult to see the discovery of parthenogenesis as anything but the product of pure observation, unaided by any kind of theoretical framework. However, Bonnet was himself aware of the value of letters in providing insights impossible to glean from formal scientific work. In a letter to Trembley, Bonnet alluded to the celebrated correspondence between Samuel Clarke (Newton's spokesman) and Leibniz over the philosophical implications of the image of God as the perfect watchmaker. He wrote: "The letters of the great Leibniz and those of Clarke have enriched us more than their books: they are in shirt-sleeves in their letters, and often rather buttoned up in their books."[8] This image of the naturalist in shirt-sleeves is an apt one. Letters allow the historian to see the informal aspects of the scientific process, to follow the patterns of investigation, and, when possible, to discover the matrix of ideas from which the observations emerged.

Correspondence for naturalists like Bonnet, Trembley, and Réaumur provided the opportunity for official communication of new discoveries. This was particularly important for those observers with serious scientific aspirations who lived outside the cosmopolitan centers that had scientific academies, such as Paris, London, St. Petersburg, and Berlin. For French-speaking scientists of Geneva like Bonnet and Trembley, contact with the prestigious Paris Academy was a means of establishing a reputation. The title of Correspondent was officially conferred by a secretary of the Academy if a particular individual's contributions were deemed worthy. An actual seat in the Academy as an *Associé étranger* carried enormous prestige, though it was extremely difficult to earn this distinction, since there were only eight such seats, elected for life. Correspondents were assigned to regular members of the Academy, and there was no limit to the number of correspondents a particular member could enjoy. Réaumur, for example, a sweet-tempered bachelor whose only diversion from his scientific research and official duties at the Academy was weekly attendance at the salon of Madame de Tencin, devoted an extraordinary amount of energy to his correspondence. Trembley and Bonnet were among his approximately one hundred correspondents whose letters were sent through the Count d'Onsenbray, Director of the Royal Postal Services, with an inner envelope addressed to Réaumur. This represented a considerable saving for Réaumur's correspondents, since he expected any serious natural history descriptions to be accompanied by actual specimens and he took pains to describe in his letters how these specimens ought to be prepared for shipping. Réaumur read the contents of letters he considered significant at regular meetings of the Academy, and such communications were recorded in the *Procès-verbaux*. Since there was usually a time lag of several years before the *Histoire et mémoires de l'académie royale des sciences* appeared, the official reading of these letters was extremely important for the progress of science.

Bonnet's letters to Réaumur are examples of official correspondence. Because of their length and restrained tone, they seldom reveal the scientist in shirt-sleeves, though Bonnet does not succeed in avoiding all metaphysical speculation, even in these formal communications. In contrast, Réaumur's responses reveal that he is the one with his coat off. He usually dashed off short responses, hardly bothering with punctuation.

Since Bonnet knew that his letters might be read to the Academy, he spared no pains in their composition. Réaumur was a venerable and reputed scientist; Bonnet was young and unknown. He appears to have transcribed passages from his journal into his letters, and he complained to Trembley that they took an excessive amount of time because he did not know how to be brief.[9] It was not unusual for Bonnet to write a letter of twenty pages of minuscule handwriting which spilled into the margins and up the side of the page. His enthusiasm to demonstrate to Réaumur his competence as an observer prevented him from leaving out the least detail. Though at the time of his investigation of reproduction in plant lice he was a nineteen-year-old student at the Academy of Geneva, he viewed his formal studies as a tedious diversion from his work on insects. In his first letter to Réaumur he claimed that "the sweetest moments, those in which I have enjoyed the pure pleasures of an innocent pastime, have been spent near my Insects."[10] None of these rapturous moments appears to have gone unrecorded.

Bonnet began the study of plant lice in May of 1740.[11] There is no indication that Réaumur proposed by letter that Bonnet apply himself to this problem. Réaumur did not communicate by letter to Bonnet between January and June, a fact which suggests that Bonnet undertook this research on his own initiative. He had read Réaumur's description of the louse in the third volume of his *Mémoires des insectes*. Réaumur stated there that both Leeuwenhoek and Giacinto Cestoni had regarded the plant louse as hermaphroditic, and he admitted that he himself had never seen a coupling. This he regarded as strange, because, unlike bees which mate in their hives, the plant louse is always within view on the stalks or leaves of plants.[12] Réaumur pointed out that an experiment could be easily designed to prove whether or not coupling was necessary: "This experiment is to observe a mother louse give birth, and to take care to bring up the new-born louse in a place where it can have no contact with other lice."[13] Réaumur had tried this experiment of isolating the offspring of a mother louse immediately after birth several times, but the longest that he was able to keep a louse alive was nine days. He suggested that other naturalists might be more successful.

Taking up Réaumur's challenge, Bonnet designed an experiment in which an isolated female louse could be kept under constant observation. He described to Réaumur the precautions which he took to prevent contact with other lice:

> During our vacation of last Spring, I made several observations to which I have not been indifferent, among others some on Lice. I attempted the experiment which you proposed for deciding if it is accorded to them to multiply without coupling. To this end, the 20th of May I filled a flower Vase with earth in the middle of which I sank a flask filled to its neck with water. I put in this flask a little branch of the spindle tree on which I had

left only five or six leaves, after having examined them attentively to assure myself that there were no lice on them. I then placed on one of these leaves a Louse whose wingless mother taken from the spindle tree had just given birth under my very eyes. I then covered the little branch with a glass Vase which fitted exactly at its opening against the surface of the earth of the flower Vase, which served me better as a place for safe keeping than the Tower of Bronze where Danaë was imprisoned.[14]

Bonnet patiently watched and recorded the births of successive generations of lice produced by his isolated female. At the end of assiduous watching and record keeping which lasted over a month, Bonnet communicated by letter of 13 July 1740 his discovery to Réaumur. As he later recalled, "I put before him a table of the days and hours of the births by my female androgenous louse, which I hardly let out of my sight from the 20th of May until the 24th of June, and for which I have been an Argus more vigilant than the one of the Fable."[15]

On the fifth of August, 1740, Réaumur wrote a letter of congratulation to Bonnet: "These are assuredly observations of a great importance in natural history since they teach us that the law of coupling is not a general law."[16] Réaumur asked Abraham Trembley, as well as two other reputed naturalists, Gilles Auguste Bazin and Pierre Lyonet, to verify Bonnet's discovery; all three, using different species of lice, confirmed Bonnet's experiment, as did Réaumur himself. Bonnet had proved that the louse which he had placed in isolation had been able to produce ninety-five offspring. While it was under observation he had not permitted any contact with other lice and had removed each newborn immediately after birth. However, did this prove that no coupling whatsoever took place? Here interpretation becomes essential, and the less formal letters which Bonnet exchanged with Trembley make it possible to discern a pattern of questions unanticipated by our twentieth-century understanding of parthenogenesis.

Throughout his life Bonnet corresponded regularly with Trembley, who was also a citizen of Geneva, though in the early years of their friendship, he resided on the estate of Count William Bentinck, not far from the Hague in Holland. Shortly after Trembley was asked to confirm Bonnet's discovery of the ability of plant lice to reproduce asexually, he discovered the curious mode of reproduction by cuttings characteristic of the fresh water hydra. The letters which the two compatriots exchanged were not complicated by the elaborate descriptions which Bonnet felt obliged to include when writing to Réaumur. Their relative brevity highlighted what was of significance — not the polished conclusions, but the unresolved questions, the ragged edge of ongoing research.

As Bonnet and Trembley carefully studied different species of lice, they became able to identify both male and female lice, something Réaumur had failed to do. Bonnet noted that the smaller male louse was "perhaps one of the most ardent that there is in Nature. It appears to me that it does nothing except have intercourse as soon as the day arrives."[17] Thus, when circumstances permitted, coupling did take place. As Trembley's letter of 27 January 1741 shows, he was not entirely satisfied that Bonnet had proved true virgin birth. The discovery of the male made him question whether no coupling at all had taken place during Bonnet's earlier experiments. Rather than an exception to natural law, Trembley proposed two possible alternative explanations of the facts. The first was one which Réaumur himself had considered: that male and female upon reaching a certain degree of maturity *in utero* might mate prior to birth. In this case, Trembley reasoned, perhaps the lice would be born in pairs like twins at short time intervals apart. The second possibility Trembley proposed as a question: "Who knows if one mating might not serve for several generations?"[18]

Bonnet dismissed the idea that lice were able to mate within the belly of the mother louse. The physical state of the embryos prevented it. Moreover, he was not sure that Réaumur himself accepted this explanation, even though he had been the one to propose it first. He wrote:

> This conjecture does not agree with the state of the Lice enclosed in the womb, where they are not only washed in a fluid which does not permit them to unite, but also where they are enclosed by a membrane which keeps all their parts better bound up than those of chrysalises. Unless you desire that the coupling of Lice happens as Swammerdam imagined that of Bees, or in some other analogous manner, I do not see that it is conceivable that it is carried out in the Bosom of the Mother.[19]

Surprisingly, Trembley's second hypothesis, that one coupling might serve to produce several generations of plant lice, Bonnet found worthy of serious consideration. "With respect to yours [your idea], it pleases me a great deal and assuredly merits study," he wrote.[20]

Trembley's idea stimulated Bonnet to undertake the most arduous observations of his career. Experimenting on several species of plant lice he succeeded in bringing up nine generations of lice—a representative of each successive generation was selected at birth and kept in isolation until producing offspring. As Bonnet described the effect of Trembley's letter on him: "If this excellent friend had been able to foresee all the evil that his 'who knows' did to my eyes, I am very sure that his tender friendship for me would not have permitted him to express it. It was, however, on this simple 'who knows' that I undertook a new study which was much more laborious than the preceding one. I was young and full of ardor: it seemed that these two words reduced to nothing all my previous work."[21] Bonnet, driven by Trembley's letter, ruined his eyesight from the strain of keeping day and night and hourly vigil of his lice for a periof of three months.

Regardless of the dismal consequences for Bonnet's career as a natural historian, Trembley's "who knows" affords a fortuitous glimpse into the metaphysical issues which surrounded reproduction in the eighteenth century. Without the benefit of effective microscopes and cell theory, the roles of egg and sperm were not fully understood. Prior to the 1740s the idea of Preformation (or, more correctly, the preexistence of the germ) dominated eighteenth-century thought. *Emboîtement*, the idea that miniature individuals were "encapsulated" one within the other and placed by God (at Creation) either in the egg (Ovist position) or sperm (Spermaticist), ensured that the generation of animals was subject to the regular, mechanical laws laid down by God. Bonnet's discovery seemed to support the Ovist position that the miniature preexisted within the egg of the female.

Given the general acceptance of the idea of preexistence, Trembley's question was perfectly logical. He apparently reasoned that if the egg carried the encapsulated miniature, though the male role must be vastly subordinate to that of the female, a coupling every few generations might still be necessary to ensure the continued unfolding of the preordained genealogy of lice. At first, Trembley seems to have been reluctant to admit for lice an exception to a natural law which held for all other species of animals; even snails and other hermaphrodites needed both male and female organs to reproduce, and in plants the stamens and pistils were yet another example of generation which depended on the union of male and female.

For both Bonnet and Trembley as well as Réaumur, the facts of observation were to be weighed against the general rules. Once Bonnet's second set of observations established beyond any doubt that nine generations of offspring could be produced without any male contact, it seemed pointless to argue that the male role was indispensable. However, do Bonnet's experiments and Trembley's question demonstrate that they began their experimental work as convinced Ovists? Here a study of the letters urges caution. While one is able to catch a tantalizing glimpse of metaphysics in Trembley's question, there is nothing in the letters to indicate that Bonnet framed his experiments in order to prove a preconceived idea of the supremacy of the egg over sperm. However, after his experiments were successful, it seems likely that he began to consider the Ovist position seriously. The failure of Bonnet's eyesight coincided with what appears to have been a spiritual crisis. Though he did not give up his study of natural history entirely, in the late 1740s he turned increasingly to philosophy. In his later writings such as *Contemplation de la nature* (1764), Bonnet became the champion of the female *emboîtement* principle.

Bonnet's early letters are important precisely because they show the intriguing and delicate relationship between theory and observation which constitutes the process of discovery. The study of an eighteenth-century scientist's published work is the starting point, but letters are indispensable to show

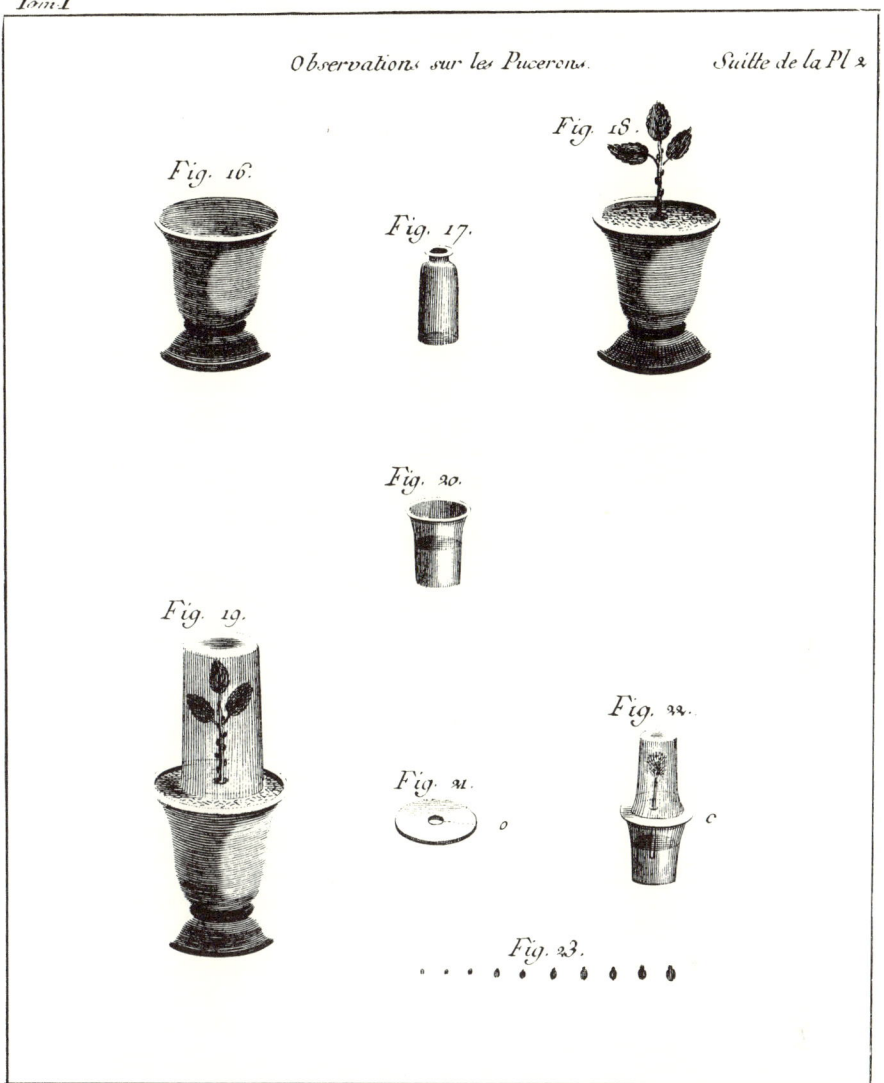

Bonnet's experimental apparatus for studying the reproduction of plant lice (figs. 16–19). Permission to reproduce plate from Charles Bonnet, *Oeuvres d'histoire naturelle et de philosophie* (Neuchâtel: S. Fauche, 1779), vol. 1, courtesy of the Department of Special Collections, Case Western Reserve University Libraries.

the scientist in shirt-sleeves, sharing his perplexities as well as his triumphs as he carefully balances his presuppositions with observed fact.

NOTES

[1] Alexandre Koyré has argued in "Concept and Experience in Newton's Scientific Thought," *Newtonian Studies* (Cambridge, Mass.: Harvard Univ. Press, 1965), p. 35, that the proper translation is "I do not feign hypotheses." Andrew Motte's translation of the *Principia* (1729) was "I frame no hypotheses," a misinterpretation which may have given impetus to the seemingly blind empiricism of early eighteenth-century scientists.

[2] Jacques Roger, *Les Sciences de la vie dans la pensée française du XVIIIe siécle* (Paris: Armand Collin, 1963), p. 164.

[3] Roger, p. 238.

[4] Charles Bonnet, *Oeuvres d'histoire naturelle et de philosophie* (Neuchâtel: S. Fauche, 1779–1783), I, rpt. (*Traité d'insectologie*), xxvi.

[5] *Journal de Trévoux* 46 (1746; Geneva: Slatkine Reprints, 1968), 106–10.

[6] "J'y ai notté jusqu'à ses moindres mouvemens et à la moindre bagatelle. Non seulement j'ai observé jour par jour et heure par heure, mais encore plusieurs fois dans la même heure, et toujours à la loupe pour rendre l'observation plus exacte . . . Mais si j'ai pris beaucoup de peine et si je me suis extrêmement gêné, par contre, j'ai lieu de croire que ce n'a pas été inutilement." Letter from Bonnet to Réaumur, 13 July 1740, Fonds Réaumur, Academy of Sciences, Paris.

[7] The word "parthenogenesis" appears to have been first used by Richard Owen, *On Parthenogenesis, or the Successive Productions of Procreating Individuals from the Single Ovum*, 1849; see OED.

[8] "Je ne scais si vous pensés comme moi, mais, il m'a toujours paru, que des semblables correspondances montroient mieux la marche de l'Esprit dans la Recherche du Vrai, que des Traités en forme. Les Lettres du grand Leibnitz, celles de Clarke nous ont plus enrichis que leurs Livres même: c'est qu'ils étoient en chemise dans leurs Lettres, et souvent assés boutonnés dans leurs Livres." Letter from Bonnet to Trembley, 21 Oct. 1768, Collection of George Trembley, Toronto, Ontario. I am deeply indebted to Professor Trembley for opening his family archives to me.

[9] "Des Etudes de Droit, d'Histoire Naturelle et des Observations ne laissent Guères de momens vuides, et la Correspondance avec Monsr. de Reaumur me prend plus de tems qu'elle n'en prendroit peut-etre a un autre. Aussi faut-il avoir autant de patience et de complaisance qu'en a Monsr. de Réaumur pour ne s'en pas lasser." Letter from Bonnet to Trembley, 24 Mar. 1741, Collection of George Trembley, Toronto, Ontario. Though the Réaumur-Bonnet correspondence has never been published, it was discussed by Jean Torlais, "Un Maître et un élève. Réaumur et Charles Bonnet (D'après leur correspondance inédite)," *Gazette Hebdomadaire des Sciences Médicales de Bordeaux*, 9 Oct. 1932, pp. 641–55 and 16 Oct. 1932, pp. 657–59; Raymond Savioz, "Un Maître et un disciple au XVIIIe siècle (Charles Bonnet et Réaumur)," *Thalès* 4 (1940), 100–12. Bonnet's letters to Réaumur conserved at the Academy of Sciences, Paris are incomplete. In contrast, none of Réaumur's letters to Bonnet at the Public and University Library of Geneva appears to be missing. For a comprehensive listing of all extant letters in this correspondence, see Virginia P. Dawson, *Nature's Enigma: the Problem of the Polyp in the Letters of Trembley, Bonnet and Réaumur* (American Philosphical Society). In press.

[10] "Je puis vous l'asseurer [sic] Monsieur, depuis que je me suis procuré la lecture de vos Livres, depuis que je leur ai donné toute mon application, les plus doux moments, ceux ou j'ai jouï des plaisirs purs d'un Amusement innocent, je les ai passés auprès de mes Insectes." Letter from Bonnet to Réaumur, 4 July 1738, Fonds Réaumur, Academy of Sciences, Paris.

[11] See H. Ehrard, "Die Entdeckung der Parthenogenesis durch Charles Bonnet," *Gesnerus* 3 (1946), 15–27. This is the only scholarly article on Bonnet's discovery in the secondary literature.

[12] René Antoine Ferchault de Réaumur, *Mémoires pour servir à l'histoire des insectes* (Paris: Imprimerie Royale, 1734–1742), III, 327.

[13] Réaumur, *Mémoires*, p. 329.

[14] "Pendant nos Vacances du Printems dernier j'ai fait quelques observations qui ne m'ont pas été indifférentes, entr'autres sur les *Pucerons*. J'ai tenté l'experience que vous proposés pour decider s'il leur est accordé de se multiplier sans accouplement. Pour cet effet, le 20me. May je remplis de terre un Vase à mettre des fleurs, au milieu duquel j'enfoncai jusqu'au col une fiole pleine d'eau. Je mis dans cette fiole une petite branche de Fusain à qui je ne laissai, que cinq à six feuilles, aprés les avoir examinées attentivement pour m'assûrer qu'elles n'avoient aucun Puceron. Je plaçai ensuite, sur une de ces feuilles, un Puceron dont la Mère depourvue d'aîles et prise sur le Fusain, venoit d'accoucher sous mes yeux. Je couvris enfin, la petite branche d'un Vase de Verre qui l'appliquant exactement par son ouverture contre la surface de la terre du vase à fleurs, me repondoit mieux de depôt que la Tour d'Airain ou Danae fut renfermée." Letter from Bonnet to Réaumur, 13 July 1740, *dossier biographique*, Fonds Réaumur, Academy of Sciences, Paris.

King Acrisius of Argos imprisoned his daughter, Danaë, in a tower because the Delphic oracle had predicted that his death would be at the hands of his daughter's son. This isolation was not successful in preventing Danaë from conceiving. Zeus was able to visit in the guise of a shower of gold, and she bore Perseus.

[15] Charles Bonnet, *Mémoires autobiographiques de Charles Bonnet de Genève*, ed. Raymond Savioz (Paris: Vrin, 1948), p. 59.

[16] Bonnet, p. 59.

[17] "Ce mâle est peutetre un des plus ardens qu'il y ait dans la Nature. Il ne semble qu'ait [sic (que?)] faire autre chose que s'accoupler dès que le jour est venu." Letter from Bonnet to Trembley, 18 Dec. 1740, Collection of George Trembley, Toronto, Ontario.

[18] "La Première idée que j'ai suivie est celle qu'indique M^r. de R. J'ai pensé que suposé que les Pucerons s'acouplassent dans le sein de la mère, les deux qui devoient s'acoupler ne devoient pas diferer beaucoup en dégré de perfection et que si ils ne s'acouplent qu'après être parvenus à la perfection requise pour naître, la naissance de l'un ne devoit, peut être, pas [s']éloigner de celle de l'autre. J'ai donc été attentif pour voir s'ils en naitroit toûjours deux à peu de distance et comme les accouplemens ne sont pas si prochains dans cette saison, elle m'a paru plus favorable pour faire l'expérience. J'ai trouvé beaucoup de variété dans la distance des accouchements. J'ai eu cependant à trois reprises deux pucerons qui se sont suivis beaucoup plus près que les autres. Enfin je n'ai rien pu conclure et je me suis trouvé aussi savant qu'au commencement. J'ai formé depuis le mois de novembre le dessein de lever plusieurs generations de suite de pucerons solitaires, pour voir s'ils feroient toujours également des petits. Dans des cas si éloignés des circonstances ordinaires, il est permis de tout tenter. Je me disois, qui sait si un accouplement ne sert point à plusieurs générations?" Letter from Trembley to Bonnet, 27 Jan. 1741, MS Bonnet 24, Public and University Library of Geneva.

[19] "Cette conjecture ne s'accorde pas avec l'état des Pucerons renfermés dans la matrice, où ils sont non seulement baignés d'une liqueur qui ne leur permettroit pas de s'unir, mais encore où ils sont envelopés d'une membrane qui tient toute leurs parties mieux emmaillottées que ne le sont celles des Crisalides. A moins qu'on ne voulut que l'accouplement des Pucerons se fit com̄e Swammerdam l'avoit imaginé de celui des Abeilles, ou de quelqu'autre maniere analogue, je ne vois pas qu'on put concevoir qu'il s'executa dans le sein de la Mere." Letter from Bonnet to Trembley, 24 March 1741, Collection of George Trembley, Toronto, Ontario. Swammerdam believed that bees did not copulate but spawned like fish. See *The Book of Nature*, trans. Thomas Flloyd, rpt. ed. (New York: Arno, 1978), Part I, p. 187, column b.

[20] "A l'égard de la vôtre elle me plait beaucoup, et merite assurement d'être suivie. Amassons Toûjours bien des faits, il sera ensuite assés tems d'imaginer." Letter from Bonnet to Trembley, 24 March 1741, Collection of George Trembley, Toronto, Ontario.

[21] Bonnet, *Mémoires autobiographiques*, p. 63.

LINGUISTIC AND BIOLOGICAL CLASSIFICATION IN THE EIGHTEENTH CENTURY

W. KEITH PERCIVAL

What I propose to do here is to compare and contrast taxonomy in the two areas of natural history and language study.[1] I shall focus my remarks on the differences between the way taxonomy manifested itself in these two areas. I shall also broach the difficult question as to why there are these differences, i.e., how they arose historically. Finally, I shall try to show that despite their apparent logical incompatibility some contact between the two taxonomies did take place in the eighteenth century.

To put the problem in a nutshell, students of language in the eighteenth century classified languages into families, and subdivided individual languages into dialects; natural historians, on the other hand, situated animals and plants on a unidimensional *scala naturae* ("nature's ladder"). The linguistic taxonomy was, moreover, evolutionary and genetic, whereas the taxonomy employed in natural history was purely static or morphological. Languages were known to change and, in doing so, to give rise to dialects, which in the course of time became separate languages; in contrast, species and genera in the world of natural history were presumed to be immutable. Both superficially and fundamentally, therefore, the two conceptions of taxonomy were quite different. What accounts for this difference, and how did it arise?

Let us first look at genealogical taxonomy in the area of language study. That the genealogical perspective had become widely accepted by the eighteenth century is especially clear if one examines the etymological dictionaries which were written in that century. Thus, Johann Georg Wachter (1663–1757) in his *Glossarium Germanicum*, which was published in Leipzig in 1737, has a lemma MUTER-SPRACH (literally, "mother language," that being the term used to denote what linguists nowadays call a protolanguage). He translates *Muttersprache* as Latin *lingua matrix* and then goes on to say: "Such is, for example, the primordial language of Germany, which was at first uniform, and, as is the fate of languages, was subsequently divided into several dialects: the Gothic, the Anglo-Saxon, the Franconian, which in turn have their own daughter languages, similar both to their mother languages and their sister languages. However, it is not the original language of the whole human race, but arose from the most ancient languages, which were close to the original language."[2] A statement of this kind would seem to be clear enough not to require detailed analysis and commentary on my part.

The genealogical model was forced on students of language partly by observation and partly by what they commonly assumed concerning the origin of linguistic diversity. Let us consider the second point first. While scholars in the period we are considering held divergent views on the origin of human language, there was virtual unanimity about two other important questions. Everybody agreed, first, that linguistic diversity resulted from the direct intervention of God in confounding the tongues at the Tower of Babel (Gen. 11: 1-9), and, second, that the whole human race was descended from Noah, each ethnic group being a set of descendants belonging to some particular sublineage of the sons of Noah.[3] From this it followed, supposedly, that the languages spoken by the groups in question were analogously related. However, in addition to the firm belief that the primeval language was confounded as a result of the Tower of Babel exploit and its unfortunate aftermath, it was also widely assumed that all subsequent languages were degenerate forms of that primeval language, which was assumed to have been perfect. Furthermore, many scholars hypothesized that all extant languages contain remnants of the primitive language. The two key notions were then confusion and corruption, *linguarium confusio et corruptela*, as Goropius Becanus expressed it.[4]

The element of observation, the first factor I mentioned, was just that. People had been aware since antiquity that languages change (see, for instance, Plato's *Cratylus*, 421D). Then from the sixteenth century on, scholars in western Europe became increasingly familiar with the major languages of Europe and the Mediterranean basin, and it was soon discovered that they fall into a small number of well-defined groups: the languages descended from Latin, the Germanic languages, the Slavic group, the Greek dialects, and so forth. Outside Europe, a striking case of a set of related languages was provided by the Semitic family, as revealed by the study of Hebrew, Aramaic, and Arabic, which Christian scholars began to take up seriously in the sixteenth century. (Here it may be noted that the fact of relationship had been known to medieval Jewish and Islamic scholars and was simply transmitted to their Christian counterparts.)

All this empirical evidence, together with the Biblical perspective, gave rise to the idea that the languages in each group had descended from a number of so-called "mother languages" (*linguae matrices*). To my knowledge, the first suggestion on these lines, and one which was repeatedly cited afterwards, was made by Joseph Justus Scaliger (1540-1609) in an essay which appeared in Paris in 1610.[5] Various attempts, none of which commanded unanimous approval, were then made to link these mother languages to Hebrew, or to some other ancient language, using the information about the geographical distribution of ethnic groups in antiquity and prehistory provided in the Bible and in the Greek and Roman writers. A large variety of conflicting theories resulted. However, the basic desideratum was clear, namely, a genealogy of all existing languages. The only difficulty was that scholars could not agree on the details. To this extent, therefore, the modern conception of language relationship already existed full-fledged well before the advent of comparative grammar in the early nineteenth century, as has recently been made clear by George Metcalf in a series of valuable studies.[6]

Let us turn now to the world of animate nature.[7] Here things were radically different. First of all, there was agreement on the question of ultimate origins: God created all forms of life individually, as specified in the first chapter of Genesis (esp. verses 11-12, 20-22, 24-26). No notion of corruption or progressive change was invoked: all species were thought to have been established at creation and since then never to have changed.

A serious attempt to attack the problem of biological taxonomy had been made in antiquity by Aristotle in his writings on natural history, especially the *Historia animalium* and the *De partibus animalium*, works which scholars in the early modern period studied with great care. Interestingly, however, Aristotle did not aim at a cut-and-dried classification; indeed, many historians of science today would say that he simply did not do taxonomy in the modern sense of the term. His point of departure in the *De partibus* (642b5-644b19) was an attack on Plato's procedure of successive bipartite divisions. The reason Aristotle rejected the dichotomous method was that he took for granted the existence of large natural genera (e.g., bird, fish, etc.) distinguished from each other by a number of equally distinctive features. One cannot, in his view, choose one differentia and set up two classes on that basis, move down one level and continue the process until one reached the individual species.

This conclusion was further strengthened by another consideration, namely the belief on Aristotle's part that there are similarities between species of the same genus and also homologies between genera. A related idea propounded by him was that there are species which are intermediate between genera and also species which do not fall unequivocally under any recognized genus. This whole approach would, therefore, rule out a genealogical tree or branching diagram as the only way of representing the relations among species and genera.

The nearest thing to a hierarchical system of classification in Aristotle's system was a logical derivative of his theory of the soul. In brief, he posited a plurality of functional principles for the soul: — nutritive, sensitive, rational (see *De anima* 412a27-b6, 413b11-13, 414a31-32) — and accordingly situated animate beings in a continuum with man at the apex, characterized by a rational soul, followed by the animals and birds, which have no more than a sensitive soul, then the plants, which have a nutritive soul, and so on down to the lowest form of life. This idea, bolstered by Christian and Neo-Platonic conceptions, was to play a crucial role in biological taxonomy in the post-Renaissance period, because it neatly explained the observed progression of life forms from the lowest to the highest.

Perhaps the strangest feature of this approach was the belief that the transitions between life forms are continuous. Aristotle, for instance, linked plants to animals by way of the so-called "zoophytes" (creatures such as sponges and sea anemones), which supposedly possessed the properties of both animals and plants. This notion of continuity dominated botany and zoology until the end of the eighteenth century. One seventeenth-century writer expressed the general principle as follows: "There is no gap, no break, no scattering of forms; the forms are linked to one another like one ring to another. The whole universe is embraced by this golden chain."[8] An equally eloquent eighteenth-century source, the *Encyclopédie*, states that "nature descends by imperceptible degrees and nuances from an animal which appears to us as the most perfect to an animal which is least perfect, and from the latter to the plant."[9] The notion that there are homologies between genera was also still alive in the eighteenth century. The author of the entry "plant" in the *Encyclopédie* sums up the idea as follows: "It appears that the mechanism of plants is very similar to that of animals: the parts of plants seem to have a constant analogy with the parts of animate bodies, and vegetable economy seems to be formed on the analogy of animal economy."[10] This notion of the uniformity of nature was bound up with the principle of continuity, of which the most often quoted formulation was Leibniz's adage that nature does not make leaps (*natura non facit saltus*).[11]

The entire Aristotelian system of biological classification, as transmitted in his writings on natural history, became available for study and criticism in the course of the Renaissance. For reasons which are not entirely clear, the taxonomic urge became acute in the second half of the sixteenth century. The first stirrings in the new taxonomy were obvious in a treatise on plants published by Andrea Cesalpino in 1588,[12] and then more ambitious projects followed, especially by Tournefort[13] in France, and John Ray in England, both from the late seventeenth century,[14] culminating in the monumental work of Linnaeus (Carl von Linné) in the middle of the eighteenth century.

What is interesting about the Linnaean taxonomy, and it is indeed a genuine taxonomy, is that it was still based on the static view of genera and species inherited from antiquity. In his *Systema naturae*, which was first published in Leiden in 1735, Linnaeus states his position categorically: "If we observe the works of God, it is abundantly clear to everybody that individual living creatures propagate from the egg, and that every egg produces an offspring identical to the parent. Therefore, no new species are produced today."[15] Thus, the objects studied by natural historians, unlike languages, were unchanging: Linnaeus's species, genera, orders, and classes carried on a perpetual existence. Moreover, Linnaeus explicitly asserts that the number of observable species in the world today is the same as the number created by God: "We number as many species as there were different forms initially created."[16]

At the same time, we see signs in some writers that the traditional picture was beginning to be felt as not completely adequate. One interesting indication of this fact is the increasing dissatisfaction with the metaphor of the *scala naturae*, i.e., the notion of an ordered unidimensional series embracing all forms of life from the lowest to the highest. By the middle of the eighteenth century, we find other metaphors being mooted. Thus, an Italian marine biologist named Vitaliano Donati in a book published in Venice in 1750 suggested the image of a network instead of the ladder of nature,[17] and a few years later Peter Simon Pallas, in a book on zoophytes, reviewed the question again, alluding to Donati's suggestion but proposing instead the tree model as more suitable for mirroring the complicated relations found to exist among the multifarious objects of natural history.[18] It is important to note, in this general connection, that the branching diagram has already been used to represent the relations between botanical species; see, for instance, Robert Morison, *Plantarum historiae universalis Oxoniensis pars secunda seu herbarum distributio nova, per tabulas cognationis et affinitatis ex libro naturae observata et detecta* (Oxford: Sheldonian Theatre, 1680). Indeed, Linnaeus himself was already thinking in terms of a *two*-dimensional arrangement of forms and even referred to the hominoids, on one occasion, as "man's cousins" (see Bernier, *Aux Sources de la biologie*, n. 7, p. 142).

At this point, I think we are ready to broach the question of why the taxonomic frameworks most commonly used in the study of language and in natural history differed so fundamentally. The most important factor, I should like to suggest, was the belief that languages were not part of God's creation, or, to formulate it in a slightly different way, the notion that languages did not result from the direct creative act of God.[19] Even if one believed, as did some scholars, that man's linguistic capacity was given by God, that proposition did not entail a belief that God was responsible for the character of human languages after the dispersion and confusion of tongues. The details of linguistic diversity were, thus, a product of human, not divine, agency.

The possibility that the principle of continuity might have been applied in language study in the eighteenth century has, as far as I am aware, never been discussed, but I believe I can at least indicate the sort of conception that results from an amalgam of biological and linguistic taxonomy. In the preface to Wachter's *Glossarium Germanicum*, the author deplores the fact that some scholars had proposed deriving the Germanic languages directly from the languages spoken immediately after Babel. This violates the principle, says Wachter, that "nature never makes a leap, either in space intervals or in time, or in any other matter, but instead moves from what is nearest to what is close by, from what is neighboring to what is more distant, and moves from the distant to the most remote only after a long interval of time." Accordingly, from a single unified primordial language (this is vouched for by Holy Scripture and by universal consensus), there arose first various dialects and almost as many variations as there were families, or sets of related families. Then, as these family groups separated, the dialects gradually became languages. From these languages, new languages and dialects afterwards developed, not suddenly and at one stroke but gradually with the help of geographical and temporal distances, migrations, and colonizings. For in the creation of new languages nature constantly adhered to the principle or law that the more recent languages should arise from more ancient ones, and that Western languages should arise from Oriental languages. Because of this law it was impossible that there could exist a language which was not rooted in some earlier language.[20]

What Wachter did here was to combine the notion of continuous gradation with the linguistic picture of the family tree. He used this argument, it is true, to bolster the particular kind of genealogical tree he was proposing. But this was only his ostensible motive in adducing the principle that nature makes no leaps. What is more significant, in my view, is that in doing so he was suggesting, if only implicitly, that languages obey a natural law, i.e., a principle which governs nature. Bluntly put, language, in this perspective, is not only a human institution but also part of nature, at least in this one respect, i.e., in exhibiting continuous, not discrete, differentiation.

It is clear, therefore, that the notion of continuity, which originally belonged in natural history, was transferred to and applied in the study of language, despite the apparent logical incompatibility of the taxonomic notions current in the two fields of inquiry.[21] It is surely significant that the influence proceeded in this direction and not the reverse. As is well known, the application of evolutionary notions in natural history had to wait until the work of Lamarck in the early years of the nineteenth century.[22] Meanwhile, the belief in the separate creation of each species by God remained unshaken.

Etymologists, on the other hand, were under no theological compulsion to derive the facts of linguistic diversity from the direct intervention of God. Although the initial act of making languages differ from one another was attributed to divine instrumentation, God was not responsible for the specific details, since languages were human institutions which arose by way of collective compact. Wachter's Leibnizian perspective views languages as subject to the same law of continuity as nature, and to this extent it represents a break with previous tradition. It would perhaps be an exaggeration to credit Wachter with ushering in a new "paradigm" or "*épistémè*" but it is worth recalling that his work was familiar to at least one of the founders of historical linguistics in the early nineteenth century, namely, the Danish scholar Rasmus Rask.[23]

NOTES

[1] I should perhaps warn the reader that there are two nineteenth-century (i.e. anachronistic) terms in the title of this article, namely biology and linguistics. The words *botany* and *zoology* have more respectable pedigrees, the former being ultimately derived from Greek *botane* "plant, wild herb," and the latter coming from Neo-Latin *zoologia*, which denoted the part of medicine dealing with remedies obtained from animals. The English word *zoology*, in the sense of "a treatise concerning living creatures," is first attested in the title of a dictionary by Nathan Bailey published in 1726 (see the article *zoology* in the *Oxford English Dictionary*).

[2] Since many of the primary sources we are dealing with are hard to come by, I append here a transcription of the relevant passage. For the convenience of the reader, I have modernized the spelling of the Latin quotations. The Wachter passage reads as follows: "MUTERSPRACH, lingua matrix. Talis est lingua Germaniae primigenia, primo quidem una et uniformis, postea, ut sors linguaram est, in plures dialectos divisa: Gothicam, Anglosaxonicam, Francicam, quae rursus suas habent filias tam matribus quam sororibus similes. Nec tamen est primitiva totius humani generis, sed ex antiquissimis linguis et primitivae proximis orta" (Johann Georg Wachter, *Glossarium Germanicum* [Leipzig: Joh. Frid. Gleditsch, 1737], col. 1110). Similar notions were expressed by the Swedish scholar Johan Ihre (1707-1780) in his *Glossarium Suiogothic* (Uppsala: Typis Erdmannianis, 1769), esp. pp. I-II. On Wachter's life, see the biography by Max Mendheim, *Allgemeine deutsche Biographie*, XL (Leipzig: Duncker and Humblot, 1896; rpt. Berlin: Duncker and Humblot, 1971), pp. 426-27.

[3] On the whole question of how language relationship was viewed from antiquity to the early modern period, see Arno Borst, *Der Turmbau von Babel: Geschichte der Meinungen über Ursprung und Vielfalt der Sprachen und Völker*, 4 vols. (Stuttgart: Anton Hiersemann, 1957-1963). Among more recent contributions to the subject, see in particular Hans Aarsleff, "An Outline of Language-Origins Theory since the Renaissance," *Origins and Evolution of Language and Speech*, ed. Stevan R. Harnad et al., *Annals of the New York Academy of Sciences* 280 (1976), 4-17, reprinted in Hans Aarsleff, *From Locke to Saussure: Essays on the Study of Language and Intellectual History* (Minneapolis: Univ. of Minnesota Press, 1982), pp. 278-92; and James H. Stam, *Inquiries into the Origin of Language: The Fate of a Question* (New York: Harper & Row, 1976).

[4] Ioannes Goropius Becanus, *Hermathena* (Antwerp: Ex officina Christophori Plantini, 1580), sig t1^v.

[5] Joseph Justus Scaliger, "Diatriba de Europaeorum linguis," *Opuscula varia antehac non edita* (Paris: Apud Hadrianum Beys, 1610), pp. 119-22.

[6] George J. Metcalf, "The Indo-European Hypothesis in the Sixteenth and Seventeenth Centuries," *Studies in the History of Linguistics: Traditions and Paradigms*, ed. Dell Hymes (Bloomington: Indiana Univ. Press, 1974), pp. 233-57; and the same author's article "Theodor Bibliander (1504-1564) and the Language of Japhet's Progeny," *Historiographia Linguistica* 7 (1980), 323-33.

[7]On biological taxonomy, see Réjane Bernier, *Aux Sources de la biologie,* I: *les vingt premiers siècles, la classification* (Montreal: Les Presses de l'Université du Québec & Paris: Masson et Cie, 1975), pp. 73 ff.; Rud. Burckhardt, "Zur Geschichte der biologischen Systematik," *Verhandlungen der naturforschenden Gesellschaft in Basel* 16 (1903), 388–440; Emile Callot, *La Renaissance des sciences de la vie au XVIe siècle,* Bibliothèque de philosophie contemporaine (Paris: Presses Universitaires de France, 1951), pp. 156–84; Henri Daudin, *De Linné à Jussieu: méthodes de la classification et idée de série en botanique et en zoologie (1749–1790),* Etudes d'histoire des sciences naturelles 1 (Paris: Librairie Félix Alcan [1926]); Erik Nordenskiöld, *The History of Biology: A Survey* (New York and London: Knopf, 1932), pp. 190–202, 207–15; Charles Singer, "Greek Biology and its Relation to the Rise of Modern Biology," *Studies in the History and Method of Science,* 2nd ed. (Oxford: Clarendon Press, 1921), pp. 1–101; Johannes Spix, *Geschichte und Beurtheilung aller Systeme in der Zoologie nach ihrer Entwicklungsfolge von Aristoteles bis auf die gegenwärtige Zeit* (Nuremberg: In der Schrag'schen Buchhandlung, 1811).

[8]"Nullus hiatus est, nulla fractio, nulla dispersio formarum; invicem conexae sunt velut anulus anulo. Aurea ista catena complectitur universum" (Juan Eusebio Nieremberg, *Historia naturae* [Antwerp: Ex officina Plantiniana Balthasaris Moreti, 1635], p. 29).

[9]"Cet examen nous conduit à reconnoître évidemment qu'il n'y a aucune différence absolument essentielle et générale entre les animaux et les végétaux, mais que la nature descend par degrés et par nuances imperceptibles d'un animal qui nous paroît le plus parfait à celui qui l'est le moins, et de celui-ci au végetal. Le polype d'eau douce sera, si l'on veut, le dernier des animaux, et la premiere des plantes" (*Encyclopédie, ou dictionnaire raisonné des sciences, des arts et des métiers,* I [Paris: Briasson, David, Le Breton et Durand, 1751], 472a).

[10]"Par les observations de Malpighi, du docteur Grew, de MM. Reneaulme, Bradley, et d'autres auteurs, il paroît que le méchanisme des plantes est fort semblable à celui des animaux: les parties des plantes semblent avoir un analogie constante avec les parties des corps animés, et l'économie végétable paroît formée sur le modele de l'économie animale" (*Encyclopédie,* XII [Neûchatel: Samuel Faulche, 1765], 712b).

[11]On Leibniz's principle of continuity, see Ernst Cassirer, *Leibniz's System in seinen wissenschaftlichen Grundlagen* (Marburg: N. G. Elwert, 1902; rpt. Darmstadt: Wissenschaftliche Buchgesellschaft, 1961), pp. 418–21; Arthur O. Lovejoy, *The Great Chain of Being: A Study of the History of an Idea* (Cambridge, Mass.: Harvard Univ. Press, 1936), pp. 144 ff. For discussions of Leibniz's activities as an etymologist, see Albert Heinekamp, "Ars characteristica und natürliche Sprache bei Leibniz," *Tijdschrift voor Philosophie* 34 (1972), 446–88, esp. 469 ff.; Hans Aarsleff, "The Study and Use of Etymology in Leibniz," *Studia Leibnitiana, Supplementa,* III: *Erkenntnislehre, Logik, Sprachphilosophie, Editionsberichte,* Akten des Internationalen Leibniz-Kongresses, Hanover 14–19 Nov. 1966 (Wiesbaden: Franz Steiner, 1969), pp. 173–89, reprinted in Hans Aarsleff, *From Locke to Saussure,* pp. 84–100; and L. Neff, *Leibniz als Sprachforscher und Etymologe,* Beilage zum Programm des Grossherzoglichen Lyceums zu Heidelberg für 1870 (Heidelberg: A. H. Avenarius, 1870).

[12]Andrea Cesalpino, *De plantis libri XVI* (Florence: Apud G. Marescottum, 1583).

[13]Joseph Pitton de Tournefort, *Elemens de botanique, ou Méthode pour connoître les plantes* (Paris: De l'Imprimerie Royale, 1694).

[14]John Ray, *Methodus plantarum nova* (London: Impensis F. Faithorne and J. Kersey, 1682); *Historia plantarum,* 3 vols. (London: Apud H. Faithorne, S. Smith and B. Walford, 1686–1704).

[15]"Si opera Dei intueamur, onmibus satis superque patet viventia singula ex ovo propagari omneque ovum producere subolem parenti simillimam. Hinc nullae species novae hodiernum producuntur" (Carolus Linnaeus, *Systema naturae,* 2nd ed. [Stockholm: Gottfr. Kiesewetter, 1740], p. 67).

[16]"Species tot numeramus quot diversae formae in principio sunt creatae" (*Philosophia botanica* [Stockholm: Godofr. Kiesewetter, 1751], p. 99). And he goes on in the following vein: "Species tot sunt quot diversas formas ab initio produxit infinitum ens; quae formae secundum generationis inditas leges produxere plures at sibi semper similes. Ergo species tot sunt quot diversae formae, scilicet structurae, hodiernum occurrunt" (p. 99). Compare the following comment in the *Systema naturae:* "Cum nullae dantur [sic] novae species, cum simile semper parit

sui simile, cum unitas in omni specie ordinem ducit, necesse est ut unitatem illam progeneratricem enti cuidam omnipotenti et omniscio attribuamus, Deo nempe, cuius opus creatio audit" (Linnaeus, *Systema naturae*, p. 67). The use of the word *audit* here is bizarre, but the meaning seems clear, namely that creation is coterminous with the work of God. Both the first edition and the Paris edition of 1744 read *audit*. In general, Linnaeus's Latin does not conform to classical standards (witness the curious use of *hodiernum* instead of *hodie* in the meaning 'today').

[17]". . . ad un rete piuttosto, che ad una catena le naturali progressioni si dovrebbero rassomigliare, essendo, per dir così, tessuta di vari fili, che tra loro hanno scambievole comunicazione, correlazione, ed unione" (Vitaliano Donati, *Della storia naturale marina dell'Adriatrico* [Venice: Francesco Storti, 1750], p. XXI).

[18]"Adeo ubique illustrissimis confirmatum inveniemus exemplis naturam numquam saltum facere; imprimis universum corporum organicorum exercitum continua acie disposuisse, arctissimoque affinitatis vinculo, species in genera, haec in ordines, ordinesque in classes, classes vero inter se contexuisse; et quidem non superficiariis his et idealibus quae a nonnullis in scala naturae conficienda requiruntur, verbi gratia vespertilionis in alas expansis palmis, exocoeti elongatis, volaticis pinnis, castoris palmipedis squamata cauda, similibusque; sed structura, abstractiori habitu, generandi modo, cet. A simplicissimis ordita, organa sensim pro finium ratione mutat et effingit, simpliciori fabricae nova successive inserit, adaptat. Hinc magni analogiae argumenti, quo tamen iudiciose utendum est, origo. Hinc varii auctores scalam quandam naturae concinnare studuerunt, quae talis numquam reperietur qualem Bradlejus et Bonnetus volunt. Neque minus bene, immo forte milius in figurae polyhedrae, multilocularis areolis iuxta se invicem corporum organicorum genera disponi, variique affinitatis gradus exprimi enim possent. Et iam Donati iudiciose observavit non in scalam et seriem continuata esse sed in rete cohaerere naturae opera. At omnium optime arboris imagine adumbraretur corporum organicorum systema, quae a radice statim, e simplicissimis plantis atque animalibus duplicem, varie contiguum proferat truncum, animalem et vegetabilem; quorum prior, per molusca pergat ad pisces, emisso magno inter haec insectorum laterali ramo, hinc ad amphibia; et extremo cacumine quadrupedia exsereret, aves vero pro laterali pariter magno ramo infra quadrupedia exsereret. Hac figura indicaretur simul corpora organica brutis non continua nec affinia esse, sed tantum insistere ceu arbor solo. Truncus e principaliori generum affinium serie confertus passim pro ramulis exsereret genera, quae istis laterali affinitate iuncta interseri tamen non possunt" (Peter Simon Pallas, *Elenchus zoophytorum* [The Hague: Petrus van Cleef, 1766], pp. 23-24.) On Pallas, see J. Victor Carus, *Geschichte der Zoologie bis auf Joh. Müller und Charl. Darwin*, Geschichte der Wissenschaften in Deutschland, neuere Zeit, XII (Munich: R Oldenbourg, 1872), pp. 535-39, esp. p. 536.

[19]For a clear statement of the conception of language as the result of a fortuitous compact made by the members of a speech community, see the definition of "language" in Chamber's *Cyclopaedia*, which reads as follows: "A Set of Words which any People have agreed upon, in order to communicate their Thoughts to each other . . . Languages are only to be looked on as an Assemblage of Expressions, which Chance or Caprice has established among a certain People; just as we look on the Mode of Dressing, etc." (Ephraim Chambers, *Cyclopaedia* II [London: James & John Knapton, et al., 1728], 428b).

[20]"Sunt qui linguam nostram ex campis Sinear immediate progressam et post dispersionem humani generis statim in his terris auditam arbitrantur, quos ego non refutandos sed explodendos existimo. Nam natura non facit saltum neque in locorum intervallis, neque in tempore, neque in ulla alia re, sed ex proximo tendit ad propinqua, a propinquis ad remotiora, et a remotioribus non nisi longo temporis tractu ad remotissima progreditur. Itaque ex una et primitiva lingua (quod sacrae litterae et gentium consensus testantur) suscitatae sunt primo variae dialecti et totidem paene variationes quot hominum familiae aut familiarum cognationes, quibus deinde separatis dialecti paulatim abierunt in linguas. Ex his linguis postea formatae sunt novae linguae et linguarum dialecti et dialectorum linguae, non subito et repente, sed gradatim et pedetemptim, temporum locorum, migrationum, et coloniarum adiumento. Hunc enim natura continuo servavit ordinem et quias legem in novis sermonibus producendis, ut recentiores fierent ex antiquioribus, occidentales ex orientalibus. Et vi huius legis impossibile erat ullam in toto terrarum orbe exsistere linguam quae non in aliqua priore fuerit radicata" (Wachter, *Glossarium Germanicum*, sig. a3^{rs}). There seems to be no doubt about Wachter's general indebtedness to Leib-

niz; see, for instance, Aarsleff, *From Locke to Saussure*, p. 48. There are textual similarities between the opening paragraph of Leibniz's essay "Brevis designatio meditationum de originibus gentium ductis potissimum ex indicio linguarum," published in the *Miscellanea Berolinensia* in 1710, and the preface to Wachter's *Glossarium*, see especially section II, sig. a2^{ra}.

[21] In the case of Leibniz, the concept of continuity was also extensively applied in mathematics and physics.

[22] Daudin remarks as follows: "Sauf exceptions, dont la plus considérable est celle de Lamarck, les affinités dont l'histoire naturelle s'applique à dresser le tableau sont conçues comme les témoignages d'une communauté de nature et non comme les effets d'une dérivation génétique." Henri Daudin, *Cuvier et Lamarck: les classes zoologiques et l'idée de série animale, 1790–1830* (Paris: Librairie Félix Alcan, 1926), II, 246.

[23] See Rasmus Rask, *Ausgewählte Abhandlungen* I, ed. Louis Hjelmslev (Copenhagen: Levin & Munksgaard, 1932), p. 60, line 3.

DIDEROT'S COMPARATIVE LINGUISTICS: THE PHILOSOPHE'S ENGLISH

BONNIE ARDEN ROBB

While the studies which founded Diderot's claim to the title "philosopher" involved excursions into many branches of knowledge — mathematics, medicine, and the natural sciences, as well as literature and the fine arts — one of his primary fields of investigation was certainly language itself. His interest was guaranteed, at least in part, by his work as a translator of English at the very beginning of his career. This work as a translator was a ready-made experiment with the functioning of language, providing an empirical basis for the development of his ideas and theories concerning language and the limitations and potentials of various languages, including his own.

In his *Lettre sur les sourds et muets*, Diderot appraises the strengths and weaknesses of several languages. He credits French with excellence in what was generally considered to be language's most important function, the clear and logical expression of thought. "The communication of thought being the principal object of language," he says, "our language is of all the most polished, the most exact, and the most estimable ... [its] didactic and ordered way of proceeding ... renders it [most] suitable for the sciences."[1] Despite this sincere pride in his native language, however, Diderot saw not only strengths but also shortcomings in its particular genius. He states, "We have gained clarity and precision ... and we have lost warmth, eloquence, and energy."[2] On the other hand, Diderot attributes particular strength in the affective realm to English, Greek, Latin, and Italian. To these languages he assigns the ability to persuade, move, and deceive. They should be spoken in the pulpit and on the stage, whereas French should be spoken in society and in schools of philosophy. Common sense would choose French; imagination and the passions would give the preference to English and the classical languages.

Diderot knew all the languages of which he spoke; his personal experience with them must have had considerable bearing on his theories concerning language. English especially must have influenced him, since during the years that preceded the *Lettre sur les sourds et muets*, he had been immersed in

English, translating Temple Stanyan's *Grecian History* and Shaftesbury's *Inquiry concerning Virtue or Merit*, and collaborating on a translation of Robert James's *Medicinal Dictionary*. At the beginning, in fact, Diderot's career as a man of letters—his first claim to some fame—had consisted primarily of his translations of English into French. This translating experience, affording an intimate, practical contact with English and inevitably a fresh, objective view of his own language, almost certainly helped shape his thinking and helped determine the influence exercised on him by the linguistic theories of his time.

Locke and Condillac had, for instance, already put forward many of the ideas developed by Diderot in the *Lettre sur les sourds et muets* concerning the origins of language and the question of "natural" word order. Nevertheless, Diderot's discussion seems to show the imprint of his personal experience with English. A case of particular interest is Diderot's analysis regarding word order of noun and modifier, destined to be thought-provoking to speakers of French, whom he addresses as follows:

> If someone asks you what is an object, you'll answer that it is "a substance extensive, impenetrable, shaped, colored, and mobile (*une substance étendue, impénétrable, figurée, colorée, et mobile*)." But take away from this definition all the adjectives, what will remain for this imaginary being that you call "substance"? If you wanted to arrange the terms of this same definition according to natural order, you would say "colored, shaped, extensive, impenetrable, mobile substance." That seems to me to be the order in which the qualities of matter would strike a man seeing the object for the first time. First his eye would perceive the shape, color, and size; then, approaching the object, he would discover by touch its impenetrability; finally, both sight and touch would reveal its mobility. In examining the question of whether the adjective should be placed before or after the substantive, it will be seen that *we* often reverse the natural order of ideas.[3]

It is interesting that, according to this reasoning, English is the only one of the languages referred to in the *Lettre* which habitually observes the "natural order" of adjectives and noun. Without denying Locke's influence on the ideas expressed here, it would seem very likely that Diderot's views on word order were sharpened by his experience as a translator whose work in moving from English to French would necessarily have involved rearranging nouns and adjectives, that is to say (borrowing Diderot's terminology), converting natural order to conventional order.[4]

Diderot's opinion on the order in which adjectives and nouns were inverted was likewise inspired by the sensualism of Condillac. He states it as follows in the *Lettre sur les sourds et muets*:

> First, perceptible objects struck the senses, and those which possessed several percepti-

ble attributes at once were the first named: these are the various objects which compose the universe. Then the perceptible attributes were distinguished from one another and given names; these are . . . the adjectives. Finally, making abstraction of these perceptible attributes, something common to all objects was found or thought to be found . . . and metaphysical, general nouns were created, along with almost all the substantives. Little by little, men became accustomed to believing that these nouns represented real things (beings); the perceptible attributes came to be considered as mere incidentals.[5]

From this, the relative importance Diderot accords to adjective and substantive follows easily: "Men have imagined," he says, "that the adjective is subordinate to the substantive, whereas, the substantive is actually nothing and *the adjective is everything.*"[6] (Emphasis is Diderot's.) This conclusion, as Jacques Chouillet has pointed out,[7] was Diderot's alone; nobody before him had gone so far as to claim that the adjective was everything.

The more interesting, perhaps even shocking, side of Diderot's theory may actually be his contention that the substantive is nothing. We have seen him condemn the fact that "little by little men came to believe that [metaphysical, general] nouns represented real things." The "little by little" presumably refers to the gradual progression, theorized by the sensualists, of man's original language of inarticulate but expressive sounds and gestures, to early written language consisting of pictorial, metaphorical representation of objects and actions, and finally to man's present language, so removed from its pictorial beginnings. In the article "Encyclopédie" of the *Encyclopédie*, Diderot extols the qualities of words when new: "They were clear, energetic and necessary . . . they painted."[8] It is interesting to note that Diderot attributes a splendid capacity for "painting" to English (along with Italian, Greek, and Latin), in the *Lettre sur les sourds et muets*. He characterizes these languages as "varied, abundant, full of images . . . suited to painting."[9]

In addition to this, English is singled out in the article "Encyclopédie" in an interesting, although ostensibly critical, way. Diderot, director of the huge, dignified French Encyclopedia project, proclaims the superiority of the French nation over the English in the arts and sciences on the basis that the French have a fully "formed" language, whereas the English haven't even thought about "forming" theirs.[10] This assertion by Diderot is significant, because it suggests that in his view the English language had not evolved as completely (was not as "perfect," in the etymological sense of the word) as French. That would presumably leave it closer to its pictorial origins and thus be consistent with Diderot's view of English as a "painting" language, rich in images.

Diderot's appraisal has its echo in the twentieth century. In an article entitled "Impenetrability or the Proper Habit of English," Robert Graves offered the following analysis of the relative "genius" of French and English:

> French ... [is a] reasonable codification of as much of human experience as can be translated into speech. [It gives] each separate object, process or quality a permanent label, duly docketed, and ever afterwards recognizes this object, process or quality by its label rather than by itself ... it is therefore also a rhetorical language, rhetoric being the poetry of labels and not the poetry of the things themselves. English proper has always been very much a language of "conceits," that is, except for the purely grammatic parts of speech, which are in general colourless enough, the vocabulary is not fully dissociated from the imagery from which it developed: words still tend to be pictorial and not typographic. The word "conceit" originally meant an image or pictorial idea contained in a word or juxtaposition of words. . . . It is the persistent use of this method of "thought by association of images" as opposed to "thought by generalized preconceptions," that distinguishes English proper from the more logical languages.[11]

The "labelling" of object, process, and quality in French, referred to by Graves, is favored, precisely, by the predominance of the substantive in French, a feature whose implications have been explored by J. P. Vinay and J. Darbelnet in their *Stylistique comparée du français et de l'anglais*. Vinay and Darbelnet illustrate the striking contrast between French and English in this regard with countless examples of the preferred use of noun-based constructions in French to render constructions based on many different parts of speech in English, including verbs, adjectives, adverbs, and even prepositions. In view of this, Diderot's suggestion that "the substantive is nothing" was fairly extreme for a French man of letters. He was taking issue with a prominent stylistic feature of his native language when he denied the natural primacy of the noun and called into question its preferred status and placement. Later, in the article "Encyclopédie," he may again have been influenced by his exposure to English when he called for enriching French vocabulary by constructing all parts of speech possible on each existing stem so that "each term may have all the variety of which it's capable." The appeal reflected a desire to expand and vary the means of expression in French and overcome what he identified as "difficulties caused by a scarcity (of words) which is particularly felt by writers who are exacting and concise."[12]

Some twentieth-century comparative linguists offer insights which are very helpful in identifying the possible influence of English on Diderot's French. In examining the effects of the substantive's predominance on the way things are communicated in French, Charles Bally noted that "French presents events as if they were substances";[13] André Chevrillon observed that "French renders especially forms, stills, cuts imposed on reality by analysis."[14]

As suggested by the latter, the substantive's prominence is closely related to another characteristic: the marked tendency of French to analyze rather than just present reality. Here again, Vinay and Darbelnet point out the contrast between French and English. Adopting the terminology of A. Malblanc,[15] they suggest that linguistic representation may be either on the analytical level (*le plan de l'entendement*) with the help of "sign" words, or on the real level (*le plan du réel*) with the help of "image" words. Sign words, like the abstract signs of mathematical language, speak to the mind more than to the senses. While all words are signs and therefore abstractions, image words are those which are the least abstract and the most concrete, those by which linguistic expression seems to close in on reality—whereas with sign words the mind contemplates reality at a greater remove. Vinay and Darbelnet posit that French words are generally more abstract than the corresponding English words, and less concerned with the details of reality. (For example, the French word "promenade" is habitually rendered in English by words which give more specifics: "walk," "ride," "drive," "sail.") French then tends to operate more on the analytical level, English more on the real level. Hippolyte Taine claimed, in fact, that "translating an English sentence into French was like making a pencil copy of a drawing that had been in color."[16] The French mind reduced the complexity of things to arrive at general ideas arranged in a simplified order.

In French the ideas or happenings to be communicated are analyzed and then logically arranged, which implies a subjective judgment of events on the part of the speaker. That this occurs is attested by the very extensive use—more extensive than in English—of connecting words to clarify relationships between clauses, sentences, or paragraphs; by the habitual positioning of cause before effect; by the preference for establishing a subject, in terms of which events or ideas are then presented (this is witnessed most noticeably by the typical French avoidance of the passive voice which can present an action without suggesting its origin). Vinay and Darbelnet designate this preferred arrangement as *"thème/propos"* (topic/comment) and see it as an extension of the established order of noun and adjective in French. (In the phrase *"le cheval blanc,"* for example, the topic or subject is first stated: *le cheval*; then a comment is made about it: *blanc*.)

The noun-adjective order is precisely the one seized upon by Diderot, not as being detrimental to clear communication, but as reversing natural order. On the other hand, the order adjective-noun, considered by Diderot as natural, is seen by Vinay and Darbelnet as characteristic of English's approach to reality: recounting things in the order they are observed or perceived by the senses. Since the relationships between things observed are frequently not apparent, this approach normally results in a message whose elements are juxtaposed rather than logically ordered. Thus, in contrast to the "reasoned" order of French, the English procedure has been dubbed "sensory," "intuitive," or "the film of reality." Instead of a static, pre-digested rendering of events, there is the movement generated by verbs whose every tense may be progressive, by prepositions whose kinetic usage is so fully exploited (the French "*ici*" may be rendered, according to context, as "in here," "out here," "up here," "down here," "over here," or "back here"), by adjectives and adverbs whose greater numbers and usage are both cause and effect of orientation towards concrete detail, by repetition rather than summation to express a succession of objects or actions ("tier on tier of chimneys" for "*l'étagement des cheminées*"). In contrast to the subjective order of French (in both form and attitude), the sensory view is objective; following the order of sensory experience, it has no second thoughts about the passive voice and is in fact unconcerned with a missing or incidental agent.

However, the relationship between linguistic structure and view of the world is reciprocal: "if the Englishman likes passive constructions, it's because he conceives the action as imposed on the subject, who remains passive; conversely, since each little English child receives from his parents a language he didn't help fashion, it's due to the abundant passive usage in English that he conceives the action as imposed."[17] If our first language colors our view of the world, presumably experience explored through a second language can do the same. If the structures of both French and English influenced Diderot's conception of the world, which in turn influenced his own structures, was his style a hybrid of French and English approaches? Did he in fact eschew the "metaphysical, general" noun he condemned and use other possible, though less common, French constructions? Did he attempt to achieve in French the "painting" quality he admired in English?

The possibility exists that he might have tried to — even consciously. As we have seen, early in his career, when he was translating, it was his job to do just that. And he commented a number of times on the difficulty of rendering the energy, the vivacity, the admirable painting offered by the English.

A fascinating and revealing document is the manuscript of Diderot's "Observations on the Translation of Pope's *Essay on Man* by Silhouette." Consisting of commentary, mainly criticism, of Silhouette's efforts, accompanied by Diderot's own translation of many lines, this document provides a unique opportunity to see Diderot's explicit sensitivity to the English text and at the same time contrast his rendition of it with that of another Frenchman. Silhouette's translation is extremely substantival. For instance, to render Pope's line "The same ambition can destroy or save" (Epistle II, 1.201), Silhouette wrote "*La même ambition produit ou la perte ou le salut*" ("The same ambition produces either destruction or salvation"). Diderot asks simply "*Pourquoi pas littéralement 'perd ou sauve'?*" ("Why not literally 'destroys or saves'?")".[18]

Silhouette also has a tendency to introduce abstract terms, which inspires considerable sarcasm from Diderot. For example, Pope wrote: "See worlds on worlds compose one universe" (Epistle I, 1.24). For the phrase "compose one universe," Silhouette wrote: "*former la totalité de l'univers*" ("form the totality of the universe"). Diderot comments: "*Il y a dans l'anglais* 'compose one universe' *qui se rend d'une façon littérale et sublime par 'former un univers,' et d'une façon triviale et mauvaise par 'former la totalité de l'univers'; la totalité, quelle expression!*" ("In the English it says 'compose one universe,' which is rendered literally and sublimely by 'form one universe,' and badly and trivially by 'form the totality of the universe'; totality, what an expression!")[19] Thus, Diderot advocates staying as close as possible to the English constructions and, although both men were translating poetry into prose, it is Diderot who succeeded in capturing much more of the economy of the original English verse.

However, it is worth noting that Diderot's other major criticism was that Silhouette's translation was sometimes in bad French! Diderot had no intention of ending up with an unnatural-sounding French. His goal was not to produce "pure English." At one point where Silhouette had translated a line in a particularly literal but unsatisfactory fashion, Diderot says: "it's English pure and simple; but one must be a real novice in both languages not to realize that excellent English translated word for word can give very bad French."[20]

Diderot was able to reconcile these two exigencies while translating Pope.[21] The French which resulted was correct and natural-sounding yet decidedly removed from the substantive-oriented, abstract nature of French as characterized by Vinay and Darbelnet and epitomized by Silhouette. Diderot allowed the stylistic influence of English to enhance, not distort, his translation. It seems to be in the spirit of that group of translations which, according to George Steiner, "not only represent the integral life of the original, but which do so by enriching, by extending the executive means of their own tongue."[22]

The effects of Diderot's close contact with English seem to have been durable. As we have seen, his version of current language theories appeared to bear the mark of his translating experience. More than that, the influence seems to have extended to his style in his own original works. A recent stylistic study of Diderot by J. P. Seguin,[23] although not in any way attempting to show English influence, nevertheless offers analyses that seem to support the possibility of such influence. A lexical inventory done by Seguin shows that Diderot strongly favored words of the type we have seen him hypothesize as being the earliest created, that is, those for "the perceptible objects and attributes which first struck the senses." Diderot's frequent use of these gives his reader the impression of being in the realm of the concrete. We recall that the predominance of concrete words—image words—has been seen as characteristic of English. Furthermore, it is interesting to see that even words like "*masse*" or "*point*," which were tools of abstract speculation for other French writers of the time, were invested with concrete content by Diderot—

often through the use of a carefully selected adjective, a practice certainly in keeping with his language theory.

Diderot's lexicon was enhanced by his method of presentation, which he himself described in *De l'interprétation de la nature* when he said, "I'll let thoughts flow from my pen in the very order in which objects presented themselves to me."[24] This of course is comparable to the sensory type of presentation we have seen attributed to English. Such a point of view also helps to account for the concrete quality of Diderot's philosophical writing. The elements of reality evoked by Diderot's lexicon are not mere textual decoration; it is they, rather than abstract concepts, which actually present Diderot's philosophy. The concreteness of this presentation distinguishes his style from that of his contemporaries. Seguin's study, in a series of rapprochements juxtaposing Diderot's treatment of certain common eighteenth-century themes with that of Helvétius, Condillac, La Mettrie, Castel, and others, showed Diderot's presentation of philosophical ideas using concrete images to be consistently in contrast with his contemporaries' more analytical, logically ordered type of development, which appeals to the mind much more than to the senses.

Diderot's type of presentation is consistent with his theories about how language may function most effectively. Since the writer's object is to transmit his experience and ideas to another, and the original experience is via the senses, the most successful transfer is to the senses of the other. Organized, analyzed, abstracted, the experience could not possibly be the same. The theoretical ideal, expressed in *Lettre sur les sourds et muets*, is to render in words the simultaneity with which things are experienced in the mind, achieving a synthesis belying the essentially analytical nature of language. While Diderot saw this as possible only in poetry with the magic of the poetic hieroglyph, he nevertheless seems to strive toward it in his prose and to succeed in fulfilling a part of the poet's mission. Indeed, a definition of the poet's role by Cassirer seems particulary applicable to Diderot, who, like the poet, seeks to "infuse life into the cold symbols of everyday language as well as into the conceptual language of science . . . among the words he uses, not one is dead or empty; each is brought to life, animated from within, nourished with intuitive, immediate content."[25]

Diderot indeed "extended the executive means" of his native language, and his early association with English as translator would seem to have been a contributing factor, providing empirical support of the theories of language he developed and out of which his own language evolved.

NOTES

[1] All references to the *Lettre sur les sourds et muets* are to the *Oeuvres complétes*, édition Hermann (Paris, 1970-), IV. English translations are my own. The original texts will be provided in the notes, beginning with the present: Hermann IV, pp. 164–65: "la communication de la penseé étant l'objet principal du langage, notre langue est de toutes les langues la plus châtiée, la plus exacte et la plus estimable . . . la marche didactique et réglée à laquelle note langue est assujettie, la rend plus propre aux sciences."

[2] Hermann, IV, 165: "Nous avous gagné . . . de la clarté, de la précision . . . nous avons perdu de la chaleur, de l'éloquence, et de l'énergie."

[3] Hermann IV, 135–37: "Qu'on vous demande ce que c'est qu'un corps, vous répondrez que c'est 'une substance étendue, impénétrable, figurée, colorée et mobile.' Mais ôtez de cette définition tous les adjectifs, que restera-t-il pour cet être imaginaire que vous appelez 'substance'? Si on voulait ranger dans la même définition les termes, suivant l'ordre naturel, on dirait 'colorée, figurée, étendue, impénétrable, mobile, substance.' C'est dans cet ordre que les différentes qualités des portions de la matière affecteraient, ce me semble, un homme qui verrait un corps pour la première fois. L'oeil serait frappé d'abord de la figure, de la couleur et de l'étendue; le toucher s'approchant ensuite du corps, en découvrirait l'impénétrabilité; et la vue et le toucher s'assureraient de la mobilité . . . si on examine cette question en elle-même, savoir si l'adjectif doit être placé devant ou après le substantif, on trouvera que nous renversons souvent l'ordre naturel des idées."

[4] Hermann, IV, 137: "Je dis 'l'ordre naturel' des idées; car il faut distinguer ici 'l'ordre naturel' d'avec 'l'ordre d'institution.'"

[5] Hermann, IV, 135: "Les objets sensibles ont les premiers frappé les sens, et ceux qui réunissaient plusieurs qualités sensibles à la fois ont été les premiers nommés; ce sont les différents individus qui composent cet univers. On a ensuite distingué les qualités sensibles les unes des autres, on leur a donné des noms; ce sont . . . [les] adjectifs. Enfin abstraction faite de ces qualités sensibles, on a trouvé ou cru trouver quelque chose de commun dans tous ces individus . . . et l'on a formé les noms métaphysiques et généraux, et presque tous les substantifs. Peu à peu on s'est accoutumé à croire que ces noms représentaient des êtres réels; on a regardé les qualités sensibles comme de simples accidents."

[6] Hermann, IV, 135: "L'on s'est imaginé que l'adjectif était réellement subordonné au substantif, quoique le substantif ne soit proprement rien, et que *l'adjectif soit tout*."

[7] Hermann, IV, 136, n. 17.

[8] References to the article "Encyclopédie" ("Enc.") are to *Encyclopédie ou Dictionnaire raisonné des sciences, des arts, et des métiers*, Nouvelle impression en facsimilé de la première édition de 1751–1780 (Stuttgart-Bad Cannstatt: Friedrich Fromann Verlag, 1966), V. "Enc.," 637: "ils étoient clairs, énergiques, & nécessaires . . . ils peignoient."

[9] Hermann, IV, 215: ". . . variée, abondante, impétueuse, pleine d'images . . . propre à remuer les âmes. . .à annoncer des vérités sublimes, à peindre des actes héroïques. . . ."

[10] "Enc.," 639: Diderot says: "A quelle distance les Anglois sont encore de nous par la considération seule que notre langue est faite, & qu'ils ne songent pas encore à former la leur!"

[11] Robert Graves, "Impenetrability or the Proper Habit of English," *Fortnightly Review* 720 (1 Dec. 1926), 782, and 721 (1 Jan. 1927), 63.

[12] "Enc.," 641: "il seroit à souhaiter que les termes y eussent toute la variété dont ils sont susceptibles"; ". . . les embarras d'une disette qui se fait particulièrement sentir aux écrivains exacts & laconiques."

[13] "Bien loin de chercher . . . le devenir dans les choses, il présente les événements comme des substances." Charles Bally, *Linguistique générale et linguistique française* (Paris: Librairie Ernest Leroux, 1932), pp. 470, 376.

[14] "Le français traduit surtout des formes, états arrêtés, les coupures imposées au réel par l'analyse." André Chevrillon, *Trois Etudes de littérature anglaise* (Plon, 1921), p. 222, cited by J. P. Vinay and J. Darbelnet, *Stylistique comparée du français et l'anglais* (Paris: Didier, 1971), p. 102.

[15] A. Malblanc, *Stylistique comparée du français et de l'allemand* 2e éd. (Paris: Didier, 1963).

[16]"Traduire en français une phrase anglaise, c'est copier au crayon gris une figure en couleur. Réduisant ainsi les aspects et les qualités des choses, l'esprit français aboutit à des idées générales, c'est-à-dire simples, qu'il aligne dans un ordre simplifié, celui de la logique." Quoted in Vinay/Darbelnet, *Styl. comp.*, p. 59.

[17]"Si l'Anglais aime les tours passifs, c'est parce qu'il conçoit le procès comme imposé au locuteur, qui reste passif; inversement, puisque chaque petit Anglais reçoit de ses parents une langue qu'il n'a pas contribué à façonner, c'est parce que les tours passifs abondent en anglais qu'il conçoit le procès sous un angle imposé, donc passif." Vinay/Darbelnet, *Styl. comp.*, pp. 259-60.

[18]Hermann, I, 223.

[19]Hermann, I, 194.

[20]Hermann, I, 262: "C'est l'anglais tout pur; mais il faut être bien novice dans l'une et l'autre langue pour ne pas s'apercevoir que de l'excellent anglais rendu mot à mot donne du très mauvais français."

[21]It should be noted that the situation is not identical in Diderot's other translations, where the stylistic effects of the translating process are of a somewhat different nature.

[22]George Steiner, *After Babel* (New York: Oxford Univ. Press, 1975), pp. 407-08.

[23]J. P. Seguin, *Diderot, le discours et les choses* (Paris: Librairie Klincksieck, 1978).

[24]Diderot, *De l'interprétation de la nature*, éd Paul Vernière (Paris: Garnier, 1964), p. 177: "Je laisserai les pensées se succéder sous ma plume, dans l'ordre même selon lequel les objets se sont offerts à ma réflexion."

[25]Ernst Cassirer, *La philosophie des Lumières*, trans. P. Quillet (Paris: Fayard, 1966), p. 337, quoted by J. P. Seguin, above, p. 124.

PARADIGMATIC, NARRATIVE AND GENETIC HISTORIES, OR THE PERILS OF RELYING ON THOMAS KUHN

JOSEPH MUSSER JR.

In the late eighteenth century, the picturesque was added to beauty and sublimity as an aesthetic category. The major theorists of the picturesque were Uvedale Price and Richard Payne Knight, dilettantes who came to aesthetic theory by way of landscape gardening.[1] Their theories are unusually polemical because they argue that the picturesque is healthier than the beautiful or the sublime: artists and gardeners should prefer the picturesque. Their argument rests on assumptions about perception, which in turn depend on assumptions about the nervous system's functions and its requirements for health. Those assumptions presumably depend upon some eighteenth-century theories about the operations of the nerves, and it was in seeking to understand and connect these theories that I discovered radical disagreement among historians of physiology.

Although most of the historians employ Thomas Kuhn's metaphor of the paradigm,[2] they identify a confusing array of paradigms, and they disagree vehemently about the deflecting power of different researchers. G. S. Rousseau, for example, argues that the seventeenth-century physician, Thomas Willis, is paradigmatic: Willis's locating the mind in the brain raised the interest in nerves and the nervous system, and his ideas deflected research in physiology for the next century.[3] But others identify completely different paradigms, including a shift from concentrating on nerves to concentrating on fluids and drugs as a consequence of Albrecht von Haller's research-deflecting work. Still other historians identify as paradigmatic the work of Thomas Sydenham (the English Hippocrates), or Herman Boerhaave, or Francis Glisson, John Keill, Robert Whytt, Cromwell Mortimer, William Cullen, Archibald Pitcairne, William Heberden, Georg Stahl, John Hunter, even Plato and Democritus.

Within this cornucopia of paradigms, I was relieved to discover two almost identical appraisals. One author perceives a "dramatic, indeed precipitous decline of varieties of mechanism and the rapid rise to preeminence of alternate varieties of vitalism";[4] another describes "a trend towards replacing chemical explanations by physical ones, and mechanistic or materialistic thinking by energistic and vitalistic thinking."[5] Did two experts agree? Can we start with this agreement to trace a paradigm or pattern of development? Alas, no. The first statement is made about the period, 1730–1770; the second about Thomas Willis (1621–1675). Perhaps phylogeny recapitulates ontogeny. Hansreudi Isler, in fact, claims the pattern of development is not unique with Willis: "this trend is represented in the writings of leading Iatrochemists since Paracelsus, and it seems to originate from a reaction against the separation of magic from the chemical doctrines" (p. 174). Georg Stahl was a prime example of one who "started as an Iatrochemist, and ended in an energetic, vitalistic, animistic soul medicine" (p. 174). So perhaps the paradigm is psychological and sociological, genetically or environmentally determined. Start as a chemist or mechanist, and you are doomed to end as a vitalist.

The confusion of paradigms raises an important question: If historians share Kuhn's strongly heuristic theory, why can they not use it to produce a clear, consistent history? It is possible, of course, that eighteenth-century physiology is a pre-paradigmatic science, in which case applying Kuhn would by definition fail. But it is at least equally possible that more rigorous or refined application of Kuhn's scheme would eliminate much of the confusion. It might help to define and explore different levels of inquiry among the physiologists, or to identify groups of physiologists who would have formed their own scientific community with its own unique paradigm. It seems most likely, however, that Kuhn's model itself has serious flaws, and that other metaphors might be more useful and productive for the historian of science, namely the perception of scientific development as a continuing narrative, or the application of an organic rather than a mechanistic model. By using my attempt to explain the physiological assumptions of the picturesque theorists, I may be able to suggest the shortcomings of Kuhn's theory as well as the advantages of other metaphors.

LEVELS OF INQUIRY

Applying Kuhn's scheme with more rigor might require defining various levels of inquiry. Some parts of Kuhn's book suggest that one can choose to speak of scientific revolutions on various levels, since paradigms define communities and communities can range from the whole scientific community to groups "of fewer than twenty-five people" (Kuhn, p. 181). Indeed, Kuhn argues that the change within a small community may not even appear revolutionary to those outside (p. 181). We might compare what happens as we move from larger, more inclusive communities to smaller ones with what happens as we switch lenses on a microscope, changing the power of magnification: the field remains the same size, but the area actually present to view becomes more restricted as we increase the power of magnification; the more restricted view is compensated for by the greater detail. Thus, the historian of eighteenth-century physiology must eschew the Olympian perspective like Freud's, who saw but three "discontinuities in the history of Western science— ... the revolution of Copernicus, ... Darwin's revolution, ... [and] third, in perhaps the least modest statement of intellectual history, Freud's own revolution...."[6] As we zoom in on the eighteenth century, we may begin to perceive revolutions in one large group's rejection of explanatory analogies or in its willingness to remain agnostic about ultimate causes or explanations. Conceivably Boerhaave played a role in tempering enthusiasm for mechanical medicine (iatromechanics) based upon Newton's mathematics. Albrecht von Haller, who rediscovered the notion of "irritability" for the eighteenth century, can be considered a paradigmatic thinker on another level. Perhaps even John Hunter, who, according to Theodore Brown, "completed the dismantling of the Royal Society's mechanistic physiology," produced an important paradigm for the group of late eighteenth-century physiologists who turned to "a phenomenalist vitalism" (Brown, p. 181). Possibly there are even paradigms for each of the two major varieties of vitalism current in the late eighteenth century: one system which explained "everything by the action of a *living principle*," and the other "by a principle somewhat indefinite, which they gave the name of irritability" (Brown, p. 183, note 16). Each of them must have had its paradigmatic models.

Thus, when we analyze the paradigms guiding eighteenth-century research, it may be necessary to specify the level on which we are operating. Perhaps the disagreement about paradigms merely indicates decoding on different levels, to switch metaphor momentarily. G. S. Rousseau, in identifying Willis as the paradigmatic thinker for nerve research, admits that he, Rousseau, is decoding on the deepest level; perhaps some historians analyze the structure of less profound levels of scientific inquiry. And maybe Rousseau was not aware of an even more fundamental level, described by Lester King, who argues that "the major battle lines were already clearly arrayed in the fifth century B.C., when Platonic doctrine confronted the Democritean."[7] If historians are careful to identify which power of magnification they are using, or on which level they are decoding, the apparent confusion of paradigms might turn into a pattern more nearly like a chemist's flow chart.

IDENTIFYING COMMUNITIES

In his postscript to the second edition of *The Structure of Scientific Revolutions*, Kuhn argues that "any study of paradigm-directed or of paradigm-shattering research must begin by locating the responsible group or groups" because "a paradigm governs, in the first instance, not a subject matter but rather a group of practitioners" (p. 180). To trace the relationships among researchers may reveal the extent to which those who are in touch with each other and who use one another's work can be said to form a community. This would be one way in which correspondence might offer invaluable information.

Consider the controversy between Haller and Whytt, for example, who agree that the followers of Stahl are wrong to "conceive the nerves to be like tense cords, which are put in motion by the impressions of objects."[8] They argue that a nervous fluid, the "animal spirit," flows through the nerves between muscle and brain. Whytt comes so close to Haller's ideas that Haller complains because Whytt fails to acknowledge his work and ideas. They agree on the merit of experimentation; Whytt praises Haller for his experiments, for example.[9] And Haller attacks Whytt for his failure to consult experimental results. Both trace the notion of "irritability" through a chain of physicians; that chain coincides in some respects. Both, for example, give quite a bit of space to Glisson. Yet they disagree radically (I would say) about the meaning and cause of "irritability," and Haller classes Whytt as Stahlian despite Whytt's staunch denial. Haller distinguished "sensibility" from "irritability"; the former characterizes nerves, the latter the muscles (irritability, says Haller, resides in the mucus, one of two muscular components). But Whytt insists that irritability, like sensibility, characterizes nerves, not muscles. Though Whytt and Haller agree about appropriate experiments, they disagree about interpreting the results. They agree about what they see, and they repeat one another's work. Both worked with responses exhibited by excised hearts or muscles. But Haller attributed the muscular responses after excision to the fact that irritability is a constituent of the muscle tissue, whereas Whytt attributed it to residual animal spirits. (It may be worth noting here that each accused the other of arguing the ridiculous and heretical notion that the soul can be divided, and each tried to prove that his theory did not require postulating the divisibility of the soul.)

Clearly the two can talk with each other. They do not need the translation that, according to Kuhn, representatives from different communities would require. And yet, their disagreement could be regarded as fundamental: if "irritability" is part of nervous responsiveness, then the operation of the nervous system would differ drastically from a system wherein irritability is located within muscle tissue. By carefully delineating their agreements and disagreements, it may be possible to define a scientific community governed by a discernible paradigm. In fact, it might be possible to identify a community that contains both, and then subcommunities which each include just one of them.

SCIENCE AS NARRATIVE

Let me now turn to an extra-Kuhnian approach which requires that we reject Kuhn's implication that total discontinuity is possible. Alasdair MacIntyre, in his essay on "Epistemological Crises, Dramatic Narrative, and the Philosophy of Science," points out that the theory of discontinuity requires "not just that the adherents of rival paradigms disagree, but that *every* relevant area of rationality is invaded by that disagreement."[10] This is the theory of complete incommensurability. But MacIntyre argues that "it can never be the case that everything is put in question simultaneously" (p. 68), or we would not know there is any question, any difference of opinion. In opposition to Kuhn, MacIntyre argues that what survives through revolutions or crises is a tradition, in a special sense of that word. Traditions "are the bearers of reason, and traditions at certain periods actually require and need revolutions for their continuance" (p. 63).

If I understand MacIntyre correctly, the continuity in revolution is provided by the standards of narrative. Narrative requires a coherent accounting of events and facts. The standard of narrative coherence in turn requires a comprehensive explanation not only of events but of explanations of those events. Thus, a revolution represents "a rewriting of the narrative which constitutes tradition" in such a way that the recast narrative "enables us to understand precisely why its predecessors have to be rejected or modified and also why, without and before its illumination, past theory could have remained credible" (p. 62).

The likely focus for such a narrative might be on epistemological argument. Such a focus is admirably exemplified by G. S. Rousseau's " 'Sowing the Wind and Reaping the Whirlwind': Aspects of Change in Eighteenth-Century Medicine," in which he traces the changing mixture of rational and empirical approaches to medical knowledge.[11] He argues that, although one cannot demonstrate any clear-cut adoption of empiricism in preference to rationalism, doctors and medical researchers had become increasingly skeptical about any sort of hypothesis and so "exercised greater caution in promoting systems" (p. 147); and he discovers "a new sense of the significance of induction in medical research" (p. 148). His careful exposition constitutes a narrative of epistemological change that occurred gradually and without the discontinuity Kuhn's theory requires.

An account that focuses on metaphor in medical treatises might similarly provide a continuous narrative that constitutes an argument about explanation itself, since metaphor frequently enters a conflict precisely at those points where the argument becomes epistemological. A glance at the very few instances from seventeenth- and eighteenth-century physiologists will show the relevance of metaphor to conflict and to the mapping of that conflict.

Thomas Willis, of the seventeenth century, bursts with metaphors. They spring from his pen like weeds, and in fact often seem to choke his thought. This fecundity of metaphor implies the tendency toward what C. S. Lewis calls the Master's, or teacher's, metaphor. Such metaphors are chosen to explain; they do not provide material to explore. Thus, their rapid appearance and short life, and their multiplicity. For example, to explain the structure and operation of the nervous system, Willis—within about one page—claims that the brain and its system of nerves are like a tree (with roots and branches), like the sun or a star with its "radiant or beamy concretion compassing it about," like the chest and windways of an organ, like a water system with a perpetual spring that supplies "Ponds and lakes of Waters lately diffused from the chanels of Rivers," or like "a Silver mass gilt or inriched with Gold."[12] This chorus of metaphors implies that Willis knows the physiology they represent, and that he chooses them to instruct us, his readers. He goes even further though. He sometimes relies on metaphor to prove his contentions. Thus, Hansreudi Ilser argues that "Willis attempts to *substantiate* [my emphasis] his explosion theory by comparing it to various chemical reactions between mineral acids and metals" (p. 116). (This explosion theory held that muscles operate by means of miniature explosions within the muscle fiber.) To use an analogy or metaphor as a source of proof goes beyond the normal function of a metaphor: it is taking literally a figurative illumination; it obliterates the distinction between *seems* and *is*.

George Cheyne, in the 1730s and 1740s, though he himself based his medical system on the assumption that "Nature works analogously," complains about Willis's resorting to metaphor as explanation.[13] He, more frequently than Willis, refers to the inadequacy of the metaphors he uses (he calls them "gross Similitudes" [p. 5]). One metaphor that both use—that the nervous system is like a pipe organ—helps demonstrate the difference between Willis's use of metaphor and Cheyne's. Willis limits the analogy to the mechanical similarity, specifically the conduits by which air gets from bellows to pipes. He appears to believe that the pipe organ represents an almost literal mapping of the nervous system, and he implies that, if you know how the organ's mechanism works, you will know how the nervous system works. But Cheyne introduces the same metaphor to explore a mystery, and he makes the analogy tentative and suggestive rather than exact and explanatory; Cheyne uses the metaphor where his scientific understanding breaks down. He suggests that there is an "intelligent Principle, or *Soul*" which "resides somewhere in the Brain, where all the Nerves, or Instruments of Sensation terminate, like a *Musician* in a finely fram'd and well-tun'd Organ-Case; that these Nerves are like *Keys*, which, being struck on or touch'd, convey the Sound and Harmony to this sentient Principle, or *Musician*" (pp. 4-5). For Willis, the metaphor conveys knowledge; for Cheyne it presents an intuition.

Later in the eighteenth century, analogy and metaphor become even more suspect (though liberally used by modern standards). Haller, for example, says, "I am persuaded that the great source of error in physic has been owing to physicians, at least a great part of them, making few or no experiments, and substituting analogy instead of them" (p. 8). When William Cullen mentions the possible analogy between the operation of electric and nervous fluids, both of which are said to be excitable, he expresses and counsels caution in using this analogy as a source of knowledge: "These [similarities] are some hints and analogies which may in some measure illustrate the matter; but there must be a concurrent view, and a consideration of many other phenomena, before we can apply this doctrine more strictly or specially to our nervous system; and though I have thus thrown out a conjecture, which every time I take a view of the nervous system seems to me to approach nearer to probability, yet I do not say that it will, in the present state of our knowledge, apply to all the phenomena with any consistency."[14] Note, too, that Cullen's use of metaphor comes closer to what C. S. Lewis calls the Pupil's metaphor, the metaphor by means of which we explore and from which we learn, in contrast to Willis's Master's metaphors.

In general, seventeenth- and eighteenth-century medical treatises move from metaphor as explanation to metaphor as hypothesis or suggestion. The movement towards fewer and more tentative metaphors corresponds with the transformation of physical explanation into metaphors. One such example is "motion." In the late seventeenth century, physiologists would have considered the idea of motion a concrete reality—the motion of corpuscles. But by the later eighteenth century, "motion" had become a consciously metaphorical term—"vital motion" or "the motion of the soul"—a radical change from the iatromechanism of corpuscular medicine and yet continuous with it. Just as a religious narrative may be salvaged by transforming it from literal account to myth or metaphor, a scientific explanation no longer taken literally may be reconstituted by rendering it metaphorical. The idea of "motion" remains, but its application and explanatory power have changed drastically.

Thus, analyzing metaphor in these physiologists may provide one especially illuminating way to follow the continuity of conflict, the epistemological debate which in part constitutes the tradition of physiological research, and so to produce a narrative that describes the development of physiological ideas in the eighteenth century.

AN ORGANIC MODEL

Finally, we might consider alternate epistemologies to Kuhn's, again by looking at metaphor. One characteristic of historians of ideas, perhaps because they are dealing with abstractions, seems to be the mixing of metaphors. It might be useful to examine Kuhn's mixture and compare it with other mixtures often applied to the world of ideas. Richard Vernon has done the sort of analysis I am talking about in his essay on Kuhn's political metaphor, the metaphor of revolution.[15] Another of Kuhn's key terms is "paradigm," which also carries important implications about his notion of what ideas are and how they operate upon human minds or within them. A paradigm is a model. Language teachers use it to label the patterns of conjugations and declensions that their students memorize and master. It conveys the sense of the neat orderliness of the chart. A paradigm arrogates authority and sets a standard none can quite match: what pupils ever ran through all their conjugations flawlessly? Or, if the students can match, they can never exceed the paradigm. It implies an aloof perfection that can never be surpassed, only replaced. This image of neat orderliness indicates Kuhn's view of scientists as human beings "deeply attached to order" who submerge their individual rights to the assent of a group, as Vernon argues when he describes Kuhn's revolutionaries. Thus, Vernon shows us that Kuhn's metaphors confuse different views of the revolution; they draw "ambiguously upon several different notions of political revolution" (p.264).

Other interesting confusions are introduced by scholars who adopt Kuhn's argument. When G. S. Rousseau and Roy Porter bow before Kuhn's paradigm, at the beginning of *The Ferment of Knowledge* (which in its very title introduces an image with its own special implications about how ideas work, implications which would have special relevance for those who favor symposia), they twice within a few sentences use an apparent synonym to "paradigm" for the action or behavior of ideas. That apparent synonym, however, has much different implications: they talk about the "seminal writings of anthropologists and psychologists" and argue that Kuhn's *Structure of Scientific Revolutions* not only "exert[ed] a seminal influence in shaping research within its own field but also . . . offer[ed] a paradigm widely appropriated by other disciplines."[16] "Seminal" is a much sloppier term than "paradigm." It is most familiar to us as an organic fluid of passionate ejaculation, as little formed by the intellect of its originator as the fate of its constituent spermatazoa is controlled by him. It is the product of physiological processes and is introduced into a social context by emotional or instinctual rather than rational behavior (usually, that is) and it requires ovarian contribution to produce full-fledged offspring. (Its etymology, however, indicates that the sexist, homuncular view informs it.) It gives us an entirely different conception (so to speak) of important ideas: that they grow, that they must be tended, that they are often unfulfilled (or that the seeds are ungerminated), that they can be hybridized. "Seminal" conveys an entirely different image of how ideas function. "Paradigm" implies a perfect model from which there is an inevitable falling away until the next paradigm (attrition by error), even though Kuhn's discussion modifies his primary impression. It allows little influence to the mere technician in shaping or altering it. "Seminal," on the other hand, implies that ideas can be influenced by environment, that the stock can be improved (perhaps with only the slightest bit of genetic engineering), that the idea can be deflected by the minutest of influences, and, moreover, that it forms part of a continuity, a genetic narrative, that can define and contain its own revolution.

The "seminal" metaphor might best be considered part of the general notion that ideas are like genetic material that can be transmitted by germ cells or by viruses. Ideas can thus be spread rapidly by infection or more slowly by insemination. If the idea is virulent or the host susceptible, it can move rapidly through the scientific community, producing feverish speculation and experimentation. The slower, more gradual propagation of ideas may be more nearly like fertilization. Biologists especially favor this metaphor. Jacques Monod compares "the evolution of ideas and that of the biosphere."[17] Like organisms, ideas "tend to perpetuate their structure and to breed; they too can fuse, recombine, segregate their content; indeed, they too can evolve, and in this evolution selection must surely play an important role" (p. 165). In *The Selfish Gene*, Richard Dawkins similarly suggests that "when you plant a fertile meme (the ideational analogue to the gene) in my mind, you literally parasitize my brain, turning it into a vehicle for the meme's propagation in just the way that a virus may parasitize the genetic mechanism of a host cell."[18] Dawkins suggests that, like genes, which can mutate, memes can vary or become distorted, and ideas may frequently have to vie with their mutations for mental and even physical resources ("radio and televison time, billboard space, newspaper and magazine column-inches and library shelf space," p. 212).[19] This emphasis on evolution of ideas by selection would encourage the study of the idea's context, which many have come to agree is requisite to understanding the development of science.

Thus, the argument between Whytt and Haller (see above) displays the competition between mutations of the idea, or meme, "irritability." Both men's accounts of the idea's provenance largely correspond: they acknowledge a similar heritage owing much to Glisson. And they agree about the manifestations of irritability and even design similar experiments to study it. But they disagree about whether it characterizes the nerves or the muscles, and their conclusions—the implications they draw from their observations—consequently differ significantly. Tracing the natural history of the meme, "irritability," thus helps explain both the similarities and possibilities of communication between Whytt and Haller, as well as the differences and perhaps even the keen sense of rivalry and competition that both felt: they (or their ideas) were mutants vying for the same niche in their environment.

This image has the additional advantage of emphasizing the continuity of tradition: as Lewis Thomas points out, "We still share genes around, and the resemblance of the enzymes of grasses to those of whales is a family resemblance."[20]

CONCLUSION

The paths that remain within Kuhn's paradigmatic theory — specifying levels of inquiry or identifying scientific communities — may help eliminate some of the present confusion about eighteenth-century physiology by making the relationships among scientists and physicans clearer. But those paths remain within a theory based on metaphor having limited congruence with the world of ideas and so have limited promise. The other two metaphors — science as narrative, ideas as seminal — have their own limitations, as metaphors inevitably do. But they would be more help in tracing the tortuously complex development of neurological theory and experimentation from the seventeenth through the eighteenth centuries, and their application would yield a more thorough and reliable account in which literary and other scholars could explore influences and discern informing patterns. Both metaphors can accommodate digression and interruption, while postulating an ultimate unity that allows the historian to perceive an intelligible pattern of developing ideas. They can allow minor characters to have more crucial roles than Kuhn's paradigm will allow, and they can explain more successfully deflections, as well as particular ramifications, of the original idea or hypothesis. The organic metaphor, in addition, implies that the seminal idea carries an innate informing, or shaping, power that is realized only in the particular manifestation or application of the idea. Historians might be most succcessful combining the two metaphors to write a narrative that records the fertilization, growth, propagating, and death of seminal ideas.

NOTES

[1] Sir Uvedale Price published his *Essay on the Picturesque* in 1794 and added a second volume in 1798. Richard Payne Knight responded with *An Analytical Inquiry into the Principles of Taste* in 1805. For detailed accounts of picturesque theory, see Christopher Hussey, *The Picturesque: Studies in a Point of View* (New York: G. P. Putnam's Sons, 1927), Walter J. Hipple, *The Beautiful, the Sublime, and the Picturesque in Eighteenth-Century British Aesthetic Theory* (Carbondale: Southern Illinois Univ. Press, 1957), and Martin Price, *To the Palace of Wisdom: Studies in Order and Energy from Dryden to Blake* (Garden City: Doubleday, 1964).
[2] Thomas Kuhn, *The Structure of Scientific Revolutions*, 2nd ed. (Chicago: Univ. of Chicago Press, 1970).

[3] G. S. Rousseau, "Nerves, Spirits, and Fibres: Towards Defining the Origins of Sensibility," in *Studies in the Eighteenth Century III: Papers Presented at the Third David Nichol Smith Memorial Seminar, Canberra, 1973*, ed. R. R. Brissenden and J. C. Eade (Canberra: Australian National Univ. Press, 1976), pp. 137-57.

[4] Theodore M. Brown, "From Mechanism to Vitalism in Eighteenth-Century Physiology," *Journal of the History of Biology* 7 (Fall 1974), 179.

[5] Hansreudi Isler, *Thomas Willis, 1621-1675: Doctor and Scientist* (New York: Hafner, 1968), pp. 173-74.

[6] Stephen Jay Gould, "Will Man Become Obsolete?" a review of Robert Jastrow's *The Enchanted Loom: Mind in the Universe*, in *The New York Review of Books* 29 (15 April 1982), 27.

[7] Lester Snow King, *The Philosophy of Medicine: The Early Eighteenth Century* (Cambridge, Mass.: Harvard Univ. Press, 1978), p. vi.

[8] Albrecht von Haller, *A Dissertation on the Sensible and Irritable Parts of Animals*, intro. Owsei Temkin (1755; rpt. Baltimore: Johns Hopkins Univ. Press, 1936), p. 20.

[9] Robert Whytt, *Physiological Essays* (Edinburgh: John Balfour, 1766), pp. 91-92.

[10] Alasdair MacIntyre, "Epistemological Crises, Dramatic Narrative, and the Philosophy of Science," in *Paradigms and Revolutions: Appraisals and Applications of Thomas Kuhn's Philosophy of Science*, ed. Gary Gutting (Notre Dame, Ind.: Univ. of Notre Dame Press, 1980), p. 68.

[11] In *Studies in Change and Revolution: Aspects of English Intellectual History 1640-1800*, ed. Paul J. Korshin (Menston, Yorkshire: Scolar Press, 1972), pp. 129-59.

[12] Thomas Willis, *The Anatomy of the Brain and Nerves*, ed. William Feindel (1681; rpt. Birmingham, Ala.: Gryphon Editions, 1978), pp. 125-26.

[13] George Cheyne, *The English Malady: Or a Treatise of Nervous Diseases of All Kinds, as Spleen, Vapours, Lowness of Spirits, Hypochondriacal, and Hysterical Distempers, &c.* (London: G. Strahan, 1733), p. 84.

[14] John Thomson, *An Account of the Life, Lectures, and Writings of William Cullen, M.D.* (Edinburgh: William Blackwood and Sons, 1859), II, 317-18.

[15] Richard Vernon, "Politics as Metaphor: Cardinal Newman and Professor Kuhn," in *Paradigms and Revolutions*, pp. 246-47.

[16] G. S. Rousseau and Roy Porter, eds., *The Ferment of Knowledge: Studies in the Historiography of Eighteenth-Century Science* (New York: Cambridge Univ. Press, 1980), pp. 1-2.

[17] Jacques Monod, *Chance and Necessity: An Essay on the Natural Philosophy of Modern Biology*, trans. Austryn Wainhouse (New York: Knopf, 1971), p. 165.

[18] Richard Dawkins, *The Selfish Gene* (New York: Oxford Univ. Press, 1976), p. 207.

[19] Douglas R. Hofstadter discusses these ideas in "Metamagical Themas: Virus-like Sentences and Self-Replicating Structures," *Scientific American* 248 (January 1983), 14-22.

[20] Lewis Thomas, *The Lives of a Cell: Notes of a Biology Watcher* (New York: Viking, 1974), p. 3.

CONTRIBUTORS

SOPHIA B. BLAYDES, Professor of English at West Virginia University, is author of *Christopher Smart as Poet of His Time* (1966) and co-author of *Sir William Davenant* (1981) and *Sir William Davenant: An Annotated Bibliography, 1629-1985* (1986).

THEODORE E. D. BRAUN, Professor of French and Comparative Literature at the University of Delaware, is author of *Un Ennemi de Voltaire—Le Franc de Pompignan* (1972), co-editor of Pompignan's opera *Prométhée* (1976) and of *Teaching the Eighteenth Century* (1979), and editor of *Alzire* for the *Complete Works of Voltaire* to be published shortly.

MELISSA A. BUTLER is Associate Professor of Political Science at Wabash College.

SPENCER DAVIS, Assistant Professor of History and Honors Program Coordinator at Peru State College, is author of *America: An Analytical Workbook* (1986).

VIRGINIA P. DAWSON, Contractor Historian for the National Aeronautics and Space Administration, is author of *Nature's Enigma: the Problem of the Polyp in the Letters of Trembley, Bonnet, and Réaumur* to be published shortly.

LESLIE FRIEDMAN GOLDSTEIN, Associate Professor of Political Science at the University of Delaware, is author of *The Constitutional Rights of Women* (1979).

COLETTE HALL, Assistant Professor of Modern Languages at Ursinus College, has published articles on French feminists and French women writers.

MANFRED KUEHN, Associate Professor of Philosophy at Purdue University, is author of *Scottish Common Sense in Germany, 1768-1800* (1987).

DAVID R. LACHTERMAN is Associate Professor of Philosophy and Greek at Pennsylvania State University and has published studies of Descartes, Spinoza, Vico, Kant, and Hegel.

BRIAN MCCREA, Associate Professor of English and Director of Graduate Studies at the University of Florida, is author of *Henry Fielding and the Politics of Mid-Eighteenth-Century England* (1981).

SYLVIA KASEY MARKS, Associate Professor of English at Polytechnic University (New York), is author of *Sir Charles Grandison: The Compleat Conduct Book* (1986).

JAMES E. MAY, Assistant Professor of English at the Pennsylvania State University-DuBois, is completing a descriptive bibliography of Edward Young.

DONALD C. MELL, JR., Professor of English at the University of Delaware, is author of *A Poetics of Augustan Elegy* (1974), *English Poetry, 1660–1800* (1982), and is co-editor of *Contemporary Studies of Swift's Poetry* (1981).

JOSEPH MUSSER, JR., Professor of English and Chair of Humanities-Classics at Ohio Wesleyan University, is completing a study of the rhetoric of eighteenth-century philosophers.

LUCIA M. PALMER, Associate Professor of Philosophy at the University of Delaware, has co-edited *Thought, Action and Intuition: Reflections on the Philosophy of Benedetto Croce* (1976), and translated and edited Vico's *Liber Metaphysicus* (1710) to be published shortly.

W. KEITH PERCIVAL is Professor of Linguistics at the University of Kansas, and has published widely on the history of linguistics in the High Middle Ages and the Renaissance.

PETER PERRETEN, Professor and Chair of the English Department at Ursinus College, teaches eighteenth-century literature and is working on a study of the relationship between the popular press and canonical literature of eighteenth-century England.

JANE PERRY–CAMP is Professor of Music Theory and Music History (Historical Musicology) at Florida State University's School of Music, and as a pianist performs in frequent recitals.

BONNIE ARDEN ROBB, Assistant Professor of French at the University of Delaware, is publishing articles on Diderot.

JANE SHINEHOUSE, Associate Professor of Biology at Ursinus College, teaches Anatomy, Physiology, and Histology.

HILDA SMITH is Associate Professor, Department of History and Director of Women's Studies, University of Cincinnati, and author of *Reason's Disciples: Seventeenth-Century English Feminists* (1982).

GIORGIO TAGLIACOZZO, founder and director of the Institute for Vico Studies, has edited *Vico: Past and Present* (1981), *Vico and Marx: Affinities and Contrasts* (1983), and has co-edited *Giambattista Vico: An International Symposium* (1969), *Giambattista Vico's Science of Humanity* (1976), and *Vico and Contemporary Thought* (1979).

ROBERT W. UPHAUS, Professor of English at Michigan State University, is the author of the *The Impossible Observer* (1979), *Beyond Tragedy* (1981), and *William Hazlitt* (1985).

DONALD PHILLIP VERENE is Professor and Chair of the Philosophy Department at Emory University and author of *Vico's Science of Imagination* (1981) and *Hegel's Recollection* (1985).

DERK VISSER, Professor of History at Ursinus College, is author of *Zacharias Ursinus: The Reluctant Reformer* (1983) and editor of *Controversy and Conciliation: The Reformation and the Palatinate, 1559–1583* (1987).

DAVID WHEELER, Associate Professor and Director of Graduate Studies in the English Department of the University of Southern Mississippi, has edited *Domestick Privacies: Samuel Johnson and the Art of Biography* (1987).

INDEX

Addison, Joseph, 108, 174, 176; *Cato*, 173, 174
Aeneid, The (Virgil), 115
Agrippa, Cornelius, 13
Akenside, Mark, 177
Allen, Ralph, 125
Allestree, Richard, *Whole Duty of Man*, 166
All for Love (Dryden), 174
Alsop, George, 108
Andrews, Mr. and Mrs. (portrait by Gainsborough), 116
Antidote (Henry More), 58
Antony and Cleopatra (Shakespeare), 174
Apel, Karl-Otto, 20, 21
Apprentice's Vade Mecum (Richardson), 164, 165
Aristotle, 60, 155, 174, 207-8; *De anima*, 208; *De partibus animalium*, 207; *Historia animalium*, 207
Arrow, Kenneth, 40
Astell, Mary, 75-83; *Serious Proposal to the Ladies*, 80
Austen, Jane, 188, 190
Autobiography (Vico), 3

Bacon, Francis, 80, 134; *New Atlantis, The*, 37-44
Baker, Daniel, 151, 152, 153, 154, 155, 156, 158
Baker, Keith Michael, 41
Bally, Charles, 218,
Bampfylde, Coplestone Warre, 115-16
Bannister, John, 109, 110
Barlow, Captain Arthur, 108

Barnett, George L., 183, 184
Barrow, Isaac, 167
Bartram, John, 107, 108, 109, 110
Bartram, William, 110
Barzun, Jacques, 113, 114
Basilikon Doron (James I), 166
Bayard v. Singleton (North Carolina Supreme Court, 1786), 144
Bazin, Gilles Auguste, 198
Beasley, Jerry, 183-84
Beattie, James, 26, 33
Becanus, Goropius, 206
Bedford, Wriothesley Russell, 3rd Duke of, 110
Belgioioso, Princess Cristina, 3
Bentinck, Count William, 198
Bergson, Henri, 15
Berkeley, George, 28, 33
Berlin, Isaiah, xii, 4, 13, 14, 15, 17, 18, 21; "The Counter-Enlightenment," 13-15
Bernier, Réjane, 209
Bernstein, Richard, 19
Betti, Ugo, 20
Betulia liberata, La (Mozart), 86, 87-88
Beverley, Robert, 109
Bible, 77, 151, 164
Blackmore, Sir Richard, 151, 152, 153, 154, 155, 156, 158
Blackstone, Sir William, 141
Blackwell, Anthony, 155
Blair, Hugh, 174
Bodin, Jean, 13
Boerhaave, Herman, 225, 227
Book of Job, paraphrases of, 151-59

Bonnet, Charles, xiv, 26, 193–202; *Contemplation de la nature*, 200; *Letters on Parthenogenesis*, 193–202; *Oeuvres*, 201; *Traité d'insectologie*, 195
Boucher, François, 112
Boucicault, Dion, 180
Boyle, Roger, 184
Bradshaigh, Lady Dorothy, 163, 164, 166, 168
Brickell, John, 108
Brissenden, R. F., 189
Broome, William, 151–52, 154, 155, 156, 159
Brougham, Henry, 130
Brown, Theodore, 227
Buffon, Georges Louis Leclerc, comte de, 26
Burke, Edmund, xiv, 65, 179, 180; *Philosophical Enquiry*, 112, 174
Burlington, Richard Boyle, 3rd Earl of, 115
Bushe, Amyas, 156
Butler, Melissa, xii
Byrd II, William, 116

Camillo, Giulio, 9
Carlyle, Thomas, 15
Carter, Elizabeth, 164
Cassirer, Ernst, 21, 222
Castel, R. P. (Louis-Bertrand), 222
Cato (Addison), 173, 174
Cebes, 5, 7; Tablet of Cebes, xi, 1–10
Cesalpino, Andrea, 208
Cestoni, Giacinto, 197
Chalmers, Alexander, 186
Chardin, Jean-Baptiste-Siméon, 113
Charron, Pierre, 13
Chesterfield, 4th Earl of, 166
Chevrillon, André, 218
Cheyne, George, 230
Childe's Patrimony (Hezekiah Woodward), 76
Chouillet, Jacques, 217
Clarissa (Richardson), 185, 188, 190
Clarke, Samuel, 166, 195, 196
Clemenza di Tito, La (Mozart), 86, 91
Coke, Sir Edward, 140, 141
Coleridge, Samuel Taylor, 3, 15

Collins, William, xiv, 177, 180
Collinson, Peter, 110, 116
Compton, Henry, Bishop of London, 109
Condillac, Étienne Bonnot de, 26, 28, 29, 31, 32, 222; *Traité des sensations*, 28
Condorcet, Jean Antoine-Nicolas de Caritat, Marquis de, 134; *Esquisse d'un tableau historique*, 39, 42, 45; *Essay on the Application of Analysis*, 40; *Fragment sur l'Atlantide*, xii, 37–45; "On the Influence of the American Constitution," 37; *Sketch*, 65
Conjectures on Original Composition (Young), 174
Congreve, William, 173, 181, 184
Considerations Concerning Free Schools (Wase), 76, 78
Contemplation de la nature (Bonnet), 200
Copernicus, Nicholas, 227
"Counter-Enlightenment, The" (Berlin), 13–15
Crane, R. S., 174, 175
Cratylus (Plato), 206
Cressy, David, 78
Critias (Plato), 37, 38, 39
Critical Dissertation on the Poems of Ossian (Blair), 174
Critique of Pure Reason (Kant), xii, 25, 33, 34
Croce, Benedetto, 3, 8
Cromwell, Oliver, 53
Cullen, William, 225, 231
Culler, Jonathan, 20

Dante Alighieri, 178
Da Ponte, Lorenzo, 86, 91
Darbelnet, J., 218, 219, 221
Darwin, Charles, 227
Davenant, Sir William, 53, 54; *Gondibert*, 53, 54
Davis, Spencer, xiii
Dawkins, Charles, 233
Dawson, Virginia, xiv
De anima (Aristotle), 208
De antiquissima (Vico), 4, 6
Defoe, Daniel, 164, 185, 188; *New*

Index

Family Instructor, 164; *Roxana*, 190
De la Tour, Quentin, 114
De l'interprétation de la nature (Diderot), 222
Democritus, 225
Dennis, John, 151, 158
De partibus animalium (Aristotle), 207
De Sanctis, Francesco, 4
Descartes, René, 16, 18, 26, 27, 29, 30, 31, 32, 37, 54, 57, 62, 80
Diderot, Denis, xiv, 38, 107, 110–16, 215–22; *De l'interprétation de la nature*, 222; "Encyclopédie," 217, 218; *Essays on Painting*, 112; *Letters to Sophie Volland*, 111; *Lettre sur les sourds et muets*, 215–22; "Observations on the Translation of Pope's *Essay on Man*," 220; *Salons*, 107, 110, 111
Digby, Sir Kenelm, 55, 62
Dilthey, Wilhelm, 21
Diritto Universale (Vico), 16
Divine Comedy (Dante), 178
Donati, Vitaliano, 209
Don Giovanni (Mozart), 90
D'Onsenbray, Count, 196
Doria, Paolo Mattia, 7
Douglas (Home), xiv, 173–81
Dryden, John, 174

Ecclesiasticus, 157
Economics of David Ricardo, The (Hollander), 129
Eighteenth-Century British Novelists (Barnett), 183, 184
Elizabeth I, 76
Elements of Political Economy (Mill), 129, 130
Elements of the Philosophy of Mind (Stewart), 134
Ellsworth, Oliver, 142
Elstob, Elizabeth, 79
Émile (Rousseau), 66–73
Encyclopédie, 208
"Encyclopédie" (Diderot), 217, 218
Epicurus, 115
Esquisse d'un tableau historique (Condorcet), 39, 42, 45
Essay of the Impolicy of a Bounty (Mill), 129
Essay of Dramatic Poesy (Dryden), 174
Essay on Man (Pope), 107–8, 220–21; (translated by Silhouette), 220–21
Essays on Painting (Diderot), 112
Essay on Taste (Gerard), 174
Essay on the Application of Analysis (Condorcet), 40
Essay on the Genius and Writings of Pope (J. Warton), 174, 176
Eusebius, 152

Fasts and Festivals (*Companion for the Festivals and Fasts*, Nelson), 166
Feder, Johann Georg Heinrich, 33
Federalist 78, 144–45
Félibien, André, 112, 114
Fénelon, François de Salignac de la Mothe, 80
Ferment of Knowledge, The (Porter and G. S. Rousseau), 232
Fichte, Johann Gottlieb, 15
Fielding, Henry, 123, 185, 186, 188; *Joseph Andrews*, xiii, 123–27; *Tom Jones*, 185, 190
First Treatise (Locke), 78
Fisch, Max, 7
Fontenelle, Bernard Le Bovier de, 179
Fordyce, James, 65
Foscolo, Ugo, 3
Four Dissertations (Hume), 174
Fragment sur l'Atlantide (Condorcet), xii, 37–45
Freud, Sigmund, 20, 227
Fried, Michael, 111
Frye, Northrop, 124

Gadamer, Hans-Georg, 20, 21
Gainsborough, Thomas, 116; *Portrait of Mr. and Mrs. Andrews*, 116
Galileo (Galileo Galilei), 16
Gamerra, Giovanni de, 86
Gardner, John, 188
Garin, Eugenio, 4, 16, 17, 18, 19, 21
Gaspard, Leon, 114
Gassendi, Pierre, 54
Gaston-Granger, Gilles, 41
Geertz, Clifford, 20

Gellert, Christian, 166
Gerard, Alexander, 174
Glisson, Francis, 225, 228, 233
Glossarium Germanicum (Wachter), 205, 210-11
Goethe, Johann Wolfgang von, 15
Goffman, Erving, 20
Goldsmith, Oliver, 124, 173
Goldstein, Leslie, xiii
Gondibert (Davenant), 53, 54
Göttingische Anzeigen von gelehrten Sachen (Feder), 33
Gouge, William, 166
Grassi, Ernesto, 5, 18
Graves, Robert, 217-18
Gray, Thomas, xiv, 174, 177, 180
Grecian History (Stanyan), 216
Gregory, John, 65
Greuze, Jean Baptiste, 112
Grimm, Jacob, 17
Grounds of Natural Philosophy (Duchess of Newcastle), 60-61

Habermas, Jürgen, 20, 21
Hall, Collette, xiii
Haller, Albrecht von, 225, 227, 228, 231, 233
Hamann, Johann Georg, 14, 15, 16, 17, 18
Hamilton, Alexander, 144, 145; *Federalist 78*, 144-45
Hartley, David, 134
Hawkesworth, John, 184
Hazard, Paul, 3, 10
"Health, Tenderness, Warmth, Feet" (Locke), 77
Heberden, William, 225
Hegel, Georg Wilhelm Friedrich, 8, 15, 17, 20
Heidegger, Martin, 20, 21, 22
Helmont, Jan Baptista van, 57, 58
Helvétius, Claude Arien, 222
Henry, Matthew, 151, 152
Herder, Gottfried, 14, 15, 17, 18
Hill, Aaron, 165
Histoire et mémoires (Réaumur), 196
Historia animalium (Aristotle), 207
History of British India (Mill), 131
History of the Present State of Virginia (Beverley), 109

Hoare, Henry, 110
Hobbes, Thomas, 37, 53, 54, 55, 57, 62; *Leviathan*, 53, 54, 57
Hogarth, William, 114, 115
Hollander, Samuel, 129
Home, John, xiv, 173-81
Homer, 6, 188
Hoole, Charles, 76; *Children's Talk*, 75
Horner, Francis, 134
Hume, David, xiii, xiv, 13, 33, 38, 131-32, 134, 135; *Four Dissertations*, 174; "Of Tragedy," 178-79
Humphry Clinker (Smollett), 190
Hunter, John, 225, 227
Hurd, Richard, 174
Husbands, John, 152
Hyams, Edward, 116

Ibsen, Henrik, 178
Idomeneo (Mozart), 86, 88, 89-90
Inferno (Dante), 178
Inquiry concerning Virtue or Merit (Shaftesbury), 216
Inquiry into the Colonial Policy (Brougham), 130
Iredell, James, 144-45
Irene (Johnson), 175
Isler, Hansreudi, 226, 230

Jacobi, Friedrich Heinrich, 14, 15
James I, King of England, 166
James, Robert, 216
Janes, Regina, 81
Jenyns, Soame, 186
Jerome, St., 152
Jerrold, Douglas, 180
Johnson, Samuel, xiv, 164, 176, 179, 181, 184; *Irene*, 175; *Rambler 4*, 165, 185-89; *Rasselas*, 185
Joseph Andrews (Fielding), xiii, 123-27
Journal de Trévoux, 195
Journal of Public Instruction, 41
Joyce, James, 3

Kames, Henry Home, Lord, 179-80; *Elements of Criticism*, 174
Kant, Immanuel, 18, 25-34, 38; *Critique of Pure Reason*, xii, 25, 33,

Index

34; "Postulates of Empirical Thought in General," 25; "Refutation of Idealism," 25–34; *Prolegomena*, 32–33
Kaplan, Marcie, 55
Keill, John, 225
Kennicott, Benjamin, 164
Kent, William, 110
King, Lester, 227
Kinnaird, Joan, 81
Kip, J., 114, 115
Knight, Richard Payne, 225
Knyff, L., 114, 115
Kuehn, Manfred, xii
Kuhn, Thomas, xiv, 225–34; *Structure of Scientific Revolutions*, 227, 232

Lacan, Jacques, 20
Lachterman, David, xii
La Mettrie, Julian Offray de, 38, 222
Laws, The (Plato), 38
Leeuwenhoek, Anton van, 194, 197
Leibniz, Gottfried Wilhelm von, 25, 26, 27, 41, 195, 196, 208
Le Nôtre, André, 116
L'Estrange, Roger, 164
Letters on Parthenogenesis (Bonnet), 193–202
Letters on Chivalry and Romance (Hurd), 174
Letters to Sophie Volland (Diderot), 111
Lettre sur les sourds et muets (Diderot), 215–22
Leviathan (Hobbes), 53, 54, 57
Lévi-Strauss, Claude, 22
Lewis, C. S., 230, 231
Lillo, George, 173, 175, 178
Lincoln, Earl of, 110
Linnaeus (Carl von Linné), 109, 208–9; *Systema naturae*, 208
Locke, John, 29, 56, 62, 78, 143, 216; *Some Thoughts Concerning Education*, 77–78; "Health, Tenderness, Warmth, Feet," 77; *First Treatise*, 78
Lodoli, Father Francesco, 5
Lodovico, Domenico, 5
Logan, James, 109
London Merchant, The (Lillo), 173, 175, 178

Longinus, 151
Lorrain, Claude, 110, 111
Loudon, John Claudius, 116
Loutherbourg, Jacques-Philippe, 111, 112
Lucio Silla (Mozart), 86, 88
Lyonet, Pierre, 198

Mably, Gabriel Bonnet de, 13
McCrea, Brian, xiii
MacIntyre, Alasdair, 229
Mackenzie, Henry, 184, 187
Macpherson, James, 186
Makin, Bathsua, 75, 79
Malblanc, A., 218–19
Malebranche, Nicolas de, 27, 29
Malpighi, Marcello, 194
Manley, Mary Delarivière, 184
Marks, Sylvia Kasey, xiii
Marx, Karl, 3, 20, 22
May, James, xiii
Mayo, Robert, 185–86
Mazzolà, Caterino, 86
Medicinal Dictionary (James), 216
Megill, Allan, 15, 18
Mémoires des insectes (Réaumur), 195, 197
Merchant, Caroline, 52
Merleau-Ponty, Maurice, 22
Metamorphoses (Ovid), 115
Metastasio, Pietro, 86, 87
Metcalf, George, 207
Michelet, Jules, 3, 13
Mill, James, xiii, 129–31, 134, 135; *Elements of Political Economy*, 129, 130; *Essay of the Impolicy of a Bounty*, 129; *History of British India*, 131
Mill, John Stuart, 130
Milton, John, 158; *Paradise Lost*, 157, 159, 174; "Tractate of Education," 77
Monod, Jacques, 233
Montaigne, Michel de, 13
Montesquieu, Charles Louis de Secondat, Baron de La Brède et de, 13
Moralists, The (Shaftesbury), 157
More, Henry, 57, 58, 62; *Antidote*, 58
Morison, Robert, 209
Morris, David, 159

Mortimer, Cromwell, 225
Möser, Justus, 14, 15
Moses, 155
Mozart, Leopold, 86
Mozart, Wolfgang Amadeus, xii, 85-93; *Betulia liberata*, 86, 87-88; *Clemenza di Tito*, 86, 91; *Don Giovanni*, 90; *Idomeneo*, 86, 88, 89-90; *Lucio Silla*, 86, 88; *Nozze di Figaro*, xii, 86, 90-91; *Zaide*, 86, 88-89; *Zauberflöte*, 86, 88, 89, 91-92
Mulso, Hester, 168
Musser, Joseph, xiv

Narratives of Early Virginia (Percy), 108
Natural History of North Carolina (Brickell), 108
Nelson, Robert, 166
New Atlantis, The (Bacon), 37-44
Newcastle, Margaret Lucas Cavendish, Duchess of, xii, 51-62, 75, 79; *Grounds of Natural Philosophy*, 60-61; *Observations upon Experimental Philosophy*, 53, 59, 60; *Philosophical Fancies*, 52, 53; *Philosophical Letters*, 51, 53, 57, 59; *Philosophical and Physical Opinions*, 52, 55; *Poems and Fancies*, 52
Newcastle, William Cavendish, Duke of, 52, 55, 56
New Family Instructor (Defoe), 164
New Science (Vico), xi, 1-10, 16, 18
Newton, Sir Isaac, 41, 132, 133, 193, 195, 227
Nicolini (Niccolo Grimaldi), 3
Nietzsche, Friedrich Wilhelm, 20, 22
Night Thoughts (Young), 177
Norfolk, Edward Howard, 9th Duke of, 110
Novak, Maximillian, 185
Novel and Romance (Williams), 183, 185
Nozze di Figaro, La (Mozart), xii, 86, 90-91

Observations on the Fairy Queen of Spenser (T. Warton), 174

"Observations on the Translation of Pope's *Essay on Man*" (Diderot), 220
Observations upon Experimental Philosophy (Duchess of Newcastle), 53, 59, 60
Of Domesticall Duties (Gouge), 166
"Of Tragedy" (Hume), 178-79
Oeuvres (Bonnet), 201
On Deconstruction (Culler), 20
"On the Influence of the American Constitution" (Condorcet), 37
Osborne, Dorothy, 52
Oswald, John, 26, 33
Otis, James, 141
Otway, Thomas, 179
Ovid, *Metamorphoses*, 115

Paine, Thomas, 65
Pallas, Peter Simon, 209
Pamela (Richardson), 165
Paracelsus, Philippus Aureolus, 226
Paradise Lost (Milton), 157, 159, 174
Pascal, Blaise, 38
Patrick, Simon, 151, 152, 153, 154, 155, 158
Pepys, Samuel, 52
Percival, W. Keith, xiv
Percy, George, 108
Peri Bathos (Pope), 151
Perreton, Peter, xiii
Perry-Camp, Jane, xii
Petre, James Robert, 8th Baron Lord, 110, 116
Phaedo (Plato), 7
Philosophical Enquiry (Burke), 112, 174
Philosophical Fancies (Duchess of Newcastle), 52, 53
Philosophical Letters (Duchess of Newcastle), 51, 53, 57, 59
Philosophical and Physical Opinions (Duchess of Newcastle), 52, 55
Piaget, Jean, 22
Pilkington, Laetitia, 164
Pitcairne, Archibald, 225
Pitt, Christopher, 152
Plantarum historiae (Morison), 209
Plato, 7, 8, 39, 60, 207, 225; *Cratylus*, 206; *Critias*, 37, 38, 39; *Laws, The*,

Index

38; *Phaedo*, 7; *Republic*, 8, 38, 39; *Statesman, The*, 38; *Timaeus*, 38
Pliny, 155
Plutarch, 39
Poems and Fancies (Duchess of Newcastle), 52
Pope, Alexander, xii–xiii, 174, 176, 180; *Essay on Man*, 107–8, 220–21; *Peri Bathos*, 151; Preface to *Iliad*, 174; Prologue to *Cato*, 174; *Windsor Forest*, xii
Porter, Roy, 232
"Postulates of Empirical Thought in General" (Kant), 25
Poussin, Nicolas, 110, 111, 115
Practice of Piety, 166
Preface to *Aesop's Fables* (Richardson), 164
Preface to *The Iliad* (Pope), 174
Price, Uvedale, 225
Priestley, Joseph, 33
Procès-verbaux (Réaumur), 196
Prolegomena (Kant), 32–33
Prologue to *Cato* (Pope), 174
Puffendorf, Samuel Freiherr von, 140

Quesnay, François, 42

Raleigh, Sir Walter, 108
Rambler 4 (Johnson), 165, 185–89
Rask, Rasmus, 211
Rasselas (Johnson), 185
Ray, John, 208
Reading Clarissa (Warner), 188
Réaumur, René-Antoine, xiv, 195–200; *Histoire et mémoires*, 196; *Mémoires des insectes*, 195, 197; *Procès-verbaux*, 196
"Refutation of Idealism" (Kant), 25–34
Reid, Thomas, 26, 29–30, 31, 32, 33, 129, 131–33, 134, 135
Religious Sublime (Morris), 159
Repton, Humphry, 116
Republic (Plato), 8, 38, 39
Reynolds, Sir Joshua, 114, 116
Ricardo, David, xiii, 129, 131
Richardson, Samuel, 123, 175, 184, 185, 188; *Apprentice's Vade Mecum*, 164, 165; *Clarissa*, 185, 188, 190; *Pamela*, 165; Preface to *Aesop's Fables*, 164; *Sir Charles Grandison*, xii, 163–71
Richmond, Charles Lennox, 2nd Duke of, 110
Ricoeur, Paul, 20
Rights of Man (Paine), 65
Robb, Bonnie, xiv
Robert, Hubert, 111, 112
Roger, Jacques, 194
Rosa, Salvator, 112
Rousseau, G. S., 225, 227; *Ferment of Knowledge*, 232; "Sowing the Wind," 229
Rousseau, Jean Jacques, xii, 3, 13, 14, 17, 65–73; *Émile*, 66–73
Roxana (Defoe), 190
Ruysdael, Jacob van, 114

Sacks, Sheldon, 188
Said, Edward, xii, 21
Salons (Diderot), 107, 110, 111
Saussure, Ferdinand de, 20
Savigny, Friedrich Karl von, 17
Scaliger, Joseph Justus, 206
Schachtner, Johann Andreas, 86, 89
Schelling, Friedrich Wilhelm Joseph von, 15
Schikaneder, Emanuel, 86
Schlegel, August Wilhelm, 17
Schlegel, Friedrich von, 17
Schopenhauer, Arthur, 15
Schurman, Anna van, 79
Seasons, The (Thomson), 154
Second Characters (Shaftesbury), xi, 7
Seguin, J. P., 222
Selfish Gene, The (Dawkins), 233
Serious Proposal to the Ladies (Astell), 80
Shaftesbury, 3rd Earl of, 7; *Inquiry concerning Virtue or Merit*, 216; *Moralists, The*, 157; *Second Characters*, xi, 7
Shakespeare, William, 176, 178, 179, 180, 181, 187; *Antony and Cleopatra*, 174
Sherbo, Arthur, 175
Sheridan, Richard Brinsley, 173
Shinehouse, Jane, xiii
Siddons, Mrs. Sarah, 180
Silhouette, Étienne de, 220–21

Sir Charles Grandison (Richardson), xiii, 163–71
Skelton, Philip, 163
Sketch (Condorcet), 65
Smith, Adam, 129, 134
Smith, Hilda L., xii, 53
Smith, William, 151, 158
Smollett, Tobias, 184, 185, 188; *Humphry Clinker*, 190
Snowiss, Sylvia, 144
Socrates, 7, 156
Some Thoughts Concerning Education (Locke), 77–78
Sources de la biologie (Bernier), 209
"Sowing the Wind and Reaping the Whirlwind" (G. S. Rousseau), 229
Spaight, Richard, 144
Spender, Dale, 82
Spenser, Edmund, 180
Spinoza, Baruch, 37
Stahl, Georg, 225, 226, 228
Stanyan, Temple, 216
Statesman, The (Plato), 38
Steiner, George, 221
Stewart, Dugald, 129, 133, 134, 135; *Elements of the Philosophy of Mind*, 134
Storace, Nancy, 91
Structure of Scientific Revolutions, The (Kuhn), 227, 232
Struever, Nancy, 19
Stylistique comparée du français et de l'anglais (Darbelnet and Vinay), 218, 219, 221
Swammerdam, Jan, 194
Swift, Jonathan, 164
Swinton, Joseph, 164
Switzer, Stephen, 116
Sydenham, Thomas, 225
Systema naturae (Linnaeus), 208

Tablet of Cebes, xi, 1–10
Tagliacozzo, Giorgio, xi–xii
Taine, Hippolyte, 219
Tasso, Torquato, 180
Taylor, Jeremy, 78
Temple, Sir William, 52, 115
Tencin, Madame de, 196
Thales, 60
Thomas, Lewis, 234

Thompson, E. P., 123–27
Thompson, William, 151, 153, 154, 156, 157–58, 159
Thomson, James, 164, 173; *The Seasons*, 154; *Winter*, 155–56
Tillemans, Pieter, 114
Tillotson, Archbishop John, 166, 167, 169
Timaeus (Plato), 38
Tom Jones (Fielding), 185, 190
Toulmin, Stephen, xii, 21
Tournefort, Joseph Pitton de, 208
"Tractate of Education" (Milton), 77
Traité des sensations (Condillac), 28
Traité d'insectologie (Bonnet), 195
Trembley, Abraham, xiv, 195–200
Trevett v. Weeden (Rhode Island Supreme Court, 1786), 142
Tucker, Thomas Tudor, 143
Turgot, Jacques, 42

Universal History (Swinton), 164
Uphaus, Robert W., xiv

Vaihinger, H., 33, 34; "Zu Kants Widerlegung des Idealismus," 25–26
Valletta, Francesco, 7
Varesco, Giambattista, 86
Varnum, James, 142
Vattel, Emer de, 140
Vernet, Joseph, 111, 112, 113
Vernon, Richard, 232
Vico, Giambattista, xi–xii, 1–10, 13–22, 38; *Autobiography*, 3; *De antiquissima*, 4, 6; *Diritto Universale*, 16; *New Science*, xi, 1–10, 16, 18
Vinay, J. P., 218, 219, 221
Vindication of the Rights of Woman (Wollstonecraft), 65–73
Virgil, 115
Visser, Derk, xiii
Volland, Sophie, 110, 111
Voltaire, François Marie Arouet de, 38

Wachter, Johann Georg, 205, 210–11
Warner, William Beatty, 188
Warton, Joseph, 177, 178, 180; *Essay on the Genius and Writings of Pope*, 174, 176

Index

Warton, Thomas, 152, 177; *Observations on the Fairy Queen of Spenser*, 174
Wase, Christopher, 76, 78
Wasserman, Earl, 180
Watt, Ian, 183, 186, 188
Watts, Isaac, 151
Wesley, John, 153
Wheeler, David, xiv
Whigs and Hunters (E. P. Thompson), 123–27
White, Hayden, xii, 21
Whitefield, George, 166
Whole Duty of Man (Allestree), 166
Whytt, Robert, 225, 228, 233
Williams, Ioan, 183, 185
Willey, Basil, 153
Willis, Thomas, 225, 226, 227, 230–31
Wilson, James, 142, 144, 145
Winch, Stephen, 20
Windsor Forest (Pope), xii
Winter (Thomson), 155–56
Winthrop, John, 108
Wittgenstein, Ludwig Josef Johan, 20, 22

Wolff, Christian, 25, 26, 27, 28, 29, 31
Wollstonecraft, Mary, xii, 65–73; *Vindication of the Rights of Woman*, 65–73
Women of Ideas (Spender), 82
Woodward, Hezekiah, 76
Woolley, Hannah, 79
Wordsworth, William, 15
Wright, Georg Henrik von, 20
Wycherley, William, 173, 181

Yates, Frances, 9
Young, Edward, 151, 153, 154, 155, 156, 157–58, 159, 165; *Conjectures on Original Composition*, 174; *Night Thoughts*, 177

Zaide (Mozart), 86, 88–89
Zauberflöte, Die (Mozart), 86, 88, 89, 91–92
"Zu Kants Widerlegung des Idealismus" (Vaihinger), 25–26